PULANI

A MEMOIR OF A YOUNG WOMAN IN APARTHEID SOUTH AFRICA

BY

RUCHEL LOUIS COETZEE

Suzy Sterling
Enjoy
Ruchel

HEROIDES

HEROIDES PUBLISHING LLC

Library of Congress Control Number: 2010936391

Pulani/by Ruchel Louis Coetzee

1. Coetzee, Ruchel Louis. 2. Apartheid. 3. Memoir. 4. South Africa. 5. Afrikaner.
6. Young Adult 7. Woman's Literature

ISBN 978-0-982-98030-9

*   *   *

To my husband and my mother,
two great lions on opposite sides of the jungle

*   *   *

People in America asked me where I was from
I replied, South Africa
They asked me where I was born
I replied, South Africa
They asked what it was like living there
I told them stories
They said, you should write a book
I replied, no one would read it
They said, you should write a book
I replied, I don't know how to write a book
They said, you should write a book
I wrote a book

*   *   *

CONTENTS

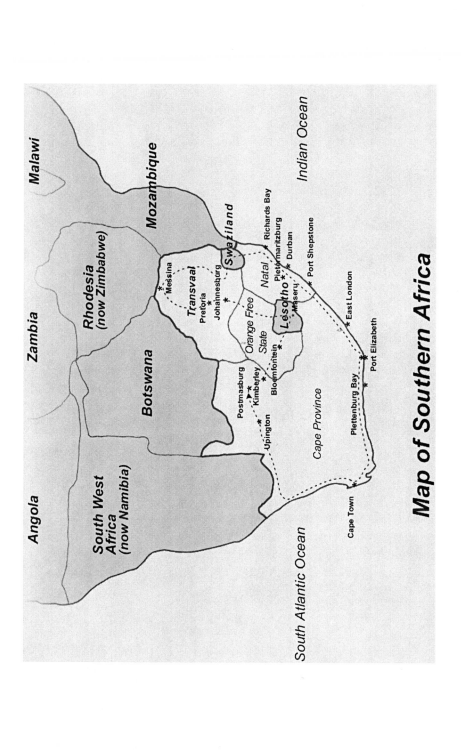

Map of Southern Africa

CHAPTER ONE

——————

1993: *Reports of horrific violence continue to come from the South African townships in the wake of the assassination of South African Communist Party (SACP) leader Chris Hani. "Killer," a township comrade, tells a Newsweek reporter the story of how he helped "necklace" a 62-year-old woman from a neighboring tribe, Mary Skhosana, who worked in a funeral parlor. Her crime was that she sold funeral insurance—"Killer" considered her part of 'the system'. "We knew she was a police informer," he said. "We did not need proof. She was pleading for mercy and crying and screaming. She said she'd pay us 7,000 rand [$3,080] if we let her go. We told her we did not need her money, we needed her life. Then we put a tire around her legs and another around her neck and shoulders. We forced her to drink petrol. We poured the rest into the tires and onto her and set her alight. But the fire went out. Another tin of petrol was fetched and it took about an hour."*

O kay, stop panicking. Just because it's close to midnight and I totally misjudged the time needed to get there does not mean I have to turn this highway into my own personal *Kyalami* (race track).

Take a left turn at the exit after the gas station with the zebra statue on the roof. Zebra statue on the roof? I switched on the overhead light and grabbed the envelope where my hastily scrawled directions now look like Chinese. Cars whiz by on either side. Exit 57. Or is it Exit 59? The envelope is about an inch from my nose, I can barely see in the dull yellow light. The exit number must be 59 because I just passed 57 and a zebra is nowhere in sight.

As pitch dark as it is, the chances of seeing that zebra are almost zero. In South Africa, the nights are black. Not gray black or blue black or mauve black. Just black.

The clock on the dashboard says 11:45 PM. Fifteen minutes late already and I have not even left the highway. The night swallowed up the city lights an hour ago and I can only see scant branches of bush reflected now and then in the headlights.

Exit 59. I swerve the wheel to the left and the envelope goes sailing. The road veers down a steep embankment toward a bullet-ridden stop sign. Why would someone shoot up a stop sign?

11:55 PM. I am not afraid. I am late.

As I retrieve my envelope, I know I am going to be another fifteen minutes late. I am so dead.

Why couldn't I have plotted the journey out in the daylight like a normal person? Of course, I know the highway. I travel the road often. The suburb outside the city is a place I have been to before. Okay, once before and in daylight, but still, how difficult could it be to reach at night with proper directions?

I study my Chinese scrawl again while idling at the stop sign. Not another car in sight. Do I turn left or right at the stop sign? I look outside the window. Black.

My heart skips a beat.

I wait a minute to see if another car will venture off the highway behind me. Nothing. Just black.

Logic kicks in. I make a left.

Once you climb back up the next hill into the town, you will see an old Anglican church with a huge parking lot next to it, I had been told. Can't miss it. After the parking lot, make an immediate left and go straight until you see a fork in the road. At the fork, veer right and the house will be at the end of the cul de sac, number 154.

Nowhere in sight does the road look like it is going up a hill. Instead, the car is moving further downhill. I try to turn around but the road is so narrow. I can't see if the hill I'm on has steep slopes on either side. Maybe I still have to go down before I go up again. I go forward slowly.

12:05 AM. I am lost and late.

12:06 AM. I am lost and late, and afraid.

Wait. What is that noise? Sounds like a crack in the air.

I open the window cautiously. Cold night air and insect noise fill the warm interior. I roll the window further down to try to see more. Who am I kidding? Black. The temperature in the car begins to drop in tandem with the temperature of my blood. Ice starts to form around my heart as if preparing it for cold storage.

How could I possibly have thought of attempting this journey to the middle of nowhere by myself at this late hour? What was I thinking? Why did I not leave much earlier, like at sunset? I could have sat in the lounge of a hotel until the appointed hour. But no, I am superwoman, I am brave and fearless. I am an utter moron.

A scream. Did I really hear it?

Wait—there is another one!

The car engine suddenly stalls. Thank God I'm on flat ground.

A loud rumble is shaking the earth, as if it is thundering. Voices buried deep in the belly of the mountain begin to chant in angry unison. *"Aaaaaaaie! Aaaaaaaaie!"*

A shot is fired. *Crack!*

What is that light in the distance? I smell something. Something is burning. Is that a fire? Smells like burning tires.

Oh God, this can't be! Please tell me this is not true. I have to get out of here. I should have turned right at the stop sign. I have to start the car again. The voices are still far away—no, wait, they are getting louder. I can't start the engine. My hands are shaking too much. I can do this. Just concentrate. I have to start the engine and turn around.

I hear more shouting. I roll the window up. Are the car doors locked?

Crack! More gunfire.

What is this place? There is no house, no gas station, only this single road with bush on either side. How do I turn around?

Wait! What is that in the headlights? Do I see something moving? Oh please God, let my hands stop shaking so I can start this car again. Use the bright lights. Is something there in the distance? Switch it on, flip it up, hurry!

Something is moving and it's coming closer. What is it? I can't see. Squint your good eye.

Crack! Who is shooting? That thing has stopped moving. Wait, it is moving again. Don't open the window.

"Aaaaaaaaie!" Open the window. *"Aaaaaaaaie!"* Close the window!

Reverse! Reverse the car! Get out of here! I can't start the engine.

What is that? It is coming closer, closer! It is a person—wait, looks like a woman...a Zulu? Roll down the window again.

"Help me, madam!" she screams.

What is that on her face? Blood? Blood is dripping from her forehead and running over her eye and her cheek. She's wounded. I have to help her. I must help.

In the distance the shouting and chanting from an angry crowd fill the air. Kill! Traitor! Kill! The words are becoming indistinguishable between the gunshots and the chanting.

Am I hearing what I think I am hearing? Is that a violent stampede rising from the deep ravine? A stampede, yes, the sound of it made worse by the echoes in the still night air.

"Help me, please help me. They will kill me!" The woman sinks to the ground in pain. A spear sails over her head, narrowly missing. A spear? If I had not caught the glint of the metal in the headlight, I would swear I was hallucinating.

Clarity overtakes my frozen brain. I have to get out of here immediately. Now.

But I have to help the woman first.

I can't get out of the car... there are gunshots and spears slicing the sky. Yes, I must. She is injured and I have to take her with me.

"Wait! I am coming to help you," I say, opening the car door.

Who is grabbing my arm? Someone is pulling me out of the car. Oh God! Oh no!

CHAPTER TWO

1958: *Hendrik Verwoerd, the ruthless mastermind of apartheid and fierce member of the ruling National Party becomes prime minister of South Africa. The African National Party (ANC) tries to prevent this "general" election in which only three million whites are allowed to vote. The ANC joins with the South African Congress of Trade Unions (SACTU) to plan a three-day strike. Pamphlets shouting "NATS MUST GO" are distributed in factories, beer halls, townships, and bus and railway stations urging thirteen million blacks not to go to work. The government learns of this plan four days before the planned strike and issues a ruling that no more than ten blacks are allowed to gather in an urban area at any one time. This ruling sends most ANC leaders—including Nelson Mandela—underground while waiting to see who will heed their call. The feedback from comrades at strategic bus and railway stations on the first day is dismal. Most workers fear retribution and go to work.*

I was born on Nelson Mandela's birthday that year: 18 July 1958. Such joy, such celebration in the household! Such praise to God!

Telegrams arrived in Bloemfontein from across the ocean, flowers threatened to cover every surface, and champagne ran through every vein. A beautiful daughter had been born.

Please God. A name. With what name will she be blessed?

Ruchel Anne, proclaimed Mother from beneath the roses in her hospital bed. "*Rukhel*" said my Jewish grandmother Gussie, giving my name the traditional pronunciation. *Pulani*, proclaimed Evelyn, Mother's half Xhosa, half Bushman head cook. "Pulani" means "rain" in Sotho but translates roughly into "happiness because the crops are growing", which brings an abundance of smiles.

The family and townsfolk went overboard, but after the death of my sister, ten days after her premature birth a year earlier, who could blame them? I was now officially the firstborn of the whole family from both sides. Mother was not going to relinquish the name Ruchel—it really belonged to my deceased sister. So technically I was the second Ruchel. Evelyn said that according to Xhosa tradition, I was accountable for the spirit of my dead sister as well as mine, and that I was to carry both spirits with responsibility, vigor, joy, and happiness throughout my life. Not twenty-four hours on this earth and already my soul was burdened with the weight of two spirits.

Evelyn would not let me forget that I was carrying two spirits. She called me Pulani whenever I was in her presence.

Bloemfontein is the Afrikaans word for "fountain of flowers," named for the wild, colourful cosmos that line the sides of its roads. Situated slapbang in the middle of South Africa, it is the judicial capital of our country. Naval Hill dominates the city. On one side it has rocks painted white, shaped to resemble a horse. It was used as a landmark for horsemen coming in from the plains during the Anglo-Boer War. Now it is home to the Franklin Game Reserve—the world's only game reserve in the middle of a city. Today the world knows my city and the Free State Stadium as host to the 2010 FIFA World Cup soccer matches.

So who were my parents?

Father's family, of French origin, arrived in Bloemfontein in the early 1900s. In 1916 my grandfather, Michel Louis, and his brother started a small trading store that was to become the largest wholesale store in the province. My father, George Michel Louis, and his brothers took over Michel Louis and Sons Ltd when my grandfather died in 1960.

Father's mother, Margo, was from Paris. Aloof, dignified, and sophisticated, she spoke only French to her children. When it was time for Father to attend school, the teacher sent him home with a note saying the child must be deaf and dumb as he answered to neither English, Afrikaans, nor Sotho.

"What do you mean you have no French at this school—impossible!" Margo exclaimed in the headmaster's office the next day. "French is the only civilized language. I demand my son be taught in French!"

"Madam," replied the headmaster patiently to this tall, robust, auburn-haired woman in her fur coat and hat. "All pupils are taught in English at this school, with Afrikaans being the obligatory second language according to government regulations. Your son would find it very difficult to communicate if he were to speak only French. I suggest you speak to him in English at home so that he can catch up with the rest of the children."

"As long as I live, I will speak to my son in the only civilized language known to man!" So Father relied on his grandfather, his friends, and the maids to help him master English.

Although Father's family came from France, the family lived for many years in Beirut, Lebanon. As both the French and the Lebanese rate food right up there with God, the traditions of the Arab and French aristocracy were transported to our table in South Africa. Silver platters of kibi, baba ghanoush, mamoul, terrines, and other delicacies were introduced to new friends. Numerous maids each had their specific tasks. No matter what mealtime it was, the table was always set with the full complement of silverware even if only a slice of toast was eaten. Of course, this tradition had to be carried through to our household. No question. Mother made sure that the maids carried out Father's instructions to the precise letter. God forbid Evelyn burnt or undercooked the meal. *Sacré bleu!*

But what was Father really like?

It was Father who tucked me under his arm before running into the surf on our annual vacation. It was Father who knelt beside me each night before bedtime so we could recite the Lord's Prayer together. It was Father who would peel his black-rimmed glasses off his wide forehead to rub his tired eyes while he read to me. It was Father who gave me the big bear hugs, the multitude of kisses on the forehead, and the total adoration any young girl would wish upon herself.

Mother might have been Father's queen but I was his undisputed princess.

Mother was indeed queen of the household and of all the land that was known as Bloemfontein. She was a petite, bubbly, chic, beehive-haired brunette. And she was intelligent, quick witted, and iron willed. No lie went undetected and no story was ever forgotten.

Mother ruled the household and the household trembled in her wake. Although she was unshakably firm on cleanliness, she was also extremely compassionate to the maids' families and needs. No one could ever dislike Mother, no matter how angry she got. She was like a summer storm on a tropical island that blew over in minutes. Men flocked around her energy.

It was her large dark brown eyes that attracted Father when he saw Mother's debutante photo in the local English newspaper *The Friend*. He took that photo to his own mother and said, "This is the woman I am going to marry."

My maternal grandfather Tanous, who I affectionately called Oupa (the Afrikaans word for grandfather), was a quiet, dignified Lebanese gentleman twenty-three years older than my grandmother, who I affectionately called Gussie. Gussie was of Russian Jewish descent. She married Oupa not long after she began working for him in his general trading store. Oupa also owned several buildings and small farms in the Free State. Together they had two children, Mother and my uncle Cedric.

"Why is it that you spend your time in your bedroom writing fan letters to movie stars in America?" sighed Gussie as a teenage Mother tore open yet another autographed photo of an American movie star. But Mother was also somewhat of a realist, and Bloemfontein was a long way from Hollywood. So she set about becoming her own star in Bloemfontein. With her European roots, chutzpah and Middle Eastern sophistication, Mother became a dominant player in the tight-knit English society. Bishops and artists, gays and straights, ministers and judges—they all sought invitations to her many soirees. All were treated equally. To Mother, no one was more important than another.

Our local newspaper, *The Friend*, documented when the Louis family went on vacation, when a diamond soiree or art exhibition was held at the home of Mr. and Mrs. George Louis, and when Mother was invited by a national magazine to join the editor and team on a six-week tour of Europe.

But what was Mother really like?

It was Mother who instilled the confidence in me to tackle the world head on and never be afraid. It was Mother who made the world better when I was teased unmercifully or was ill in bed. It was

Mother to whom I always ran first no matter the circumstance. And it was Mother who taught me compassion and taught me to share with those less fortunate. But to describe Mother as a stay-at-home mom is truly an understatement. She was anything but that. She would be better described as a tiger in a cage, a butterfly in a net, or a lawyer struck dumb.

These were the parents to whom I was born, and heaven help me if I did not perform according to their expectations.

CHAPTER THREE

1959: The Government creates eight separate ethnic "Bantustans" (known as tribal or black homelands). Under the new law, seventy percent of the people of South Africa will now call only thirteen percent of the land their own. No independence or voting rights are granted and pass books become a requirement. Pass books must be signed by an employee outside the homelands, and housing or travel accommodations are either in townships or in hostels at the mines. Tribal chiefs around the country protest in anger and send impis (traditional spear-fighting warriors) to kill government enforcers. The protesting impis are arrested, brutally beaten, or murdered. The only witnesses in these remote areas are white farmers. It is a silent massacre. Closer to the larger metropolitan cities, some Youth League members of the ANC become disillusioned with the ANC's multiracial membership and form the Pan-Africanist Congress (PAC), which accepts only blacks. At the Sharpeville township, thirty-five miles south of Johannesburg, the PAC organizes some twenty thousand demonstrators to gather outside the local police station to protest the pass law. They are controlled and unarmed. The police call for reinforcements and armored cars. Demonstrators, including women and children, turn and run in fear; sixty-nine are killed. Liberal South Africans plead with the government to offer concessions to the blacks, others plan to emigrate only to be discouraged by the government's strict currency controls after a heavy bleeding of capital.

Mother gave Gussie a tour of her empty, newly purchased four-story brick home at the foot of Naval Hill in the leafy suburb of Waverley. Deer had ambled down to the fence to observe the midnight-blue forties Chevrolet parked on the dirt path.

"You will have to pave the driveway," announced Gussie as she stared out the bedroom window at the rolling lawns and old-fashioned swimming pool. "My car is already full of dust. You would think the owners would have had more sense!" Gussie was on a roll. "By the way, Shirley, the two acres at the back of the house have plenty of room for the servant's quarters and an orchard. Very important for the children to have fresh fruit every day. And don't destroy the old walnut tree when you start construction. It will come in handy when I make mamoul."

Gussie heaved up the final flight of stairs to the master suite, commenting on every step how dusty the place was. All Mother could do was sigh and mumble some half-hearted agreement.

"You must show the maids how to clean a toilet properly. Two separate cloths—one for the outside, and one for the inside bowl. Now, I have to be back at my house this afternoon to roll the vine leaves for the dolmades."

Back in the large kitchen on the split-level second floor, Gussie lifted her aching feet out of her shoes. "You have to make sure the plans for the servants' quarters include a lounge and at least two bathrooms. Remember, you must always treat the servants with respect, as they will become your right hand. In my house, you were taught never to disrespect any human being. Show kindness to people and they will show kindness back to you."

"I know that, Mom, how different can it be? The maids in our house know what to do."

"They know what to do," replied Gussie, "because I spent many hours teaching them how to do it. You cannot just expect them to know what to do. Many of these young women live in one-room huts on farms or in shanty tin rooms in townships and don't know the first thing about cleaning a toilet. Most have never even had proper toilets, never mind refrigerators. It will take weeks of patient education. Don't forget, many of them speak very little English.

Mother began to interview young hopefuls, all eager to work for this madam because she seemed kind and the room they were going to live in looked like a palace.

Father had instructed the contractors to build several rooms for the servants' quarters, including a small kitchen, the lounge and two bathrooms. A laundry, separate ironing room, and several storerooms were also added. The whole compound was planted neatly beside the tennis court and pavilion at the back of the house.

"Tell me, Evelyn...," Mother pondered how to phrase her sentence delicately. Evelyn was a gentle yet confident young woman. A doek [headscarf], common to the Sotho, covered her short curly black hair. She was lightskinned, but she had the characteristic short squat body of a Bushman. "You say you are half Xhosa and half Bushman. I have never met anyone from either tribe. The only black people I know are the Sothos who live here in the area. What language do you speak?"

"Well, Madam." She looked directly at Mother. "I was born in the northern Cape, but I speak Sotho because I have lived here in Bloemfontein with friends of my mother, ever since my parents died in a faction fight when I was young. I learnt how to cook the meals at home as a child and have learnt to read and write. I don't intend getting married. I like the rooms you have here and I know I will be good for the madam."

Most women whether black or white would not have come forward expressing what their strengths were. The interviews would typically elicit an extremely shy "Yes, Madam" or a vigorous shake of the head with a blurted out "No" if the question came up asking if she drank alcohol, smoked too much, or had a boyfriend.

"You are thirty years old," continued Mother, "older than the others I have employed. So maybe you will be good for me. At times I have a problem controlling the parties that go on at the back of the house late at night. I don't want to repeat the incident I had here when the master was away in Johannesburg."

Incident? Let's rewind.

One of the maids had decided to organize a party the instant Mother told her that she would be out for the evening at an art exhibition. As soon as Mother left it was party time!

Word spread to the township. An endless stream of strangers poured into a back room of the servants' quarters like teenagers going to a rock concert.

Was this legal? Are you crazy? Go straight to jail, do not pass go.

A party meant jail time for all those caught on the property without a signature in their pass book from Mother or their employer, giving them permission to visit—and—a huge fine for Mother.

But what a party! Loud, drunken, and aggressive, they partied like there was no tomorrow. That is, until Mother pulled up the driveway, running over beer cartons and empty brown paper bags. Volcanic anger engulfed Mother as she flew up the stairs to get her gun. She tried to speak calmly when the telephone rang.

"Hello, Shirley, this is Maureen from next door. I have been phoning all night. Is everything okay?"

For the neighbor to hear the noise, it must have really been something. Her house was at least a quarter mile down.

Mother stormed out the house, nearly tripping over a half-unconscious body sprawled in the yard. The air was clogged with the sour-sweet smell of fermenting homemade *sorghum* (African beer). When Mother saw one of her silver teapots on the ground outside the maid's quarters, the volcano erupted. She raised the gun and fired a shot into the night sky.

Boom!

Comatose bodies sprang back to life. "*Hauw,* Madam, don't shoot!" they screamed. "Sorry, Madam, we leave now, sorry, Madam, don't shoot!" they begged, arms flailing in all directions. Two heavy-bosomed women rose from the floor and ran screaming toward the entrance.

Mother lowered the gun and yanked another woman out the doorway. "You're fired!" Mother shouted as the maid and her friends staggered down the driveway.

That incident.

"Evelyn," Mother sighed, "you strike me as someone who could organize the staff and help me select who will be hardworking and honest. I spend so much time teaching them, only to get into situations where I have to fire them and start all over again. It is exhausting."

"That is no problem, Madam," she replied, knowing the job was now hers. "I am happy to help the madam and I will help translate for the madam so that they understand what the madam wants."

And with that Evelyn became queen of the household, after Mother.

What a household it was! For things to run according to Mother's obsession with cleanliness and orderliness, it took a minimum of one head cook, one kitchen person to wash dishes, two cleaning women, one clothes-washing woman, one ironing woman (even our underwear was ironed), three garden staff, and a nursemaid for each child.

Cleaning was an organized operation. A serious military exercise. Crystal chandeliers were dusted delicately while marble floors were scrubbed blue. Tuesdays were windows and Thursdays were bedroom walls and doors. The furniture from the two lounges was carried out to the patio each and every morning. Why? Because an amazing amount of dust escapes into the air when you beat a chair to death with your hands. Normal people had alarm clocks or roosters to wake them up in the morning. Not at our house. The beating of cushions at the crack of dawn was our wake-up call.

Oh, and let us not forget the treasured Persian carpets, especially the large deep-red one that lay on the marble floor at the entrance. If you opened the front door and stepped onto the carpet with your dirty shoes you were dead. Very dead. Everyone, which meant the maids and the children—no argument—had to walk around that carpet.

But cleanliness obsessions aside, my childhood home was magical. Fairies with pink tutus and sparkling wands resided under the petunias at the bottom of the garden and elves with pointy ears and green suits chased ghosts that mumbled and creaked in Mother's attic closet. Tea was available the length and breadth of the house. I served tea to the fairies and my dolls under the old oak tree at the bottom of the garden while Mother served tea to her ever-growing circle of eclectic friends in the pavilion and Evelyn served tea to the neighbor's maids in her sitting room. Sugar was in high demand.

Sipping Earl Gray one morning with her friends, Mother complained what a nuisance it was to constantly write notes when one of her maids wanted to visit a friend at night.

"You know that most of these poor women cannot write legibly in English and if they decide to go out without a note they risk the chance of being picked up by one of the roving police vans and thrown in jail for the night. It is the most ridiculous thing you have ever heard. It seems we are going downhill ever since we became a republic," she said as she placed her bone china teacup back on its bone china saucer.

"Downhill!" exclaimed Cyril, the pompous head of the History Foundation. "We are sinking faster than the Titanic. Becoming a republic was just the confirmation that we struck an iceberg! It all started when these bloody Afrikaner dutchmen came into power."

Father John sighed sadly.

"Well!" interjected mother's friend Juliet, "Everyone [translation: English liberals] is talking about how the government deceived us last October when they said we would be much better off as a republic instead of being tied to England. We all voted in favor, thinking we would still be part of the Commonwealth but no, each time the government instituted another apartheid law, South Africa got another strike against itself. We smelled worse than a skunk. So Verwoerd tries to keep his inflated ego intact by telling the Commonwealth in London to go to bloody hell."

"He had no choice," said Cyril, "They were going to expel him anyway. The Afrikaners hate the English so much that they most probably rejoiced at the new government's decision!"

"I know," agreed Mother, "it is just awful. The rest of the world thinks we are all barbaric. Because of apartheid, they won't even allow us to participate in the Olympic Games."

I can vaguely remember the day South Africa became a republic. The appointed day was 31 May 1961, and the parade downtown was a kaleidoscope of dancing girls and marching bands. Sitting high on Father's shoulders while Mother held my new year-old sister in her arms, I waved at the swirling skirts and stiff black suits as they performed the traditional *volkspele* (Afrikaans dance) down the main street of Bloemfontein. Orange, blue, and white balloons lingered long after the white doves and army jets flew into the blue beyond. I wanted to stay longer to savor the festivities and try to coax another ice cream out of Father, but my baby sister made it known that she was extremely bored with the whole spectacle so we all climbed back into the car and drove home.

That would not be the first time I would be upstaged by the vociferous and extremely sharp Jennylind Margaret Louis, who just happened to be the spitting image of Mother in more ways than one.

CHAPTER FOUR

1961: *Mandela creates a branch of the ANC that will employ more revolutionary reactions against the government's growing apartheid policies. It is named Umkhonto we Sizwe (Spear of the Nation) but is simply known as MK. The organization adopts guerilla warfare tactics and allows revolutionary whites to join. Mandela sends letters to newspapers threatening that "a country wide campaign of non-co-operation will be launched if the state fails to hold a national constitutional convention." Many whites view this as a declaration of war, others feel the government should cooperate or risk anarchy. There is no middle ground. Homemade bombs explode at government offices and power stations in Johannesburg, Durban, and Port Elizabeth. The government and ordinary white South Africans are shocked, and the hunt for Mandela and members of MK goes into overdrive. Mandela is dubbed "the Black Pimpernel" for eluding the law. Mandela escapes to Great Britain where he receives support and funding. He then travels to Addis Ababa in Africa for military training. After eight weeks, he receives a telegram from the ANC in South Africa asking him to return and resume a leadership role within the organization. Three days after Mandela sneaks back into the country, police receive a tip and arrest him in his car outside Durban. The newspaper headline screams with relief: "Police Swoop Ends Two Years On The Run."*

J enny stole the show in every way, from personality (there was no arguing with her, she always won), weight (she was enviably thin), energy (she had more than a lightning bolt), to chutzpah (it had no bounds). And to top it all, she looked like Mother. A mini-Mother who usurped my crown with ease.

But let's go back to a time when the crown was still firmly on my head.

The kitchen was a flurry of activity with uniformed maids scurrying to and fro carrying cast iron pots and bone china platters.

Spicy aromas curled through the air like Van Gogh's twisted swirls. Cuddles, our white cat, clawed furiously at the door of the fridge.

Evelyn waved her wooden spoon in the air issuing orders in Sotho and English - diva chef in the making. "I need a bigger pan! Where is my soup spoon? *Pakisa! Pakisa*! [Hurry up! Hurry up!]. The madam will be back from the shops any minute now. *Shoh!*"

No one noticed I had crawled under the kitchen table to sit on the floor right beside Evelyn. *"Ah ba*, Evie! *Ah ba*!" I wailed, *"Ah ba, Ah ba!"*

"*Thula, thula* [Shh, shh], Pulani!" she cooed as she scooped me up onto her back and tied me securely with the blanket that she unwrapped from her waist. With me now fastened safely in my "pouch," she handed me a juice bottle and continued where she left off, wooden spoon now moving vigorously in the lamb stew. Other maids passed by, pinching me softly on the cheeks.

I knew no greater heaven than when Evelyn sang old Sotho and Xhosa ballads from centuries gone by. *"Thula, thula, thula, thula, baba..."* A quiet calm blanketed the kitchen.

I was paraded around from arm to arm, dressed in the finest hand-stitched or knitted outfits known to Bloemfontein. Evelyn and her merry troupe would dress me up in the finery of a Sotho girl with colourful beads from head to toe. But a Sotho girl had to have more than just beads, so one of the maids fastened a nappy (a diaper) on my head to resemble a *doek*.

"*Ai, Ai, Ai!*" they laughed and clapped in unison. Evelyn grabbed another nappy and tied my own "baby" on my back using one of my dolls. More clapping and dancing.

I did not have a nursemaid for quite some time, partly because Evelyn did not think anyone would be good enough for her Pulani, and partly because Evelyn wanted me all to herself. After many interviews with Mother and Evelyn, Sara was finally given the job. A tall thin sixteen-year-old Sotho farm girl, Sara had the gentle, soft-spoken, and reserved nature Mother was so desperately looking for.

As for my obesity, I place the blame squarely on the shoulders of the women of the Jewish/Lebanese/French/Sotho household who constantly reminded us that if we didn't eat the healthy food put in front of us, we would be sickly. Moderation was not an operative word when it came to cooking or eating.

Most parents become silly when trying to cajole their child to eat. But for Mother, an Oscar should have been awarded for the performance she choreographed with the talented Sotho song and dance troupe.

The fat contented star sat in her scrupulously scrubbed high chair. Beside her was the supporting actress, played by Mother, who was inspecting the finely hand-sifted preboiled mixture of unsalted lamb chop, carrot, and potato. To the left and right of the star were four actresses, played brilliantly by Evelyn, Sara, and two cleaning staff.

Evelyn started off with the first note, followed by Sara who clapped her hands and added the second note. The two cleaning staff began to sway their hips and tap their toes. The show had begun!

The star, taken in by the performance, turned her head from side to side, mouth wide open in amazement. That was Mother's cue to shove the first spoonful of mashed food into the star's mouth. Tumultuous praise and clapping from the other supporting actresses. This was repeated over and over again until the plate was empty. The fat cells in the star's body desperately tried to warn the brain that they were bursting at the seams but the fat cells finally just gave up and multiplied into more fat cells. Let's give everyone a round of applause!

"*Tlo, Pulani* [Come, Pulani]," called Sara as I waddled toward where she was sitting under the shade of the oak tree at the bottom of the garden. Spread out on a Merino wool blanket was an enormous assortment of toys and stuffed animals. Sitting next to Sara was my younger cousin Michael's nursemaid, Veronica. She was crocheting and watching Michael at the same time. He had an immense fascination with throwing our juice bottles into the rosebushes.

A few feet away, Mother sat under the shade of the umbrella with her sister-in-law Babs, a former beauty queen. Both were heavily pregnant.

"You know, Babs, sometimes it is so difficult to understand what they are saying. So Father Patrick has offered to teach me some Sotho."

"Are you serious, Shirley? You are going to learn Sotho?"

"Of course! How can one earn their respect if one doesn't make an effort to learn their language? By the way, did you hear that Princess Margaret is actually going to marry Lord Snowden next year? He is just a fashion photographer but so good looking. I wonder what the Queen thinks of her marrying a commoner?"

Any self-respecting citizen of the Colony was consumed with interest in the British royal family. For Mother it was more than that. Gussie and Oupa had been personally invited to a tea party at the governor's mansion to meet Princess Margaret and Princess Elizabeth when they visited South Africa in 1952.

"Stephen," called Mother to the old gardener carrying tulip bulbs down the driveway. "I bought your tobacco this morning. It should be with Evelyn in the kitchen."

"*Kea laboha* [thank you], Madam," said Steven, smiling, while tipping his hat and nodding his head. His black face wrinkled with joy like a wizened prophet. Tobacco and pipe were all he needed to take in the African sunset while sitting under the huge old walnut tree.

"You know," Mother commented, turning back to Babs, "he is the nicest person I have ever met. Always courteous and kind and even takes Ruchel for rides in the wheelbarrow."

"Is he not the husband of your laundry maid?" asked Babs, who was now seeing if she could prevent her son from throwing any more juice bottles into the rosebushes.

"Yes, he lives with Miriam in one of the rooms at the back, and let me tell you, she can wash and iron like you have never experienced. Never burns a thing! They are both like gold to me."

Let's pause the home movie.

Jennylind Margaret Louis announced her arrival the day before Christmas, lest anyone forgot then or forevermore. Mother, Father, Gussie, and Monica (her nursemaid) wheeled her pram morning, noon, and night. Tiny, with dark brown hair and brown eyes, Jenny was vocal from day one. The spotlight immediately shifted onto her and stayed there, shining brightly, even after my brother Wayne was born two years later.

That someone so tiny had invaded my kingdom was an absolute shock to my system. To the outside world, Mother and Father included, I was still a princess of the Louis kingdom but to my inside world, I was now second best. I never really blamed my sister, but from then on I constantly second-guessed myself. She received such praise that it made me blame myself for being inadequate, because really, if you think about it, how else could someone so tiny usurp your position on the throne?

The disparity was made even clearer when Wayne was born because he just faded into the background, content to laugh and play with his friends. Wayne resembled a miniature Father but with red-blond hair, lots of freckles, and a consistently happy-go-lucky disposition. Before he could even walk properly he was rallying the garden staff, old Stephen included, into a round of soccer. Rosie, his nursemaid, was the most active of the nursemaids as she was constantly running and picking up the clothes he dropped everywhere.

Mother used to say I was a serious little girl, always deep in thought. I think I was deep in thought because I was constantly trying to figure out how to get the spotlight back on me, but to little avail.

Take, for example, the private pottery lessons we went to at Mrs. Rhodes-Harrison's studio in the backyard of her house. At five and a half years old, I spent a painstaking two hours decorating a flat round clay ashtray with tiny perfect clay balls while my sister haphazardly threw something together in half an hour and won first prize at the local show. At the private art lessons we had at the Varney-Cantrell School of Free Expression, my sister's art, even at age three, lived up to the school's name while mine resembled a study in concentrated composition. At four years, Jenny and a friend lit a match under the friend's mother's bed to see what would happen. The bed naturally started to burn. Mother was appropriately horrified when she learned of the incident but then just shook her head in "you can't say no to her" amusement.

With Jenny around, I never knew for sure whether the spotlight was actually slanted toward me at times or whether I was hallucinating. The constant uncertainty set me up for a rapidly developing neurosis.

CHAPTER FIVE

1964: *The highly publicized Rivonia Trial begins shortly after Mandela's arrest outside Durban. The charges against Mandela and other leading ANC members (of all races) include armed incursions, guerilla warfare, and more than 200 acts of sabotage. The accused enter the court. The spectator's gallery is standing room only as local and foreign press jockey for position. Before sentencing, Alan Paton, author of* Cry the Beloved Country *and national president of the Liberal Party, pleads that the defendants should receive clemency, "otherwise the future of South Africa will be bleak." Judge de Wet, a white Afrikaner, rises slowly from his bench as a hushed silence sweeps the courthouse. He reads from a prepared statement: "I have decided not to impose the supreme penalty, which in a case like this would usually be the proper penalty for the crime. But consistent with my duty this is the only leniency which I can show. The sentence in the case of all the accused will be one of life imprisonment." The judge takes the middle road, not bowing to his government on the one side or to the furious protests from foreign embassies and international leaders on the other side. Mandela speaks from the dock: "…I have fought against white domination, and I have fought against black domination. I have cherished the ideal of a democratic and free society in which all persons live together in harmony and with equal opportunities. It is an ideal which I hope to live for and to achieve. But if needs be, it is an ideal for which I am prepared to die." Mandela raises his hand in a thumbs-up ANC salute and smiles before he and his co-accused are transported to Robben Island, a prison off the coast of Cape Town.*

E arly dawn, the two cleaning maids were helping old Stephen and the rest of the garden staff set up long tables outside on the front lawn. Frost from the evening's chill clung stubbornly to the blades of grass under the oak tree long after the tentacles of the sun pierced its mighty branches. Cuddles, perched regally on the roof of Mother's green Ford Capri Sport, paused in her routine morning cleansing to observe the frenzied activity. She let out a faint mew before dropping her head again to lick her front paw.

"Stephen!" Mother called out from the second bedroom window. "I need you to help me with the balloons. Please bring the pump in the storeroom to the library."

"Yes, Madam," replied Stephen as he pulled his woolen army coat tighter around his body to ward off the fresh winter chill.

Just then Gussie pulled up the driveway tooting the horn for one of the cleaning maids to help her with the Red Riding Hood birthday cake she had just collected from the cake lady.

Gussie found Mother in the sunroom finishing off the last of what looked like hundreds of little straw baskets filled with cookies and party favours. "Do you have enough savories and sandwiches for the adults, Shirley?"

"I have 70 children, 30 mothers, and 30 nannies coming and right now I have not even thought of any of the husbands who might attend," Mother said as she tied yet another red ribbon on the top of one basket. "Sara, go with the old madam to the kitchen, wake Ruchel and see that she puts on the red and white dress that the master brought back from Johannesburg. Monica and Rosie," Mother addressed the other two nursemaids, "carry these baskets out to the tables outside, put the tea nets over them, and then get Jenny and Wayne dressed."

Gussie found Father in the kitchen. Both began to assess the amount of food while Evelyn continued icing cupcakes faster than an assembly line.

"Are you sure we have enough food here, mom?" Under no circumstance did the Louis household run out of food. God forbid. The supply must always exceed the demand by at least threefold. What was not used would be distributed later to the family and friends of the staff who resided in the townships.

"George?" Mother poked her head into the kitchen. "Have you set up the movie in the lounge? Evelyn?"

Evelyn paused, holding her icing knife in midair. "When Madam June drops off the roses," Mother continued, "cut the stems an inch before you put them in the vases and make sure the tablecloths are starched and ironed and that the silver is polished properly."

"Yes Madam." Only then did Evelyn refocus on the icing.

Parties were Mother's forte, and none ranked higher than birthday parties on her agenda. My sixth birthday party, like all those that preceded it, was a mammoth production. The festivities always lasted long into the night.

The crowd arrived. I had a rare moment of unbridled joy as I accepted gift after colourful gift. Michelle, my new best friend from school, arrived with her mother but no nanny. "Come, let me show you my cake," I whispered into her ear while dragging her to the long table where the cake sat proudly at the head. "Here, taste the red icing," I continued whispering as we both swiped our fingers across the bottom of Red Riding Hood's skirt and quickly licked them before anyone could catch us. "Mommy says she will have a dress made like this cake for the doll when all the cake is eaten."

Nannies organized their small charges in front of plates of food as adults talked animatedly at tables under umbrellas a few feet away. The show began. Candles were blown out. "Happy Birthday" resonated around the hill and all the children smeared frosting on some part of themselves. Nannies sprang into action wiping down hands, faces, and clothing with wet cloths before everyone was shepherded into the lounge to watch a movie Father was showing with his 16-mm projector. Bottles, cups, and napkins scattered over the freshly manicured lawn were hurriedly retrieved by the garden staff.

But my sixth birthday party became different from all my other birthday parties.

The adults continued to sip Earl Grey from bone china teacups while Mother flitted from one scene to another making sure everyone was having a good time. "Do you want another cup of tea, Dad?" Mother asked Oupa. She noticed how tired he looked, sitting under the shade of the umbrella.

"No, dear," Oupa said, "I just want to sit and take in the joy of my favorite granddaughter. Look how she runs around laughing with her friends. She has the same determination as your mother. See, she likes to gather all the children around her. She is always smiling. I am thinking of purchasing a hotel in Durban and putting it in her name so that she never has to worry about anything when she is older." He added wistfully, "I won't be around that much longer."

"That is very generous of you, Dad," replied Mother, "but I don't want you to think of things like that. This is a day you should have happy thoughts. Let me get Evelyn to get you a nice cup of tea and some birthday cake. Cedric is arriving from America tonight so you will have both your children with you. Tomorrow we will have a lovely lunch here with just the family. Evelyn will help me bake your favorite cheesecake." Mother called out to Evelyn to bring the old master some tea and cake.

Mother's brother Cedric had married an American girl two years earlier. He vehemently disagreed with the government's apartheid laws and chose to live in America instead.

The day had been planned meticulously, with party guests leaving at sunset, children put to bed, and a celebratory dinner planned for Oupa and Gussie at their house. But just like a movie script changed at the whim of the director, that evening the celebration turned to mourning when my grandfather collapsed in the kitchen and died an hour before my uncle's plane landed on the tarmac.

They said Oupa had a stroke and that he died before he fell, but that was little comfort. Nothing sad had ever confronted us before. It was the first time Mother stayed in her bedroom with the doors closed for hours on end. We could not even run to Gussie for comfort. It was as if someone had thrown a dark blanket over our house, shutting out all the bright happy light.

The home movie fades to black. Black everywhere. Even Evelyn and the staff wore black.

In the days that followed, I did not want to be left alone for even a second. I wandered over to Sara's room one afternoon, even though Mother, who was still behind closed bedroom doors, told me not to bother Sara during her off time.

"What are you doing, Sara?" I found her sitting on a chair sewing colourful thread into a white cloth. Her room was immaculate, with everything folded neatly on a very high bed. On the small bedside table there was a Bible, one of Mother's old dishes filled with candy, and an alarm clock. On the wall hung a poster of the Drakensburg mountains in Natal with their snow-covered peaks. A basket next to Sara was filled with colourful fabric and threads.

"I am making a bedspread for the bed, Pulani." She smiled as she watched me attempt to climb onto the bed.

"Why is your bed so high?" I asked. Not waiting for an answer I looked under the bed to figure it out. "Look, you have bricks under the legs of your bed. Why do you have bricks under your bed?"

"That's so that the *thokolosi* does not take me away when I sleep," replied Sara as she continued threading red and yellow in and out of the white cotton cloth.

"What's a *thokolosi*?" I was suddenly worried.

"A *thokolosi* is a little man who comes at night to try and steal you. He is very small so he cannot reach you if your bed is high," replied Sara.

What?

A small man comes to steal you at night?

Okay, that demanded an explanation from Mother as to why our beds were not on bricks. What would stop a *thokolosi* from grabbing me in my bed? I ran back into the house.

"There is no such thing as a *thokolosi*, Ruchel!" Mother answered exasperatedly, wiping a tear from her eye. "It is just a silly belief in their culture and I don't want you going into Sara's room disturbing her, do you hear me!"

But I would not let it go. If Sara said there was a *thokolosi*, who was I not to believe it?

Night took on a new, ominous meaning.

A few days later, I heard Mother calling outside, "Sara, Sara, where are you? It's late. The children have to get up for school!"

I crawled out of bed and shuffled to the bathroom window that overlooked the staff quarters, rubbing my eyes to see what the commotion was about.

"Is Sara not in her room?" I heard Mother asking.

"No, Madam," replied Monica, "she is not in her room."

"Oh, no!" I screamed as I rushed downstairs, through the kitchen, and out to the back of the house. "The *thokolosi* took Sara!" I cried. I ran to her room and found it empty. "I told you the *thokolosi* comes at night, and look, Sara is gone! She must have been sitting on her chair when the *thokolosi* came!!" I was now hysterical.

"Calm down immediately, Ruchel!" Mother ordered. "There is no such a thing as a *thokolosi*. I have told you that a thousand times! She most probably forgot her pass book and is now in jail. Monica, help Ruchel get ready for school. I am going down to the police station. You know, this government makes me sick!"

"I am coming with!" I demanded, not believing for one moment that Sara was in jail and that maybe I could persuade the policeman to help me find Sara and put the horrible *thokolosi* in jail.

"No, you are to dress for school!" replied Mother.

"I am coming with you!" I cried as I folded my arms defiantly across my chest.

"Well," Mother sighed, "go and put your gown and slippers on and meet me in the car. Hurry up!"

The police station was a one-story brick building several blocks down the road.

"Where is my maid Sara?" Mother demanded of the two policemen, who looked at her with indifference. "If you do not let her out immediately I am going to phone your superior! I am sick and tired of all this nonsense. You waste your time picking up innocent people when you could be spending the time catching the millions of thieves roaming the streets. Do you think we don't know what is going on here?"

"*Gaan haal die bliksemse meid, Jonas. Sy is in sel vyf!* [Go fetch the goddam maid, Jonas. She is in cell five!]" said the thick-set Afrikaans policeman in brown uniform, black boots, and brown cap to the black policeman dressed in the same uniform. "You know, Mrs. Louis," he continued in his heavily accented English, wagging his finger at her, "you should teach your maids to carry their pass books. Otherwise they will not be allowed to walk in the streets after nine o'clock at night. That is the law!"

"A most ridiculous law!" shouted Mother. "And don't you dare wag your finger at me. You should blame your lovely government for all the trouble we are having!" Mother stormed back to the car leaving me to hastily follow her while clutching tearful Sara's hand.

"Don't worry, Sara." I comforted her in the car. "I told the policeman that he must find the horrible *thokolosi* and put him in jail!"

Two weeks later, at Mother's insistence, Gussie sold her house and moved onto the third floor of our house. I was ecstatic. Now I would have my favorite grandmother near me. She would praise the most insignificant achievement of mine, even when my sister climbed yet another rung higher in Mother's estimation. Gussie was to become my strongest ally.

CHAPTER SIX

1966: South African Prime Minister Hendrik Verwoerd is brutally assassinated in Parliament in South Africa. The assassin, disguised as a uniformed parliamentary messenger, stabs Verwoerd four times in the chest with a dagger as his wife Betsie looks on in horror. The prime minister is rushed to hospital where he is certified dead on arrival. The police immediately arrest the assassin, who they later identify as Dimitri-Tsafendas, an illegitimate son of a Greek father and a Mozambique mother. Further investigations reveal that Dimitri-Tsafendas was shunned by the white community because of his darker skin tone. He is declared mentally unfit to stand trial.

Father Patrick dipped his fork into a slice of Evelyn's cherry pie, savoring the tartness of the cherries. After being at the Xhosa missionary for the past four years, it truly was a delicacy.

"Your Sotho lessons have been invaluable, I have sent you constant prayers of thanks," said Mother, as she sipped her tea.

"Prayers of any kind are much needed in Transkei, particularly at the missionary school. I was only too pleased to be able to help you before I left. So how are the children?"

"They are fine, thank you. The other day Jenny beat the entire swim team by half the length of the pool. There is nothing stopping that child."

"What about Ruchel? How is she doing at school?"

"What can I say," Mother sighed. "She is such a kindhearted child but she needs to lose some weight. It's a constant battle. My mother lets her eat whatever she wants. She does well at school but I don't think she stretches herself to any limit. Unlike Jenny who always takes the bull by the horns. Both George and my mother have protected and fussed over Ruchel ever since the drowning accident."

"Drowning accident?" asked Father Patrick with eyebrows raised.

"Yes, terrible," replied Mother quietly. "She was just two and a half years, a short while after you left town. She was in the pool with quite a few other children, somehow she slipped out of her tube and sank to the bottom. Thank God a boy saw her disappear under the water. A little Afrikaans boy, Johannes, his uncle is the Minister of Transport, you know. Anyway, he's shouting, and dragging Ruchel to the side of the pool. She was not breathing, just floating in his arms. You can't imagine my state of shock!"

"Is Ruchel okay?" Father Patrick was clearly concerned.

"I turned her over, forced the water out, thank God she suddenly started to cry while water was pouring out her mouth. After a trip to the hospital she was declared fine. George, of course, was horrified and ordered the maids and myself to not let her out of our sight for one minute after that incident. So as you can imagine, no matter what I say, George and my mother always let her do and eat whatever she wants."

At eight years old I did not know that all I had to do to lose weight was eat less and exercise more. Instead I continued to eat the extra slices of pie as my fragile self-esteem diminished and my neurosis grew like furry mold in some dark dank corner of my brain.

The furry mold underwent a major growth spurt when I had to perform the Mermaid Monologue in front of judges from England for the annual festival of performing arts, the Eisteddfod.

Mother had enrolled Jenny and me in private speech and drama lessons with Mrs. Fox, a pencil-thin elderly English lady whose disapproval of most everything was legendary. Mother was one of her first pupils.

Mrs. Fox turned her attention to me. "Ruchel!" I can still hear her booming over the backstage chaos, "Remember to sit up straight, open your mouth wide to project your vowels, it is AAAAAH not AAAAAY."

I could not think about projecting vowels because I was too worried about how I looked. I was perched on top of a paper mache rock, wearing a mermaid suit that made me look half-naked.

I recited the first line while looking in a handheld mirror, and brushed my hair with my other hand. As I was about to start the fourth line, I surreptitiously angled the mirror to see if any fat rolls were bulging over the top of the mermaid's tail.

That is when I saw my nipples protruding under the flesh-coloured body stocking.

"Aaaaagh!" I blurted out in horror.

The judges from England looked up from their papers, Mrs. Fox looked horrified. Mother, sitting in the front row, flicked her hand at me to continue.

"Oh God, please just give me the strength to finish this monologue," I prayed as I picked up the brush and mirror.

The furry clump of mold in my brain expanded greatly that day and for many nightmarish nights after, as I continued to press the rewind button of that fateful day over and over again.

And my angst did not end there.

Part of the Louis philosophy was that all children were required to enroll in every artistic and cultural activity known to man. Nothing would be overlooked, so Jenny and I were signed up for ballet, tap, and Spanish lessons.

I hated ballet with a passion. Mother basked in the constant praise my sister received as she pirouetted her way to Honors with Distinction.

Tap was different. I could achieve some sort of perfection with tap because it was a movement and style that could be danced with carefree abandon no matter how fat or balletically useless I was.

Tap let me join Evelyn and the maids in the backyard to clap, laugh, and sing as we danced to the African music blaring from the Sotho radio station. Tap chased the demons away for a few brief moments whenever I shuffled and ballparked on the driveway. Tap threaded its magical notes through my limbs and veins in a musical rhythm that freed my soul and smudged the furry mold as I danced lightly across the African landscape.

CHAPTER SEVEN

1966: The Government, under the 1950s Group Area Act, which confines each race group to its own residential and trading group, targets a suburb near downtown Cape Town. The suburb, known as District Six, is home to sixty thousand coloured people. The Government declares the area a crime-ridden and unsanitary slum and uses the Act to move the bulldozers in. The residents of District Six are forced to move to an area set aside for them outside Cape Town called the Cape Flats. The result is a community destroyed.

Joan placed her bone china teacup neatly on its saucer, "I can't begin to tell you what a state of panic we were all in. My husband took a while to recover from the shock."

"I nearly died." Mother turned to see her friend's Mercedes coming up the driveway.

"I am so mad with this bloody government!" Cyril was redfaced from heat and frustration.

"Hello, Cyril." Mother smiled sweetly. "Evelyn will bring us a fresh pot of tea."

"I just heard Eartha Kitt cannot perform in South Africa because our bloody Group Areas Act won't allow her to stay in any of our five-star hotels! Where in heavens name did they think she should stay? In the township with no electricity?"

"Eartha Kitt," sighed Joan, "my husband has all her records."

"Well, she won't be coming here," Cyril shot back. "Shirley tells me that your family's jewelry is now safely back under lock and key. So how is your husband, Joan?"

"Relieved, what an ordeal!" replied Joan.

"I was ready to kill George," said Mother. "I had told him a thousand times, 'be very careful when you deliver Joan's suitcase, her family's heirloom jewels are in it!' But no, he let Simon pack it on top of the car. He only realized it was gone when he got all the way to Johannesburg!"

"Amazing, a Good Samaritan saw it fall onto the road," continued Joan, "There are still honest and decent people, even in this world."

"I was so furious, you have no idea," said Mother. "When George phoned to tell me, I ranted and raved for close to an hour."

"All I heard was this deathly silence on the other end" continued Mother. "Eventually I became worried that something had happened to George so I said, 'George are you listening to me!'"

Cyril laughed, "He most probably was having a heart attack."

"I was the one having a heart attack! All I hear at the other end of the phone is this strange deep voice...'it is me, Simon, Madam, *Baas* says I must hold the phone until madam is finished shouting.'"

* * *

The school my sister and I attended was a private Anglican all-girl's school, St Michael's. It was a typical colonial school with old ivy-covered stone buildings, red tiled roofs, and a small chapel set among tall acacia trees.

Although we were technically in the middle of the African bush, that did not deter the imported Scottish nuns and teachers from thinking they were still in the middle of the Scottish highlands. Even our uniform looked like the Scottish highlands—a thick navy blue pinafore with white long-sleeved cotton blouse, striped St. Michael's tie, and navy blue sash tied around the waist. Blazers with a St. Michaels' badge sewn on the breast pocket were required at all formal events. Fine for the winter, but summers were a sweaty hell. If you tried to roll up your sleeves you were instantly slapped on the arm with a ruler, so the sweat naturally won out. By the eighth grade the short-sleeved dress with optional cardigan and blazer won hands down for the entire year.

While I was traveling through the halls of early childhood education, Mother was busy kicking up a storm on the social calendar with her much sought after soirees. Expensive European cars were always lining the brick driveway as champagne laughter echoed around the mountain.

"There's your mom," I whispered to my best friend Michelle as we sat on the stairs one night peeking between the balustrades and through the glass doors to the formal lounge. Liz, our other friend who was actually a Hungarian countess by birth, sat on the step above us. She was a year older than Michelle and me and had long blond hair and a svelte figure like Michelle.

"Look!" Liz bent down to whisper in our ears, "my dad is showing both your moms the diamond he got from the Basotho chief high up in the Lesotho mountains. Let's move closer so we can hear."

Liz's father, in his element with an audience of women surrounding him, spoke with a sophisticated European accent.

"When it came to paying for this diamond, this Basotho chief refused to take any notes or checks. Can you imagine? So my partner and I had to figure out how to get this huge sum of money in coins of fifty cents to his hut on this huge mountain peak."

Juliet bent in closer. "That would translate into a mountain of coins!"

"Correct. The bank manager thought we were joking when we asked him to put them into burlap sacks, eight to be precise."

"Burlap sacks?" asked Michelle's mother, Peggy. "Why didn't you just put it all into a steel chest with a lock?"

"This Basotho chief lives like a prophet on top of this mountain. The only way to get there is by donkey, so we had to strap the sacks on both sides of four donkeys."

"How come no one attacked you with *assegais* [spears] to steal all your money?"

"Oh, Peggy"—Mother giggled—"these natives may be uncivilized but they are not primitive. I am sure they were equally horrified at seeing these donkeys with two white men in the middle of their territory."

"I want to hear the story," interrupted Juliet.

"Here we were, my partner and I and two of my staff on donkeys, trying to negotiate the rocky terrain, antelope weaving in and out of our path, when we came upon a stream running down from the top. We got off the donkeys to allow them to drink and one of the beasts decided to gallop down the mountain with the money still strapped to its back."

"No!" Juliet exclaimed. Mother and Peggy laughed.

"We had no alternative but to get back on the three remaining donkeys and proceed up the mountain to the waiting Basotho chief. One thing you do not want to do with these people is to go back on your word and not arrive at the appointed time. As we approached the huts at the top of the mountain we heard this huge commotion of shouting, whistling, and drum beating across the valley. My partner and I thought that without a doubt we were now going to be attacked, slaughtered, and thrown off the mountain cliff in bits and pieces. We did not know what to think so we just kept going."

"Were you brave or just plain crazy?" Juliet said.

"The Basotho chief, he was huge, looked even taller with his cone shaped straw hat perched on top of his head. Had a huge woven blanket wrapped around his body. He emerges from this smoke-filled hut with four or five children running around his feet. His wife in her long brightly coloured robe and headdress, stands at the entrance of the mud hut holding a big black bowl of porridge. They motion for us to sit down on rocks placed in a ring in front of the hut. Bowls of this porridge were thrust into our hands—no spoon, mind you—and she gestures to us to eat."

"Can you imagine!" Peggy interjected.

"I don't normally eat with my hands," he continued, "but there was no way you could insult their hospitality. When we finished, we were ordered to help count the money, and as you can imagine, I am shaking as I have no idea how to explain to the chief that one of the donkeys had suddenly decided to retreat down the mountain, leaving us short."

"So what did you do?" asked Juliet.

"It was extraordinary. Here we were putting fifty-cent coins into piles so the money was accurately counted, but before we reached the end, the errant donkey with the burlap sacks on its back was led up the mountain by two young natives. They found him grazing at the bottom of the mountain, and all that whistling and shouting I told you about before was their signal to the tribe about discovering the donkey."

"Amazing that these natives did not steal the money and the donkey," interrupted Father.

"No, it is not amazing, George, because these people in the mountains have a huge respect for their chief. They are a very honorable and old-fashioned tribe. Their traditions are deeply rooted, it's considered a huge crime to steal from the tribe. I have heard stories of how they throw thieves off the mountain top into the valley below," he concluded. The ladies could barely contain themselves.

"Can you imagine if you came up fifty cents short?"

"You would have been thrown off the mountain yourself!"

"So what did this Basotho chief do with all his money?"

"Oh, that was interesting," he continued. "The Basotho chief took a plane to England to see the Queen. Never been in a plane before, mind you, so you can imagine. The wife, she of course persuaded her husband to give her some of the money. So she decided to buy a number of huts on the mountain slopes and she rented them out. Now who do you say was the smarter one at the end of the day?"

"See," I whispered to Michelle and Liz as we crawled back upstairs. "Women are smarter. Even Gussie says so. Liz, remember the story your dad told us about those people years ago in Kimberley digging in the ground and finding all those diamonds? Millions and millions of diamonds. Imagine what fun that would be."

"Oh, Ruchel," said Michelle, giggling. "First of all you have no idea what the right side of a shovel is, never mind how to dig for diamonds. You don't know how to run your own bath water, pack your own clothes away, or even make your own bed. How on earth would you know how to dig a hole?"

"Just wait and see!" I said. "Gussie says I can be whatever I want to be if I just put my mind to it."

CHAPTER EIGHT

1967: The first human heart transplant in the world takes place in Cape Town at the Groote Schuur Hospital. The pioneer making this medical history is a South African Afrikaner, Dr Christiaan Barnard. He and his team implant the heart of a twenty-five-year-old female accident victim into a middle-aged man. The operation is a success and the man lives for 18 days before succumbing to pneumonia.

G ussie was my safe harbor when the balance of my fragile ego threatened to rock off kilter. It was Gussie who never stopped telling me that she loved me and would always be there for me. Having her live in the same house was heaven.

We spent afternoons together in her lounge with its heavy velvet drapes and her Chanel No. 5 wafting through the air. African landscapes painted by Uncle Cedric hung between family photos on the walls. There was always a plate of homemade apricot cookies on the table. It was Gussie who helped me with my homework, especially Afrikaans, which was a required second language at school. She showed me pictures of Mother when Mother was small, listened patiently if something bothered me, sewed my teddy bear together, and read me stories of princes and princesses in faraway lands.

But the story I loved to hear again and again was how Oupa came over the ocean with two bags of gold so long, long ago.

* * *

1910: The South African Act, passed by the British House of Commons a year earlier, makes way for the four South African colonies to unite and form the Union of South Africa. Under this new Act, the Transvaal, Cape, Natal, and Orange Free State colonies will now be governed under

a "Westminster" system that allows for an all-white central parliament
consisting of a senate and house of assembly. Both English and Dutch
are to be recognized as the country's official languages and a governor
general will represent the Crown. Protesting this new Act are the blacks,
who immediately send an eight-man delegation to London. Their appeal
fails. The Nationalist Party with General Botha as its leader wins the
Union's first election.

"Please, take my sons, I beg of you, please! They are going to kill them! I have a bag of gold for you, please!" cried Rose Garzouzie as she stood on the Beirut dockside watching the sailors carrying crates up the gangplank on their shoulders. By her side were her four children, two boys aged twelve and ten and two girls aged six and seven, all clinging to their mother's skirt. The boys were dressed in neat striped shirts and short pants, as if they were going off to a birthday party.

"My eldest daughter, Lisa, is in South Africa. Look, I have her address, you just need to deliver the boys to her. They will die here. Please, I beg you!" she continued, tears streaming down her cheeks. It was 1910 and the Lebanese wars were in full swing. It was a time when boys from the age of twelve were forced by the police at gunpoint to join the armed forces. Such boys rarely made it back home, and when Rose heard the police coming through the gates early one morning she grabbed her children and ran through the back door and headed for the docks. She was frantic and kept looking anxiously over her shoulder as she pleaded with the sailors. Gunshots could be heard in the distance.

"We're going to America, Ma'am, not South Africa," replied one muscular young sailor as he paused at the top of the gangplank and looked at the smartly dressed woman with her children. This was a rare sight on the dockside; most of the women he encountered were ones who demanded money.

"Please, what's your name, sailor?" cried Rose. The sailor paused, not believing what he heard. Nobody had ever bothered to ask his name before.

"My name?" he said, lowering the crate to the floor. "My name, Ma'am, is Stanos," he said proudly, curious about the elegant woman in her long blue skirt and freshly starched white blouse, her face stained with tears. The children clinging to her were wide eyed with fear as he stepped closer.

"Stanos, sir, please, I have two bags of gold here. One is for the two boys and one is for you if you promise to take them to this address of my daughter who lives in South Africa. You need never have to work again. Please just take my two boys with you and get them to South Africa. I see you are a kind and gentle man, please, I beg you with all my heart," continued Rose, choking back the sobs in huge gulps.

The sailor stood back, confused, his mind spinning. "Stanos," "sir," and "bag of gold"—these words had never been addressed to him in his life. After his mother died when he was five, his drunken father forced him to go begging for food. They slept under bridges or behind trash bins. It was "boy" then and "sailor" later when he ran away from the beatings of his father to work on the ships, but never, never his name, let alone "sir."

"Hey sailor!" shouted the captain from the bow, "who do you think you are, standing there like that? Get your ass up the gangplank now, help pull in the ropes! The soldiers are coming and we need to leave immediately! Hurry up, you lazy good for nothing son of a bitch!"

Anger flickered across the sailor's face as he watched the captain turn his back and shout orders on the other side of the ship. "I will take them, Ma'am, but I have to leave now," whispered the sailor as he looked from side to side to see if anyone had witnessed the exchange.

"Thank you for your kind heart, sir, may God be with you always," Rose cried as she peeled the two boys off her and knelt down, wrapping her arms tightly around them. "Remember who you are, Tanous," she whispered into the ear of the elder boy, who was now shaking as he desperately clutched his mother's arm. "Remember your heritage and look after your younger brother, John. Promise me this, my son."

"Mama, I don't want to go with this man, please do not make me do this. I want to stay with you!" Tanous begged, holding her tight. She kissed their tear-stained cheeks and hugged them for the last time.

"Be brave, my son," said Rose, her heart shattering into sad fragments. "Go with this kind man. He has promised that he will take you to your sister, she will take care of you until it is safe to return here. The bad men who killed your father are looking for you and your brother. It is better that you stay safe with Lisa. Go on now, my darlings."

She untangled herself from their clutches, wiped her face, and handed the two bags of gold on the floor beside her to the sailor, along with an envelope. She pushed the two boys toward the sailor.

"Please be gentle with them, sir, and deliver them safely to the address in the envelope, I beg you. May God be with you all," she sobbed. Her two daughters were hysterical, wondering why their brothers were being swept up by this huge horrible ogre with the gruff voice. The sailor ran up the gangplank with one boy under each arm and the two bags of gold coins clutched in his hand. "Pull the gangplank up!" he shouted to one of his mates as he ducked behind the crates on deck to avoid the captain.

Rebel soldiers ran through the streets and onto the harbor front, shouting and shooting into the air as the ship eased from the dock. "There's his wife! Where are the sons?" Tanous heard them shout as he struggled to escape the sailor's grip, tears streaming down his cheeks. He heard shots ring through the air and managed to crane his head over the crate, only to see his mother fall to the ground.

"They've hurt my mother, they have shot her!" he screamed hysterically as he kicked and pounded the chest of his captor. The sailor, shocked to see the beautiful kind woman fall, dragged his two sobbing and kicking charges below deck.

"Here, stay in this cabin and don't make another sound, do you hear me!" he threatened as he unceremoniously dumped the boys on the floor. "If the captain finds you here, you will both be thrown overboard! I will bring you something to eat later, just don't make one sound!" With that he slammed the door shut.

Tanous hugged his brother, who was now crying uncontrollably. "Shhhh, John. Mama said we have to be brave and remember who we are. We are going to see Lisa soon, don't worry." A steady resolve already had begun to envelope his heart.

"They will make Mama better, won't they, Tanous?" pleaded John between sobs.

"Yes, they will," he halfheartedly promised, "but we have to be quiet now. Remember what the sailor man said. We don't want to be thrown overboard."

The hours turned into days and the days into months, as the ship slowly crossed the ocean with the two little boys hidden inside. The sailor never thought he could feel such an emotion as he fiercely guarded his two charges from the taunts and snickers of his crewmates, none of whom knew about the gold.

Arriving in America four months later, he gathered the now very subdued boys in his arms and sneaked off the ship late that same night. In his suitcase he carried the gold and the envelope with Lisa's address. That God had delivered him an angel in the shape of a beautiful woman had never left his mind since that day on the docks of Beirut, and he was determined to carry out the task. After all, he was no longer a sailor who carried crates up and down a gangplank. He was now Stanos, a wealthy merchant with a bag of gold and two boys who had to be delivered to South Africa, wherever that was.

Holding the boys' hands, he walked up and down the docks asking if any ship was going to South Africa. Finally he spotted one with a flag of India flapping in the wind.

"Are you going to South Africa?" he called out to one of the sailors preparing the ship for departure.

"We are going past South Africa on our way to India. Why?"

"I need to take these two boys to South Africa. I have a gold coin. Please ask your captain if we can sail part of the way on his vessel."

A few minutes later, the captain appeared at the top of the gangplank and surveyed this rugged person, who looked like one of his sailors, with two small, neatly dressed boys at his side. An odd combination, he thought.

"Show me your gold coin!" shouted the captain. Stanos took the coin out of his pocket and flashed it in the moonlight.

"Okay," said the captain as he beckoned them to walk up the gangplank. "The journey will take five months. It's going to be very rough before we reach South Africa. Make sure you don't let those boys run all over the ship. I run a strict and orderly ship!"

"Yes, captain, thank you, captain," said Stanos as he led the boys up the gangplank.

"I promised your mother that I would take you both to your sister Lisa," the sailor said gently to the two boys. "And that is where this ship is going, to the place where Lisa lives. You will be with her soon."

He was fascinated with these dignified little boys who nodded their heads quietly and hardly said anything except "yes, please" and "thank you." Their sad faces broke his heart and he prayed that one day he would make them smile. His own childhood, clouded in a haze of noise, brawling, and starvation, gave him no opportunity to smile. He was determined not to let the same fate befall these boys. His unexpectedly elevated financial situation made him rethink his own life as well and consider what he was going to do once he had delivered the boys to their sister. He wasn't sure what that was yet, but he knew that he had been influenced by the quiet dignified demeanor of his two charges.

Steep rocky cliffs of a majestic mountain rose up from the edge of the sea. They were nearing Cape Town.

"Sir, could you show me how to get to this address?" Stanos stopped a British gentleman in top hat and coat tails rushing past the bottom of the gangplank.

"What is it, man? Can you not see I am in a hurry? I can't understand one bloody word you are saying. Speak up man!"

"Sir, please," replied Stanos as he bowed his head up and down. "Do you know in what direction we have to walk to find this address?"

Tanous and John hid behind the legs of the sailor. Up and down the docks there was a hustle and bustle, strange looking people from all parts of the world.

"Walk?" said the English gentleman angrily. "Are you joking with me, man?"

"No, sir," the sailor said. He bowed even deeper although he wanted to punch this impertinent man—but that was the old Stanos. The new Stanos did not act in such a fashion. "This is where the two boys behind me have to go. Their sister lives there and I promised their mother, God rest her soul, that I would take them to her," Stanos continued, making a cross on his chest before stepping aside so the man could see Tanous and John.

"This address is in Bloemfontein," said the Englishman with a sarcastic laugh. "That's a two-month ox-wagon trip over harsh mountainous terrain fraught with savage natives. What was their mother thinking? You will have to ask one of the Afrikaner Boers how to get there. They are the only ones mad enough to consider it!"

Cape Town looked like a European city, with its beautiful Victorian buildings and large oak trees. Adderly Street was filled with horse-drawn buggies, ladies walking under parasols, men in bowler hats and tailored suits. Nimble natives carried suitcases or boxes from one side of the street to the other. Seagulls squawked loudly overhead, and the smell of fresh kelp washed the air. There was noisy activity everywhere.

An old black fisherman with a pipe in his mouth, sat by the water's edge gutting a *snoek*, which is a fish known to the waters of the Cape.

"Excuse me sir," said Stanos, "can you tell me where to find a Boer?"

The only word the fisherman could decipher was "Boer." "*Ja, Baas. My baas is 'n Boer. Hy is in die winkel daar met die geel vis bokant die deur* [Yes, boss. My boss is a Boer. He is in the shop over there with a yellow fish above the door]," he answered, nodding his head and pointing to a man at the fish shop behind him.

"Ja, my man!" the Boer bellowed as he studied this *uitlander* (foreigner) standing under the piercing sun with two young boys and one small suitcase. Boers were descendants of the Dutch settlers, mostly farmers, and spoke a language called Afrikaans. "My brother, he is going to Bloemfontein next week, he can give you a ride. You have money?"

So began the journey to Bloemfontein.

"Don't worry, John. We are nearly there," Tanous whispered into his brother's ear. "Lisa will be waiting for us." He tried to reassure his brother, but both were awestruck as the ox wagon rolled over the Hottentot Mountains and into the Karoo, a semi-desert region that stretched on for miles. The boys clung to each other each time an elephant or giraffe appeared close by. Never had they seen such strange creatures. They were full of questions but they kept still. Stanos, fearful that natives would eat them for traveling over their land, watched the distant bushes and saw how the natives watched the ox wagon rolling along.

The Boer's brother passed them strips of dried salted meat. "*Eet, dis biltong* [Eat, it's jerky]." The boys reluctantly chewed on the meat, hunger pains getting the better of them. This world was so very strange to them. Tanous missed his mother and hoped that someone had taken her to the hospital. In his mind he pictured his mother and sisters sitting in the lounge drinking tea and eating sweet pastries or maybe a freshly sliced pear. He missed them, their house and the food. He hugged John tighter and vowed to make his sister, Lisa, take him back to Beirut as soon as they got to her house.

Finally the landscape changed, revealing larger clumps of trees and small hills. They were entering the heart of South Africa. "We have just passed Kimberley, where they found a huge famous diamond in this big hole," said the Boer's brother to Stanos. "Many people like you have come here to dig in this hole. The people say there are lots more diamonds there."

Fascinated with the story of the diamonds, Stanos, suddenly thinking that he could now become even richer, decided that is where he would go after he delivered the two boys to their sister. He would ask the Boer's brother to drop him off in Kimberley on the return trip to Cape Town. Diamond fever rushed through his veins, and Stanos smiled.

Bloemfontein finally rose in the distance. Tanous saw a large hill in the center of town and wondered if his sister lived on that hill. A huge white German Neo-Gothic—style building with two tall towers stood in the middle of the town. The Boer's brother said, "That is the *Tweetoring Kerk* [Two Tower Church] that belongs to the Afrikaner people, and it is where the Afrikaner presidents attend church when they are in town."

"What church is that?" asked Stanos, pointing to a large square brick double-story building with a bell tower to the side.

"Oh, that is you English people's church, the Anglican Cathedral. They say it was copied from the plans of the first *raadsaal* [justice building], which is the oldest building in town, built in 1849. And that building with the dome on top and all the Roman columns is the fourth *raadsaal*. They are busy building the appeals court near it.

Can you see? It's going to be a lovely building. All those columns and domes, *lekker* [lovely], hey?"

Stanos nodded. They were nearing the center of town.

Two boys stood on opposite sides of the street corners shouting headlines from their newspapers in different languages. The English *"The Friend"* newspaper boy and the Afrikaans *"The Volksblad"* newspaper boy looked at each other with hatred. The Boer War was still fresh in their minds.

The Boer War, fought between 1899 and 1902, was a bitter struggle sparked by the Dutch descendents who resisted British control of South Africa. The British won, but the price of their victory was unforgivable. During the war the British created concentration camps where more than twenty-six thousand Boer woman and children died of disease and starvation. This was a cruel and tragic contrast to the six thousand Boer men killed on the battlefield.

The result was a simmering hatred between the Afrikaners and the English, and an undying resolve on the part of the Afrikaner Boer to control his land at whatever cost.

This hatred was nowhere more prevalent than in the town of Bloemfontein, once capital of the Boer Republic. Here social gatherings were held in separate venues. The Afrikaners attended their *Nederduitse Gereformeerde Kerk*, or NGK church, the Afrikaans version of the Protestant church with very heavy Calvinistic teachings, while the English attended their Anglican churches.

It was to this town, with its simmering animosities, that Tanous and his brother came in December of 1910, finally reaching the door of Lisa's tiny three-bedroom stone house in the predominantly English side of town. With tears streaming down her cheeks she swept the boys into her arms and praised God for the kindness of the sailor who had delivered them to the safety of her home.

May God be with you always.

CHAPTER NINE

———————

1968: *Basil D'Oliviera, a South African coloured cricketer now living in England, is omitted from the initial selection for the upcoming tour to South Africa. D'Oliviera made headlines in England with his century against Australia (100 runs—a landmark score for a batsman) and was an obvious choice for the tour. The omission causes a huge public outcry in England. D'Oliviera is then offered the opportunity of accompanying the team as a reporter for the News of the World. The prime minister of South Africa, John Vorster, refuses to accept the alternative, replying, "We cannot allow those organizations, individuals and newspapers to make political capital out of such relations or use certain people or sportsmen as pawns in their game to bedevil relations, to create incidents, and undermine our way of life." One of the English cricketers then decides to drop out of the team and D'Oliviera is asked to replace him as a full-fledged team member for the upcoming tour. The South African prime minister refuses to accept the touring team with D'Oliviera on board, stating that the team is "no longer a cricket team but a team of troublemakers for South Africa's separate development policies." The tour is canceled.*

The early dawn light made it difficult to see. We were both in our nightgowns, trying stay quiet so not to wake the neighbors. Michelle whispered to me from behind the bushes.

"Push the potato harder in the exhaust pipe!"

"It won't fit!" I whispered back. "I hear a noise!"

"Get down, get down!" hissed Michelle. "Here, catch! Try this one."

"Where, where?" I whispered, sweeping the sandy driveway with my hands.

"Next to the left tire. Shove it in and hurry back here before he opens the front door!" whispered Michelle.

Michelle pushed my head down behind the bushes just as the front door opened. Trying not to breathe, we watched as the neighbor fumbled with his keys before opening the car door.

"Now run!" ordered Michelle just as the car door slammed.

A thorn bush ripped through my nightgown.

"Just go, just go!" Michelle had turned and was running down the street.

We were barely five houses away when a loud bang frightened the birds into flight.

"Shew! That was close!" Michelle giggled. "Hey, let's play *tok-tokkie* [knock-knock] on this house!" she continued, now clearly on a roll. "You run up and ring the bell and this time don't hesitate before you run away. Last time we were nearly caught."

"What?" I asked breathlessly trying to catch up to her, all the while inspecting the gap in my nightgown, panic in my face.

"Oh, stop being such a ninny, Ruchel," said Michelle. "Tell your mother you fell off your bicycle."

"But my mother doesn't allow me to ride my bicycle in my nightgown," I replied, trying to fight the tears. "What am I going to do? This is a new one. She is going to be mad with me."

"Okay, okay," sighed Michelle. "I'll ask Lydia to see if she can patch it up for you. Besides, all this running has made me hungry. Let's go back home."

That was a time when the worldwide hippie movement had finally reached the shores of South Africa. It was 1968, and we were both age ten. Mother had just returned from London raving about the fabulous show *Hair*—Heavens! You could not believe all that nudity on stage!—and the fashions of Carnaby Street, which Mother just had to have. *Playboy* magazine was smuggled into the country and a cute 'bunny ears' logo showed up on the back of Mother's green Capri Sport. But that is where the excitement ended at our house, where life continued in its prim and proper way.

That is, until I had my first sleepover at Michelle's house.

Michelle's home was down the road, past the neighborhood shops, and over the veld. There could not have been a greater divide between the two households. In Michelle's single-story home the hippies found a kindred soul. Her free-spirited mother, tall, blond, and beautiful, had been a runway model. Her father, also tall and handsome, was from Holland. The combination resulted in Michelle, who looked like a model herself, which of course just added to my fat neurosis. She had three brothers. Billy was two years older, Michael and Jonathan were younger.

The house was always teaming with Billy's friends, which meant mean pillow fights and much giggling and slamming of doors. The radio in Michelle's house was often in various stages of disrepair on the lounge floor, thanks to Michael's fascination with how things worked. Billy's room had a huge mural of the Beatles painted across one wall by his friend Charlie, who was as weird as he was talented. Other walls had flower-power stickers and Charlie's painted psychedelic swirls.

I asked Mother if I could have a mural of the Beatles painted on my bedroom wall. Ha! I might as well have asked to move to outer Mongolia.

At Michelle's house, *Penny Lane* blared from speakers in Billy's bedroom. Clothes lay all over the house, much to the despair of their one and only maid, Lydia. Lydia never managed to stay ahead of the game but at least she had her own weapon—a wet dishcloth—to control her hooligan charges. She slapped us with it each time we messed up her kitchen. And there were many of those times.

Michelle and I and loved to bake cakes, then decorate them with vivid colours of frosting, like red and green. We'd argue about which colour should go where, which would usually lead to a frosting fight that splattered red and green across the kitchen. Fearful of Lydia, we would pour dishwashing liquid all over the floor, meaning to mop it up, but would instead end up skating on it, which was a lot more fun than mopping.

Little wonder I was attracted to the anarchy there like a moth to a flame.

But it was an innocent anarchy, set in a period that posed no threat to us as children. We could disappear on our bikes for a whole day, riding up and down the concrete culvert in the veld until we reached the other side of town, and return only when it was time to turn on the street lamps. Michelle and I could walk up Naval Hill to explore the hidden valleys and fountains, two girls alone, and never have to think that someone could be lurking in the bushes. No one needed to worry when we walked at night from one friend's house to another. Fear was not in our vocabulary.

At age eleven, my only fear was that boys wouldn't like me. I was afraid of being reviled because my bum was too big and my hair was too frizzy. So to avoid the dreaded reviling, in particular by teenage boys, I embarked on a mission of "fitting in." That did not mean fitting in with my classmates at school—those girls that buried their noses in books or slaughtered each other on the hockey field. No—fitting in meant with Michelle and her friends from the other school. Because they were cool and looked like Twiggy or Karen Carpenter in their hip clothes. Because they all had long straight curtains of hair parted down the middle and not a single fat bum. Because they got Valentine's cards and little love notes in their mail boxes. Because all the cute boys were mad about them. I thought that if I could only stay on the periphery, maybe the boys would look at me, too. Michelle and her friends were who I wanted to be, ached to be. I desperately wanted a Valentine's card, at least one.

Michelle and I walked through the veld, popping bright coloured Smarties into our mouths. They are candies, like M&Ms.

"Billy is having his thirteenth birthday party at home. He says I can invite my friends too! It is going to be our first real party with dancing." Michelle was so excited. "You are the only one who is not from my school, but you will get to know the other girls better. Mary is helping me make these foot thongs that tie around your ankle. They are so cool, so don't wear anything weird. Jeans and a flower shirt will be fine."

"What does Mary look like?" I asked, hoping she would have a long nose or pimply face.

"She is as tall as I am with long black hair and skinny," answered Michelle. "My brother is nuts about her and says he is going to dance with her most of the night. Oh, and Charlie is stealing some of his father's beer and will be hiding it in the bushes until it is dark. This is going to be so much fun!"

We sat on the edge of the concrete culvert waiting for a yellow Smartie to melt on our tongue before we put each a pink one in our mouth. A thin stream of water below was disappearing under the intense heat of the African sun. Long dry grass enveloped us, its strong herblike aroma seeping into our pores. For a while we just sat there savoring the smells and sounds of the veld. All around us crickets were hopping in and out of the grass, their chirps competing with the cries of birds perched on the black arthritic branches of the few sparse trees.

"Well," I said, "I am definitely sleeping over at your place that night since there's no way I'm having my mom fetch me from the party. She would be asking the boys about their parents, what do they do, etcetera. I will just die of embarrassment."

"Ha, ha," giggled Michelle as she lay on her back, arms folded under her head, staring at the clouds to see what shape she could find next. "Halloooo, my dear boy!" Michelle imitated Mother. "Ruchel tells me that your name is Gavin. Tell me where do you live and do I know your parents?"

"Ja, right! And watch the guy answer her and swear never to look at or speak to me again." I fretted all the way home trying to figure out how I could persuade my parents to let me go, what I would wear that would not make me look like a water balloon, and how I could transform my thick curly hair into something resembling a sleek parted curtain.

A few days later I plucked up the courage to ask Mother during lunch. Depending on how late we returned from school at noon, lunch was served either before the BBC World News on the radio began or after it ended. Either way, we all had to sit at the table and silently listen to whatever disaster or miracle had befallen the world that day. Then Evelyn and one of the kitchen staff would come into the dining room at the sound of the bell and serve the salad. That would be followed by the main course and then usually a fruit for dessert. The little silver bell was never far from Mother's reach. Questions on school, homework, and after-school activities were reserved for dessert.

So there I was sitting at the table with a starched napkin on my lap, staring at baked pears in custard sauce.

"Michelle's brother is having his thirteenth birthday at their house and Michelle is going to invite some of her friends as well," I began hesitantly. "She says they are going to decorate the garage with posters and coloured lights and that there will be some dancing."

Silence.

I quickly added, "It will be something like the dancing they have at the Ramblers Club where all the teenagers go."

The Ramblers Club was Bloemfontein's country club for the English community in town. It was home to cricket games, tennis, and lawn bowling, and had the same stuffy atmosphere as the snobby clubs in England.

"Are the parents going to be at home?" asked Father after another moment of silence.

"Of course the parents will be there, George," replied Mother, lifting her napkin to wipe the corners of her mouth. "That's not my concern. My concern, Ruchel, is who are the boys who will be attending? I am not happy for you to mix with people we do not know. Some of them might be a bad influence on you."

What! Could Mother mentally zoom all the way over the veld to Michelle's house and see crazy Charlie and his friends hiding bottles of beer in the bushes?

"I have met Billy's friends, Ma, and they are very well behaved," I lied. "Please let me go. Michelle is my best friend and she will be very upset if I don't attend."

After much discussion, and with Evelyn adding her two cents while clearing the dishes, my parents finally consented.

"George!" Mother turned to Father. "You will have to ask the factory showroom to select a sensible modern dress when you leave for Johannesburg tomorrow. Ruchel, you may attend if you promise to behave as a lady. Do not shout or laugh loudly, it is very uncouth. I think I will phone Peggy to see if she needs any help."

"Oh no!" I replied hastily. "Michelle's mother says she does not need any help"—another lie—"and besides we will not be eating that much."

Sensible modern dress! Michelle had said jeans and a flowered shirt. But if that is what it took to go to the party, how bad could the dress be?

Bad? It was so bad, it was beyond bad. Father had returned with an orange leather pinafore dress that had an even brighter orange long-sleeve knitted shirt underneath. It was hideous.

"What a lovely choice, George!" exclaimed Mother. She had made me try the dress on. "I must phone that delightful saleslady to thank her."

The orange monstrosity accentuated my fat stomach and bum.

"You look lovely, Ruchel!" she exclaimed again "I have asked Peggy to take some photos of the party."

"Photos! Now there was no way I could sneak on the jeans and shirt Sara had hidden for me at the bottom of my suitcase.

Michelle took one look at me and hauled me into her bedroom the minute Mother drove off.

"What were you thinking?" she asked horrified. "You look like those nun friends of yours at your school. Didn't I tell you to wear jeans and a flowered shirt?"

"This is the only way I was allowed to go to your party," I cried. "My father bought this dress in Johannesburg just for this party! The worst thing is, my mother told your mother to take photos. So I can't even change into my jeans. I am so dead."

"Well, let's jazz it up then," said the ever resourceful Michelle. "Here, tie this scarf around your head while I paint some flowers on your cheeks."

Just then Mary walked into the bedroom. Tall, slim, with sleek long hair, she was Karen Carpenter's double. "God, Ruchel, what are you wearing?" she asked, looking me up and down.

"Mary, check if all the posters are up in the garage," said Michelle hastily, "and tell Charlie to smoke outside, otherwise my father will have a fit! Honestly, Ruchel!"—Michelle giggled as Mary walked out of the room—"your mother!"

Have I mentioned that I had hardly any confidence in myself? Whatever I did have went straight down the toilet. Now, seeing the other girls—who looked like advertisements for *California Dreamin'* in their tight jeans and colourful shirts—it was a horrible nightmare. I felt sick.

"I think I will stay in your room the whole night." I teared up as Michelle continued to paint petals on my cheeks with her mother's eye shadow. "I look like an orange chiffon cake. No one is going to ask me to dance!"

"Don't be ridiculous!" she retorted. She chewed her gum furiously. Her long straight parted-in-the-middle blond hair hung loosely over her brightly flowered shirt. "I'll tell my brother to dance with you."

Had it not been for Michelle, I'm sure I'd have dried up and been a spinster for the rest of my life.

All in all, that year turned out to be a pivotal one in my angst-filled life. Billy's thirteenth birthday party launched my own self-consciousness movement. Before that, I was happy to have clothes chosen for me, food put in front of me, and instructions given to me that I obeyed without much thought. But that year, all that changed. I began to question the status quo. Fat became my number one enemy.

CHAPTER TEN

1971: *Aware of South Africa's increasing isolation from international sports and cultural activities, Prime Minister John Vorster embarks on a mission to become more friendly with his African neighbors. He calls this a policy of "détente" and invites Malawi's Dr. Hasting Kamuzu Banda as his first guest to South Africa. The meeting is hailed as a success in the local newspapers and during the next three years the prime minister meets the leaders of eight more independent African states. Arthur Ashe, the African-American tennis player, has his visa application denied by the South African government.*

E velyn cracked egg after egg into a large ceramic bowl with the speed and precision of a fine chef. Her rose-pink uniform and starched white apron was covered in a light shower of powder. Even Cuddles, purring peacefully at her feet, had flour dust on her black nose.

"*Hauw*, why so sad, Pulani?" asked Evelyn.

"Do you think I'm too fat?" I sighed, peeling my school blazer off before pulling up a chair at the kitchen table.

"Come, I make you a nice cup of tea and then you tell your Evelyn all your troubles. Rosie, bring me a teacup and napkin for Pulani here, my hands are full of flour

"Tell me the truth, Evie."

"Hmph! Who is telling you such lies?" she demanded.

"Well," I began, "Michelle and Mary—"

"Ai, ai, ai! Michelle and Mary," she interrupted. "They are telling you these lies?"

"No, they did not say that but today both of them were chosen to be in the boys' school play. I tried my best at the audition, really I did. Maybe it's because I am too fat or not as pretty as they are," I said, rolling the corner of the table cloth into a neat little sausage, as if that would stop the tears.

"*Hauw!* These people who choose are stupid and blind, Pulani," replied Evelyn. "They are not clever. Here in Africa if you are very thin, people think there is something wrong with you. They think you are poor and sickly. All those bones sticking out is not good. No boy likes to feel just bones. You, Pulani, are healthy and strong. Look at your rosy cheeks!" she announced, pinching my cheek. "Here, drink your tea up and forget this stupid boys' play!"

Just then Jenny burst into the kitchen. "I want to lick the bowl!" She turned to me. "And you can't have any!"

"Madam says I must not give you raw dough," said Evelyn now spooning the batter into cupcake molds.

"Mommy's not here, she won't know!" Jenny shot back.

"Ai, your sister, Pulani. She knows what she wants." Evelyn shook her head as Jenny rushed out the back door licking the wooden spoon. "Here, have some nice chocolate cake I baked this morning. It will cheer you up."

"No thanks, Evie," I said. "I think I should just stop eating so that I can look as thin as Michelle. Maybe then Basil will ask me to dance. He always asks the other girls. I just wish he would ask me, just once." Silent tears fell.

"I want to hear none of that silly talk about not eating, Pulani. Boys like girls who are healthy and have happy faces. That's who they will dance with. Not sad skeletons. So show your Evelyn a happy face," she commanded as she broke into song and dance. "Show me how you will dance with this Basil. Come!"

Evelyn grabbed my hand and pulled me up. Rosie and Sara joined in and suddenly the kitchen was alive with clapping and singing, and I slowly joined in too.

"Oh happy day…" Evelyn broke in midstep as a smile crept over my face. "Oh happy day…."

There were many of those days. Happy days when my fragile self-esteem sought refuge in the warmth of the smiles and laughter of the kitchen.

*   *   *

By age fourteen I had miraculously graduated to being French kissed by two boys.

That was huge because never in my wildest imagination did I think some half decent looking boy would ever find me attractive enough to French kiss me. A kiss, yes, but not a French kiss. It happened while we were playing Spin the Bottle at the top of Naval Hill one afternoon. One of the boys just leaned over and French kissed me the instant the bottle pointed in my direction. I was so shocked that I excused myself and ran back down the hill to my house.

That of course led to lectures from Michelle, who described in detail the art and technique of French kissing. When I told her that the second time felt like I was dropping my tongue into mint-flavored mouthwash, she just threw up her hands and said "I give up."

How was my self-esteem then? Oh, still way down in the toilet.

That same year, Michelle and I found our first summer job—at the Cool Cat, an ice cream and sandwich parlor.

The first two days we ate more than we served, the third day we tried to see how much ice cream we could sip through a straw. By the end of the week we started to notice the boys who came in. This was of major importance. It gave us the opportunity to get to know Conrad, Johan, and Alex, the hottest seniors in town.

"I doubt my mother would ever say yes to us going to Johan's party," I whispered to Michelle after serving a milkshake to a soldier.

"I have a plan," said Michelle. "Tell your mother you're sleeping at my house tonight. My parents are going out to a party, so we can walk to Johan's house after they've left."

Throughout the years this trickle of a conspiracy plan became a river of omissions and half truths.

*   *   *

I tried on half the clothes in my wardrobe before packing a pair of jeans and a white shirt into my overnight bag.

That night Michelle and I walked from one smoke-filled room to another with the bravado of clueless teenagers. Everywhere in the dimly lit house couples were intertwined in corners or on sofas. The furniture was usually either borrowed from parents or bought for pennies on the rand from questionable vendors on the outskirts of town. Beer bottles were scattered around the room. Jethro Tull and the Beatles blared over speakers rigged in every hallway. I was mesmerized but I tried to act nonchalant and really tried not to stare. At one point I saw Michelle talking with Conrad, from the ice cream parlor. He was an Afrikaner so handsome that girls fainted in his wake. I met up with Mary and another of her school friends. Then Michelle disappeared while I was having a philosophical discussion with some nerdy guy. A friend of his joined the conversation and I had to strain to hear the words over the loud music.

"Excuse me, I have to find my friend Michelle," I said, politely trying to escape before we crossed the border into boring. "Your friend is not going to run away, Ruchel," said the nerdy guy's friend, putting his arm around my shoulder. "Why don't you and I go outside and I can point out the constellation of the stars."

"That's okay, I must find my friend. Maybe another time," I replied quickly as I disentangled myself from his arm and retreated to where I'd last seen Michelle. I wasn't prepared for anything other than just being at this party. Without Michelle next to me I was way out of my league. Awkwardly I went from room to room. Then I heard her behind me.

"Let's go! I will tell you when we get home," she said as she saw my mouth about to ask why.

Her parents were, mercifully, not home so we headed straight for the kitchen. Act cool and eat nothing, then gorge yourself after the party. Michelle pulled a tin of Bully Beef (like Spam) out of the cupboard and stir-fried it with her own concoction of Mrs. Ball's Chutney and Worcestershire Sauce.

"So what happened," I asked between mouthfuls of somewhat burned meat and sweet sauce, "when Conrad asked you to follow him? I can't believe he actually asked you to follow him! I am so jealous!"

"Well," Michelle said, "we sat on the bed and he started to kiss me on the mouth—"

"Kiss you, he kissed you?" I interrupted.

"Ja, I know, and I nearly fainted from excitement. And then he started to run his hands over my breast while still kissing me."

"And then, and then, and then?" I asked, nearly choking on the meat.

"Well, then he tried to slide his hands into the top of my jeans but I pulled them out."

"Were you still kissing him?" I asked. I wondered how she could do all these things at the same time.

"Ja, we were still kissing and he kept on trying and trying. Eventually he realized that I was not going to let anything else happen so he tried by telling me how beautiful I was and that he found me so sexy blah blah and that I should just relax and go with the moment."

"Bloody hell, I most probably would have run out of the room. What did you do?" I asked.

"Well, it was all happening too quickly so I just said it was late and that I had to get home. And that's why we left in a hurry. I will say this, though. He is cute and his kisses are yummy!"

I was in awe of the events of that night. Through the following months Michelle's kitchen became time out for fantasizing while Michelle continued her infatuation with Conrad. Even though we did not see them often, it didn't stop us from discussing the "what ifs." Before we knew it, another year was over.

*   *   *

"Guess what," I whispered into Dale's ear as we waited for Mrs. Street to return to the classroom. Dale was my closest friend at school, and I spent many afternoons and weekends with her during our elementary years.

"What?" Dale whispered back, scribbling in her book.

"Mrs. Downs said that St. Andrews School across the road is joining their art department with ours. The boys will be joining our art history class on Fridays. She said—"

The classroom door swung open.

"What is this commotion, where is your teacher?" demanded Sister Bulldog—as we called her. A deathly silence settled over the room. Fran stuck her hand up. "Yes, Fran, maybe you can tell me what is going on here!"

"Excuse me, Sister. Mrs. Street has gone to the science lab to check on our bean experiments and we are waiting for her," Fran said apologetically.

"Well, if your teacher is out of the room that does not give you permission to have an afternoon tea party," she boomed, "Open your books and study for the upcoming exams. I do not want to hear a sound! Is that understood?"

We all quickly opened our books. "Yes, Sister" we said in unison just as Mrs. Street walked back in. I scribbled and passed a note to Dale as Mrs. Street turned to write our homework assignment on the chalkboard. The note said, "Let's meet behind the *tuck* shop at break."

"So what did Mrs. Downs say exactly?" asked Dale. Several of us sat under the Acacia tree behind the *tuck* shop.

"Well, apparently only a few boys are interested in art history, and our art program is stronger, so both schools have decided to join the classes. After all, they are our brother school."

"What does that mean?" asked Felicity, our resident bookworm and artist.

"It means there will be boys in our class, Felicity." Dale sighed in exasperation. "Ruchel, do you know who the boys are?"

"No, but there are about five of them. I wonder if any of them are cute?"

"I thought you said that you were only interested in boys at least four years older than you," said Dale.

"No harm in looking." I laughed. "I'm not going to marry anyone in Bloemfontein, please!"

"Pass me your palm, Ruchel," Fran chipped in as she grabbed my hand. "I will tell you who you will marry."

Fran considered herself our class psychic and insisted on reading the leaves left behind in our teacups. She peered intently into my palm. "You are going to have a shotgun wedding and you are going to marry an Afrikaner in Bloemfontein!" she announced to the world.

"Are you crazy?" I said. "There is no way I am going to marry an Afrikaner, never mind get pregnant before I am married. Besides, my mother would kill me. And I'm going to Cape Town University after I finish school. How is an Afrikaner from Bloemfontein going to find me if I am in Cape Town? No way!" I pulled my hand away as Dale and Felicity collapsed in laughter.

"You can't believe what Fran said at break this morning!" I told Michelle over the phone the minute I got home.

"Don't tell me you believe such nonsense, Ruchel, I swear, if someone told you that you were going to marry a Martian, you would believe that too! Forget about it. By the way, don't forget we are meeting at Jennifer's house this Saturday."

*   *   *

During those carefree days, parents were conveniently absent attending dinner parties, art exhibitions, or theater performances. Transportation problems were nonexistent because we all lived close to each other. We wandered like nomads from one house to another during the day and late into the night while Simon and Garfunkel, Elvis, Janis Joplin, the Beatles, the Stones, and anything else we could lay our hands on from America or London followed us. Television was unknown in South Africa, so our imaginations ran wild.

Opinions and admonitions were dished out not only by parents but by the maids who were part of all the girls' households. Maids were in on our conspiracy and often covered up for us in close shaves. But they were also our surrogate mothers. We ran everything past them, from fashion to boys to school assignments. I thought nothing could change my peaceful world.

I was wrong.

I was in my room studying for a Latin test when Sara came rushing in. "Miss Michelle is on the phone and she is crying."

I flew downstairs.

"I'm leaving!" Michelle sobbed.

"What do you mean you are leaving?" I was frightened.

"My parents are divorcing. We all have to move with my mother to Margate and start at the new school as soon as possible."

"What?" I cried. "There's no way, it's the middle of the term and we have two and a half more years of school left. You can stay with us, I'll ask my mom. I can't cope without you!"

Visions of weekends devoid of Michelle filled me with horror. Without her sage advice, guidance, and encouragement, I was a rudderless ship on a stormy sea. And the thought of her sitting sadly in some strange school with no old friends to share secrets sent my heart plummeting. It was almost worse than death.

"I can't believe this is happening!" she sobbed. And for an hour we cried on the phone.

For the remainder of that week, Michelle and I talked on the phone and spent every possible moment together. When it came to saying goodbye at the airport, we were both drained.

"We will phone each other, we will spend holidays together, promise me!" I cried as I stood hugging my best friend.

"I promise," she said. "No matter where we are, we will always remain best friends forever and ever!"

CHAPTER ELEVEN

1973: Chief Mangosutho Buthelezi of the Zulu tribe in Natal is invited to speak at Howard University in America. Answering a barrage of questions from students accusing him of working within the apartheid system, he defends his actions and decisions by replying that, although he "abhors" segregation, there is no other option for him and his tribe. He follows that by urging all American activists to please place enormous pressure on American companies in South Africa to increase their worker's wages.

With my support crutch Michelle gone, I became even more neurotic about my weight. It was not long before I was balancing precariously between reality and perception. Each time I stood naked in front of the mirror, my bum seemed to expand while the rest of my body got thinner. Food became an evil to be avoided at all costs. Lies and excuses abounded as I sought refuge in chewing gum. Considering that at age thirteen I wore size fourteen jeans, Mother, who was reed thin, was pleased that I was "losing a little weight" and therefore did not question whether I had eaten or not.

"Thank you for the compliment, Juliet, dear," Mother sighed to her friend while viewing an artist's new work at the gallery. "It is rather gratifying to see Ruchel finally lose some of that excess weight. Clothes never fit correctly on a body that is out of proportion."

Mother gave me a sharp glance from across the room—meaning 'stand up straight and pull in your stomach,' then turned back to Juliet.

"I cannot fathom the desire for worn out jeans and those horrendous T-shirts she insists on wearing every day. It was such a battle to get her to wear a skirt and blouse for the exhibition tonight."

"Maybe you should bring her back something fashionable the next time you are in London?"

"Juliet, you are a genius!" Mother laughed. "I will take Ruchel with me to Europe this July. She needs to be exposed to some sort of civilization!"

Pasty Ian kept following me around the gallery. He was the son of one of Mother's friends, which meant that he would be considered "acceptable," meaning English and from a nice family that moved in the same social circles. Acceptable, although not desirable. "Desirable" on Mother's scale was someone sophisticated and civilized, in short, a European gentleman. On my scale, Ian was a minus ten.

"So what University are you going to attend?" I tried to make conversation so he would stop staring at me.

"Definitely Wits [the University of Witswatersrand in Johannesburg]," Ian said. "They have a great medical school and I hear the parties are huge drunken fests!"

Great, I thought. Slice and dice corpses during the day and drink yourself into a stupor at night. I would not want to be his patient. I smiled and wished the night over.

*   *   *

London, Europe—I could not begin to imagine! I was over the moon when Mother told me about the European trip. In a moment of pure ecstasy I let myself eat the slice of lemon meringue pie that normally would have sat there untouched with the rest of the lunch.

"Why can't I come too?" whined Jenny as I reached for another sliver of pie.

"Your turn will come in two years," Mother said. "Ruchel, we will have to obtain permission from the headmaster for you to miss a week of school. We will be away for four weeks. I thought we could visit Uncle Habib's daughter-in-law's family in Stockholm. They have a lovely chateau on the lake. Also, Colonel Trevor said he would be delighted to show you around the Jersey Islands, I spoke with him last night."

It was getting better with each mouthful of pie. Skip school, see a chateau, Carnaby Street, Amsterdam, Madrid…. I couldn't wait.

And what delicious decadence! Forget all the obligatory art museums and historical monuments that eventually blended into one sensory overload. Mother's artistic and eclectic friends came to the rescue. One of them insisted on taking us to a fashionable gay club in London.

"Shirley," he said, "you will find the place fascinating."

"Let's go, ma!" I pleaded, fearing I would miss out.

"Well," Mother hesitated, "only for a quick look, Ruchel."

My jaw dropped as my eyes feasted on the décor, the men snuggled up to each other, and the male dancers on stage. Was that man really kissing another man? Wait till I tell Michelle!

"I want to dance!" I announced for the world to hear.

Mother sighed. "One dance, Ruchel. I will wait here at the bar for the two of you."

"May we join you?" asked two sophisticated men as they sidled up to Mother, who was drinking a glass of champagne.

"Sure." Mother smiled at the white British gentleman and his black African partner in their Savile Row finery. "My friend has been dragged onto the dance floor by my daughter and I am just waiting for them to finish dancing."

"Where are you from? You don't sound as if you're from London," asked the British gentleman, smoothing his hair before summoning the barman.

"South Africa."

"Oh, South Africa," they nodded slowly. After a pregnant pause, the African gentleman spoke. "You must find our relationship rather strange," he said, looking her in the eye.

"Quite the contrary!" Mother countered. "It is all rather refreshing. Not everyone agrees with the country's politics!"

"Let's drink to that!" They all laughed.

And so it went. The further we traveled, the more people we met. They were drawn to Mother's effervescent personality. We were never short of something new to experience. It was an education in itself, as new and old friends of Mother introduced me to a more global way of thinking.

Going through customs in Europe was another type of eye opening experience. There, I felt like a visiting leper. The minute we gave customs our South African passports to be stamped, the immigration officers would look at us with suspicion and contempt. After glaring for a while, they would reluctantly stamp the offending South African green book before flinging it back across the table to us. Because we were white, they assumed we supported apartheid. It was completely unfair.

"It might be unfair," Mother explained while we waited to retrieve our luggage, "but unless our government abolishes the apartheid system, we will be forever tarred with the same brush." The second we reached home I ran upstairs to phone Michelle and spill out all the news.

"Then we walked into this pink store in Carnaby Street and I thought, cool, another place to buy clothes. Believe me, Mali"—I went on like a bullet train—"I was on this mission to buy as many cool clothes as I could. So I went in and immediately walked slapbang into this huge pink rubber thing. I was just about to grab hold of it when I looked up and saw that it was actually a giant pink plastic penis. The look of horror on my mother's face as she marched me out of the store was classic!" I giggled.

"So what shows did you see?" asked Michelle.

"Well, my mom's friend who is this member of Parliament in London took us to see *Hair*. I had to see it after I heard they were nude on stage. Then we saw *Godspell* and went onstage after to meet the actors. That was cool. Lots of *Playboy* magazines on the street, you can buy them anywhere, amazing, and they have TV. I watched Coronation Street, it was really funny."

"Did you meet any interesting guys?"

"Well, remember I told you we were going to visit this colonel friend of my mother on the Jersey Islands?"

"Ja, the one we had met when we were on the Windsor Castle ship last year," replied Michelle.

"Well, his chauffeur comes to pick us up in the colonel's little red sports car. Now he was *kinda* cute. Dark hair, Italian, nice accent."

"Italian accent," Michelle giggled.

"Anyway, after driving us around the whole island, he says to the colonel and my mother that night that he would like to take me to this party his friends are having."

"And your mother let you go?!"

"It took a bit of a persuasion but the colonel said he had better look after me, otherwise he's in trouble, so my mother let me go."

"You've got to tell me what happened!"

"Well, we drove out to this house in the middle of the island. There were a lot of people there, a little older than us. I got drunk on Pimms No. 1. You gotta taste that drink, it is made with a lot of fruit."

"So what happened?"

"Nothing, we just talked, giggled, I met some interesting people, and then he took me home. Oh… he gave me a kiss when he said goodbye but nothing else happened. See, I am fine on my own."

"You are bloody lucky! The chauffeur was most probably afraid of losing his job. In any other circumstance, these guys would have taken advantage of a young drunk girl."

"Oh rubbish!" I laughed. "They would not do that!"

"What?" said Michelle. "Don't you remember when we were on that ship and one of the officers, what was his name?"

"Julian."

"Ja, Julian, you really liked him. Then, he invited you to his cabin and you thought it was just for another party and having fun. I had to drag you away when we found out it was just you, him, another guy, and me. Honestly, Ruchel, when are you going to get it? I won't always be there to bail you out."

* * *

Michelle was right. I never anticipated anything bad in any situation. I never had any reason to. My life was uncomplicated and my innocence prevented me from thinking further than the immediate situation. I had just turned fifteen for heaven's sake!

Fifteen, and no one decent to ask to Liz's sixteenth birthday party.

"She decided to have this formal dinner and we all have to invite a partner," I moaned to Michelle one afternoon after school. "Conrad has agreed to go with her, can you believe it! And Ineka is going to ask Johan. And everyone else is asking first year students at the University. Everyone but me."

"Conrad is going with Liz? Shit! I am so jealous! I hate being here in Margate. I wish I were back there with you guys."

"You have no idea how much I wish you were back here." Since the beginning of the year, Conrad and his friends had attended the

University of the Orange Free State (UOFS, or *Kovsies*, as it was better known), an all-white conservative Afrikaans university in town. Alex had decided on University of Cape Town, called *Ikeys*. It was a more liberal, all-English university. That's where I wanted to go.

Kovsies was one of the largest universities in the country. The buildings, surrounded by lush gardens, were modern and impressive. It was clearly one of the government's favorite institutions. Its students were being groomed as the country's future leaders in business and sports, a veritable factory for making conservative Afrikaner citizens who could be counted on to deliver the votes. But not everyone there felt the same.

Liberal Afrikaner students like Conrad and his friends, found mainly in the architecture, art, and drama departments, tried their utmost to buck the establishment.

After a party one night in the beginning of the year, Conrad took five of us girls to visit campus and view the architectural model he was building. Two students were busy working on their projects when we arrived.

"This is Carl and Pieter," Conrad said. "Say hi to Liz, Ineka, Mary, Susan, and Ruchel, guys!"

"Hello," they replied in unison, glancing up from their drawing boards.

What was it with this place? Good-looking guys seemed to emerge from the woodwork!

Michelle would not accept that I could not find a date, and reminded me of that day at the architectural school. "What about that guy you met with Conrad? You said he was good looking. Why don't you ask him?"

The subject of who to invite morphed into monumental proportions.

"I don't know, Mali, Pieter is very good looking but his English is *vrot* [bad] and you know how my Afrikaans is. When we spoke, I did most of the talking. I'm not sure he even understood half of what I was saying. He just nodded and smiled a lot. And that was three months ago. He won't even remember me. I am too embarrassed to ask him, he will most probably say no, and then I will just die of shame."

"Don't be silly, Ruchel, what have you got to lose?" said Michelle. "If you don't try you will never know."

"Okay, okay," I told her the next day. "You win. I'm so desperate I'm willing to make an utter fool of myself. I'll let you know what happens. My mother would have a fit if she knew I was asking an Afrikaans boy to be my date. You know how she is. In her mind Afrikaners are not part of our culture."

"You are not marrying him, so stop worrying!"

She was right—it was just a party, and as that party was in two weeks I did not have much time to pluck up additional courage. I knew that every Saturday, Conrad and his friends met for brunch at the Bloemfontein Hotel, which bordered the FVB Shopping Center. So the following Saturday morning I took two hours to get ready.

"Hurry up, Ruchel!" Mother called from the bottom of the stairs. "If you want to go to town, then you have to come with me now. The hairdresser won't take me later. I still have to pick up the cakes for the tennis party this afternoon!"

The indoor atrium of the FVB Center was a hive of activity as I waved Mother goodbye. Ineka was waiting for me in front of the Cool Cat.

"Can you believe Johan said yes? I am so psyched, I have no clue what I am going to wear," Ineka squealed. Gusts of wind blew my carefully styled hair in all directions.

"How do I ask Pieter to go with me? Do you think I should ask him?" I asked anxiously, trying to coax my thick, tangled, and totally screwed up hair into something that resembled a parted curtain.

"Maybe I should just forget the whole exercise and just go with pasty Ian."

"Don't be ridiculous, Ruchel!" Ineka said. "If I can pluck up the courage to ask Johan, then you should be able to do the same. Besides they all hang together. Oh, here comes Conrad and, look, that Afrikaans guy is right behind him."

"Oh hell, I am so nervous," I whispered as they walked toward us.

"Hello," drawled Conrad as they approached.

"Hi," I said, patting down my hair. I would have had better luck getting a nervous dog to lie down.

"So Johan tells me he is going with you," Conrad said to Ineka, leaning nonchalantly against the store window. "Where is this farm?"

"It is just outside Tweespruit, about an hour and a half out of town. Liz's aunt has this huge double-story farmhouse next to a river, so it should be fun," she answered, scanning the area for Johan. "She is going to have this very fancy dinner for us, so you better wear your tux."

"And who is going with you, Ruchel?" asked Conrad.

"I, I don't know yet," I stammered, "I thought maybe I could ask Pieter?"

"What's this?" Pieter asked. My bloody hair was flying in all directions.

"*Sy wil weet of jy saam met haar gaan na Liz se partytjie volgende naweek* [She wants to know if you will go with her to Liz's party next week]," said Conrad.

Not exactly the way I had imagined.

"Well…" I tried to redeem myself. "We have to take a partner to this party and I thought you might want to come. It will be fun."

"Sure," Pieter said.

I nearly died.

"Okay then," I said before he changed his mind. "You can get the details from Conrad, and I will meet you next Saturday. Have to rush, I have to fetch some cakes for my mother." A lie. "I'll phone you later, Ineka."

"He said yes! Sara!" I shouted as I leaped up the stairs to my bedroom where Sara was busy packing away the laundry. "Can you believe it? I have to phone Michelle. Don't tell mommy who I am going with. I am just going to tell her that a group of us are going together."

"But you don't even know how to speak a proper Afrikaans," Sara said.

"Who cares?" I said. I kicked my shoes off and bounced onto my bed. "He speaks some English but the best thing is, he is so handsome. You should see his eyes. The most amazing green eyes. His shoulders are huge! He is even taller than Conrad. And his hands! I have to phone Michelle. Warn me when mommy comes back."

I ran down the stairs again, passing my brother Wayne. He was playing Cowboys and Indians with one of his irritating friends. He had on a black cowboy hat and was squinting to take aim at his friend, dressed in an Indian headdress complete with ostrich feathers, courtesy of Father's store. As far as I was concerned, my brother at age eleven was from another planet.

"Go play outside," I commanded. "Mommy says you are not to play inside. I need to use the phone."

"Bang, bang, you're dead!" Wayne shouted as he and his friend ran out the front door.

"Yes, he said yes!" I squealed into the phone to my psychiatrist-cum-best friend. "Actually, he said 'Sure.' But anyway we are going next Saturday. I was so bloody nervous afterward that I just fled the scene. I hope he goes next Saturday."

"You have to tell me *everything*," said Michelle. "Take photos so I can see what this guy looks like."

CHAPTER TWELVE

1973: In Heidelburg, in the Transvaal, the charismatic and radical Afrikaner orator Eugene Terre'Blanche forms the extreme right wing Afrikaner Weerstandbeweging (AWB) party together with a few of his colleagues. Many staunch National Party members defect to the new party because of their growing distaste for the government's relaxation of some of their apartheid policies.

S aturday could not come early enough. Ineka's house was the departure point, so all the girls slept over on Friday night. To say my heart had gone into overdrive would be an understatement.

Ineka's mom knocked on her door the next morning at nine.

"The boys are here and they are ready to go," she shouted above the chatter of six excitable fifteen year olds.

"Where are my contacts?" Susan squinted as she groped through a pile of clothes strewn across the floor. "How many guys are there?"

I stuck my head through the crack of the door. Tall and buxom with graying blond hair pulled back in a bun, Ineka's mom was Earth Mother personified.

"Six, and yes, the Afrikaans guy is with them," she said. "My, he is good looking. Looks a bit shy to me though?" She smiled and winked as I quickly shut the door.

"Oh hell, oh hell," I moaned as I wriggled on the floor trying to pull on my new jeans. It usually took me a good ten minutes lying down to get them past my bum, and now everyone was stepping over me in their hurry to walk out the door as casually as possible.

"Hurry up, Ruchel, what's taking you so long?" whispered Liz. She climbed over me to brush her hair in front of the only mirror in the room.

"I finally fit into a size eight pair of jeans, even if it takes me forever to pull them up. I am nearly done."

I sauntered out of the room as though the past few hours had been spent in quiet meditation.

"Hi!" I said as I walked up to Pieter. Oh my God, I thought to myself, he is so damn good looking, how am I ever going to stop from going numb every time he looks at me?

"Hello," he said in his thick Afrikaans accent. His smoldering eyes bore into mine. I could barely speak.

"Six of us into each car," Liz ordered. "I'll go with the guys and you girls can squeeze into Johan's Volksie."

Whew! I was relieved that further conversation could wait until we reached the party.

We drove for an hour and a half over the dusty roads of the Free State. Open vistas of ploughed wheat fields competed with small sparse hilltops. Black women in long colourful skirts walked back to their townships balancing baskets of store-bought food on their heads. Pink and yellow cosmos blossomed along the roadside. It was a scene so familiar that it passed by in a blur of comforting silence.

Tweespruit was a cluster of small homes with a larger township to one side. With all the nervous conversation going on, both cars shot right past the wooden sign at the entrance to the farm. Two screeching U-turns were made with only a cursory glance at oncoming traffic. Thank heavens Mother was home, unaware. We turned into a narrow dirt road where smiling black farm children swung on an open gate and waved as the cars went down the rocky driveway to the farmhouse. They scrambled off the fence gate and rushed to the cars as we parked.

"*Dumela, dumela* [Hello, hello]!" we greeted them as we climbed out of the cars and hugged them. The customary bags of candy and toys were distributed to eager outstretched hands as Aunt Fay ambled down the garden path toward us.

"Hello everyone!" she said as she walked up to hug Liz. Aunt Fay was a tall strong woman dressed in a long skirt, hair pulled back at the nape of her neck. You could sense that she was a woman who was at home inspecting the cows and wheat fields of her farm with her two black Labradors at her side. Aunt Fay, a widow, lived alone in her large two-story stone farmhouse. She was much respected by the farm workers. The loyalty of the staff made her feel secure. Her late husband's shotgun stayed silently in its case—no unwelcome invaders.

"The girls' rooms are upstairs, the boys will sleep downstairs," Aunt Fay instructed as we handed the maids our baggage. The smell of cow dung blended with freshly cut hay as we climbed up the steps to the front porch of the farmhouse.

From the porch you could see the African landscape for miles around: straw *rondavels* (round huts) dotting wheat fields and cow pastures, and bubbling streams appearing like cracks in the rocky earth. The sounds were distinct: cows, dogs, birds, crickets, dry grass, and crackling wood fires. The smell was a mixture of all this as it baked under the sun.

Inside the house was a huge lounge, furnished in Cape Dutch mahogany and Persian rugs. The two Labradors ran free through the kitchen. Anticipation of how the evening would progress made me nervous.

"Great dress, Ruchel," Jennifer said as I stepped in front of the mirror to view my simple black Chanel-looking dress.

"You have no idea how I had to persuade my mother to buy this," I replied. "She wanted the dressmaker to let it out over the hips so that it would hang loose like a tent. You cannot imagine the argument."

"You are too much, Ruchel," giggled Jennifer, who never in her life had to go through having fat bum. "Come, they're waiting."

I opened the door and walked to the top of the stairs, hoping I would not fall.

Bum and stomach in, shoulders back, chin up, smile. Check!

Move slowly down the stairs like a lady. Check!

Practice witty conversation while descending stairs. Check!

"You look lovely, Ruchel." I had walked blindly into the tuxedoed chest of some giant.

"What—oops, I am so sorry, the room is a bit dark," I stammered. I prayed, God let this chest belong to one of the serving staff, but as my gaze traveled up past the shoulders I saw intense green eyes staring back at me. Strikingly handsome, he looked like a movie star.

"Oh my gosh! Pieter," I said as I took a step back.

Just then Liz called all of us to the lounge for cocktails.

"Th-thanks for coming." I tried to make my brain operable.

"We saw some cows while you were getting ready," said Pieter as we walked toward the lounge. "My uncle has a farm and I have milked cows myself."

That called for some remark that would lead to an interesting conversation about the trials and tribulations of milking cows in the African bush. But I knew nothing about cows.

"That's nice," I said.

Just then Johan joined in, telling us how he went horseback riding on his cousin's farm. I wanted to tell them how I was nearly thrown off a horse during a riding lesson when it took off at a furious gallop. But I just smiled stiff as a mummy.

The dining room table was set with bone china and silverware fit for a queen. Place cards indicated where we were to sit, which eliminated one source of anxiety. Dinner started off with birthday toasts. Then the staff replaced the hardly eaten asparagus soup with succulent roast lamb, baby potatoes, peas, and mashed pumpkin. Liz and Conrad dominated the conversation while I nervously pushed baby potatoes from one side of the plate. By the time the peach Melba arrived, I was clutching my wine glass for support.

"Coffee and port is being served in the lounge," Liz announced. I knew if I drank any more I would be drunk.

"I think I need some fresh air," I whispered to Pieter.

"Okay, I will come outside with you," he said.

I wanted nothing beyond just standing outside to clear my befuddled brain. My conversation so far had consisted mainly of one- or two-syllable words.

We walked under the full moon, hearing the distant drum beat of the farm laborers as they wound down from the long day's work. It was a comforting, familiar sound. The silhouette of Africa was cut from the night sky by the spotlight of a full moon. Smoke from wood fires wafted like veiled gray shadows across the pointed roofs of straw huts. The blues and purples of night washed over the canvas backdrop. A lone dog's bark echoed through the valley.

"Let's walk down to the river." Pieter's voice was soft and lyrical.

"Okay," I said. If Pieter had said "let's do a somersault," my response would have been the same. On the way to the river our hands brushed together and before long they were intertwined like a vine around a branch. My heart pounded with the beat of the far-off drums. I felt my whole body turning within itself.

I did not know what to think. Was he being polite? Polite! Maybe I had grabbed his hand, and now he had no idea how to untangle it without being rude. Rude! Maybe he thought I was drunk and might trip and he needed to hold me upright. Upright! Was this really happening?

Soon we heard water gurgling over smooth pebbles.

"Here we are," said Pieter. "I saw the river this afternoon and it looked so peaceful. Look how the moon shines on the water."

"It's magical!" I had visions of fairies dancing on sparkling moonlit bubbles. I felt like a child because I had never been so nervous in all my life.

Pieter gently put his arm around my shoulders and drew me close to him. He put his arm around me. Oh please, can the butterflies in my stomach stop fluttering for one second. I need to think.

His hands found my burning cheeks and his lips touched mine. The butterflies rioted and flew out of every pore. My brain shut down. I was immersed in a sensation that I did not want to end. If Pieter's hands had not been holding my face, I would have flowed right into the river below, never to be retrieved.

The lion on top of the African mountain surveyed the world below. He spied a nervous lioness drinking at the water hole. He saw how her hips swayed as she adjusted her position among her friends at the water's edge. A submerged hippopotamus sent a spray of water over the lioness. She shook her head in annoyance. The lion smiled. He let out a powerful roar. He had marked his territory.

CHAPTER THIRTEEN

——————

1973: *South African boxer Arnie Taylor wins the world bantam weight crown after defeating Mexican boxer Romeo Amaya in a knockout in the fourteenth round. On the home front, South Africa's apartheid policies are ignored when African-American boxer Bob Foster fights against South African boxer Pierre Fourie. Fourie, an Afrikaner, had won both the South African Middleweight and Lightweight Titles but could never beat Foster. After the match, Foster became a hero for many Black South Africans.*

Mother headed up the ramp to the rooftop parking of the FVB Center. "*Dumela*, Miss Shirley, your parking spot is open," said the smiling attendant.

"Thank you, Mary, I am so late for the hairdresser and I still have to pick up the rest of the groceries before the shops close at twelve." Mother smiled. "Make sure John looks after my car and I will bring you a Coke and a packet of chips when I come back."

Before the large black woman in the booth could say thank you, Mother went screeching past the rows of cars, waving frantically when she saw the attendant standing at her spot. No one had a dedicated parking spot on that roof top but there was an unspoken understanding that Mother would always have her favorite place a short step from the escalators.

"Thank you, John, see that no one steals anything," Mother said, handing him a tip with one hand, locking the car with the other. Then Mother was gone in a flash.

"Shirley!" Celeste stood in the doorway of her boutique and waved. "I have a new collection of clothes from Italy, just arrived this morning."

"Hello, my friend," Mother replied, barely slowing down. "I am late for Mia and you know you can never offend your hairdresser! Keep some things aside for me."

* * *

"Mia, wait till I tell you about the new group I've joined."

Mother checked her makeup before leaning back into the salon chair. Mia was the only one who could perfect Mother's beehive hairdo, which she wore long after it was out of fashion.

"Esther and I have joined the IZWE arts and culture group," Mother said. "We meet once a month and learn all about the banned artists and authors. It is a branch of the ANC—so interesting! Each month they come out with a magazine for its members that contains an original lithograph by one of the banned artists. Something else I learned—did you know Tolkien was born here?"

"The one who wrote *Lord of the Rings*?" asked Mia while teasing Mother's hair to unimaginable heights.

"Yes, can you believe it?" Mother continued. "He just recently passed away, in England somewhere. They are going to lay a cornerstone where his house once stood. None of this information is ever published in the newspapers."

"There's barely any interesting news that comes out in the papers." Mia was spraying nearly a whole can of hairspray to shape the beehive.

"And, the members...." Mother smiled. "These are very educated blacks who certainly come to the table with interesting and refreshing perspectives."

"Now that's unusual. The only blacks one sees here in Bloemfontein are the staff, who certainly don't elicit in-depth conversation. But then again," Mia reflected, "I don't think we attempt to have any in-depth conversation with our staff."

"That is what I am talking about!" Mother was adamant. "If only our government could have a constructive dialogue with these people we would not be so ostracized around the world."

"On another note, Shirley, did you hear that Bruce's boyfriend was murdered last night?"

"No! What happened?"

"Apparently, while Bruce was on a business trip the boyfriend went to a bar in town and picked up some young guy and brought him home. The next thing you know, the young guy murdered the boyfriend, stole all the clothes and the car, and disappeared into the night."

"That's terrible!"

"It is too terrible!" continued Mia. "Bruce came home this morning to find the boyfriend still in his pink nightie and slippers, stone cold. Blood everywhere."

On the way back to the parking garage Mother passed a beggar sitting outside a store with a small child attached to her bosom. Mother opened her purse and dropped a few coins into the palm of the outstretched hand. The woman nodded a silent thank you. Then a small black child rushed up and tugged at Mother's skirt as she stepped onto the escalator. Mother opened her purse again and handed a bag of sweets to the smiling little face. The child dashed off again.

It was impossible to satisfy the hunger of all the beggars who swarmed around you, but something was better than nothing. The guilt of starving children was embedded in every South African psyche. It was anathema to waste even one scrap of food.

* * *

The story of my love for a true Afrikaner began with that earth-shattering kiss at the farm. I was fifteen. Pieter was five years older than me. That he found me even remotely attractive was so impossible to imagine that I wondered when I would wake up from the dream. Thank heavens for Mother's hectic social schedule and Father's frequent trips to Johannesburg—they called for few explanations from me. My only conscience was in the guise of Sara and Evelyn, who never failed to remind me that Madam would not be happy if she knew I was seeing an Afrikaner.

I saw Pieter on Saturdays at the Bloemfontein Hotel for coffee. These graduated to lunch at Sylvano's Pizzeria. This was a major deviation from eating nothing, but starving in front of Pieter was not an alternative.

Slowly, I learned about another culture that had been off limits to me.

Home was Postmasburg, a mining town two hours north of Kimberley. I learned that Pieter's father liked to listen to boxing on the radio. He had his own contracting business, and had built all the schools, hospital, and houses in the surrounding area.

Pieter's mother was a housewife and was pregnant with her seventh child. I could not begin to imagine Mother pregnant now.

Our conversation mostly centered around mutual friends, architecture, and my life, which he seemed to find fascinating, heaven knows why. Too shy to ask more about his life, and I was happy just to be with this handsome Afrikaner and answer his questions.

I was smitten with everything about him, from the smell of his aftershave to the feel of his soft hair. And when he drew me into his arms to kiss me? Forget it. I was ensnared by the lion.

Gradually we extended our hours together on Saturdays to include the afternoon rugby matches at the university. We had an unspoken agreement that each Saturday we would see each other. The rest of the week could not pass by quickly enough.

Where was Mother? Secure in her belief that her darling daughter was with her girlfriends while she, Mother, perfected her social scene.

The rugby field below us was burned yellow by the African winter sun.

"Look what he is wearing, it's hysterical! Plaid pants and a yellow tie?!"

Male and female cheerleaders screamed through handheld loudspeakers, "*Gee vir my a V!*" [Give me a V]

"V," the students shouted back.

"It's Leon's Shuster's signature style," Pieter said, watching the ball dart from player to player. "*Gryp die bliksemse bal, jou donner!*" [Grab the goddam ball, you idiot!]

"*Gee vir my 'n R!*"

"R!"

"The students there." I yelled and pointed. "Why are they in church clothes?"

"*Wat se dit* [What does it say]?" screamed Leon.

"*Vrystaat* [Free State]!" screamed the students.

"What?" Pieter was focused on the field.

"They look like they are going to church." I pointed, yelling louder as they screamed *Vrystaats* again.

"Oh," he laughed, "first-year students, the one who obey the rules. We are all supposed to wear these stupid suits for the first eight months on campus. Our group at the architectural department said screw that!"

Was it Pieter's rebellious stand against the staid bastion of Afrikanerdom that drew me to him, or his dark incredibly good looks? Maybe both. We were like the two currents off the tip of Africa, drawn together by the forces of the moon.

The call of the jungle echoed over the plains.

* * *

That December Pieter went to Cape Town with his family. I visited Michelle at Port Elizabeth while she stayed with her father for the holidays.

"Pieter said he might swing by here and drive me back to Bloemfontein instead of me flying back," I whispered to Michelle. She peered into a handheld mirror while curling her eyelashes.

"Your mother will never allow a guy who she has never formally met to drive you through the Transkei all the way back to Bloemfontein. If she knew how often you were seeing him, she definitely would not allow it."

"Eeuw, how can you put that curling thing on your eyelash?" I said.

"Don't be such a baby, Ruchel. All the girls in my school curl their eyelashes. Some even wear makeup to school, would you believe it?"

"What? You must be joking! The nuns would kill us. So what's it like here?" I asked, turning sideways to support my head. "Have you made any friends?"

"Ja, some, but I miss you guys. I was so angry with my parents for divorcing and leaving Bloemfontein. And I'm still jealous that I wasn't at Liz's party. You have no idea how I cried over not being able to go to that party."

With the comfort of best friends, we talked long into the night and drew strength from each other as the days slowly peeled away.

While I was in Port Elizabeth with Michelle, Mother decided to travel with Father to Johannesburg to visit one of her friends, leaving Jenny and Wayne with Gussie and the staff.

"So what's happening at home?" I asked Jenny over the phone one afternoon. "Nothing much," sighed my sister. "Wayne and his friend Timmy are being annoying as usual. Janet and I are begging Evelyn to help us make lemon curd."

"Why don't you ask Gussie to help?" I suggested. "She'd like that."

"Gussie went to Daddy's store to check the books and Evelyn says we don't have any milk for Cuddles and no lemons for the lemon curd. Wayne is always complaining that there is no Coke in the fridge. I am thinking of taking Mommy's car to the shops. If I get them some chocolate they will shut up and get out of our hair. Janet and I discovered where Mommy left money in one of her drawers in the bedroom." Jenny continued, warming up to the idea of taking the green Capri Sport to the store down the road. Jenny was fourteen.

"Are you crazy?" I shouted over the phone, big sister asserting authority. "First of all you are too young to drive and have no clue how to drive, and secondly, mommy will kill you if she knew you were going through her drawers."

"We found some *Playboys* there as well," Jenny giggled. "And it's not true that I don't know how to drive. Mommy let me drive on the road to Thaba Nchu when the road was quiet."

"She did?" I yelled. "I don't even know how to drive, how come she let you?"

What am I saying?

"That's beside the point—you can't go! Mali, come talk some sense into my sister."

"Talk sense into your sister?" asked Michelle from the other side of the room. "You forget it was your sister who put a voodoo curse on me some years back by sticking pins into my Barbie doll. Bloody hell. I am still trying to figure out if she was successful."

"You can't go!" I yelled again to Jenny.

"Watch me!" she said. She slammed the phone down.

When Jenny got an idea in her head, it was almost impossible to change it.

She called to Wayne and his friend Timmy from the top of the stairs, "If you want Coke and chocolate, then hurry up and get into Mommy's car and keep your mouths shut as I have to concentrate on driving. Janet, you can sit in the front with me and don't tell your mother either."

Blond and quiet, Janet was Jenny's best friend and under her spell. She never questioned Jenny's take-charge attitude. So the four of them, aged fourteen and under, piled into Mother's green Capri. The maids looked on, horrified, as Jenny put the car into drive and rolled down the driveway. She could hardly see over the steering wheel.

Miraculously they reached the corner café a mile and half down the road.

Jenny gave the orders. "Hurry and choose which chocolates you want. Wayne, not the *Flakes*, they mess all over. Don't open it before you get home. If you mess, Mommy is going to know about it. Janet, grab the milk from the back. Try and choose the one with the tightest lid."

Milk was sold in bottles with a tinfoil lid that always burst open if the milk bottle suddenly became horizontal. Jenny was not going to take chances. As they climbed back into the car, she ordered Wayne to hold the bottle tightly. But on the way home, Wayne got into a punching battle with Timmy, hitting him with one hand while clutching the bottle in the other.

"Stop it, you stupid idiot!" screamed Jenny as the commotion intensified in the back seat.

"It's Timmy, he started it!" whined Wayne. He threw another punch, and milk poured all over the floor. Jenny let go of the steering wheel for a second to turn around and slap Wayne. That second was all it took for Mother's green Capri Sport to slam into a tree on the side of the road. Boom!

Because of the long nose that housed the engine of the sports car, the four of them managed to climb out with just a sense of shock. Mother's car was not so lucky.

"See what you have done now, Wayne!" Jenny screamed before she yelled at them to follow her. They left the accident and ran all the way home. Then all four jumped on their bicycles.

People and police cars surrounded the area by the time Jenny and company arrived.

"Jenny, darling!" Mrs. Burton, Mother's friend from the Arts Council, ran to Jenny. "Where is your poor mother, how badly is she hurt? Who took her to the hospital?"

"Oh, my mother is in Johannesburg, she is fine." Jenny replied as if this were a normal conversation.

"Then who was driving the car?" Mrs. Burton exclaimed.

Jenny shrugged her shoulders innocently and said, "I don't know, why don't you ask them?"

"Yes, I'll see what the police have to say!" Mrs. Burton turned to make her way through the crowd, then paused to look back at Jenny. "And your grandmother?".

"She is okay, Mrs. Burton, she is resting at home."

Gussie's and Mother's reactions were a whole different matter. A few days later I phoned home and told her that Pieter, a friend of Conrad and Johan, was passing Port Elizabeth and offered to give me a lift home. Mother was still so aghast at what Jenny had done that all she said to me was "that's fine, as long as he drives safely."

"She didn't argue?" Michelle asked when I put the phone down. "I can't believe it! My mother would have definitely said no. I suppose you can thank your sister for your mother's temporary loss of judgment."

"Thank you Jenny!" I shouted to the air. "I am so psyched! You can finally meet him in person!" I so wanted to gain my best friend's approval of him.

The next day Pieter arrived at Michelle's father's apartment in his father's yellow truck. He hugged me then offered to take Michelle and me for ice cream before leaving. I thought it was rather sweet of him. Michelle was smarter than that.

"He wants to see how much influence I have over you," she whispered as we rushed to fetch our purses.

"Rubbish!" I replied. "He knows you are my best friend."

"That's precisely the point." Michelle sighed. "I agree he is good looking and nice but he is still an Afrikaner and five years older than you *nogal* [as well]. Your mother will have a fit if she knows how much you really like him. Just don't do anything stupid, you hear me?"

In my wildest imagination I could not think of anything more than holding hands, kissing, and going to dances at the university. I assured my best friend with the full bravado of innocence that of course I would not do anything stupid and that she was just being silly.

The lion smiled sardonically and licked his paw in the shade of the Baobab tree.

The shortest route from Port Elizabeth to Bloemfontein was through the Transkei, one of the homelands that were relatively underdeveloped. On the way we stopped at a convenience store high in the hills that was run by an Indian businessman from Natal. Now, when I say convenience store it doesn't mean a 7-Eleven. This place was more like a trading post, a rectangular structure built of stone and clay from the river, with a flat corrugated-tin roof.

"Ooh, is this not interesting!" A handful of Transkei men and women sitting on thick logs watched me intently as I climbed out of Pieter's yellow truck. The women wore long dresses of sharply contrasting colours with matching turbans on their heads. Their fabric was much sought after in the stores of Johannesburg and Cape Town where city folk fashioned them into wraps, miniskirts, and other dress styles.

"*Dumela*!" I greeted them as we walked by. Clearly Sotho was not the language in the Transkei but I did not know what hello was in Xhosa. Still, they nodded their heads in greeting, smiles on their faces. Two women sitting on a thick woolen blanket were threading beads into necklaces and bracelets.

"Let me see?" I asked as I crouched on the blanket. I rolled the necklaces between my fingers, noticing how the beads formed intricate diamond shapes. "How much is this one? What about the bangle over there?"

"Don't you want to see what's inside?" asked Pieter. He was clearly not used to shopping with a woman.

"Just now. I want to pay for this set of bangles. Look how the beads form a pattern when you put them all together."

Walking inside was an assault on all the senses. The room was divided by a long wooden counter. One side had a floor of smooth hardened clay, and the other side housed shelves filled with tins of meat, bags of *mielie meel*, flour, sugar, and other staples of the African diet. The Indian owner had hung everything possible from the ceiling: pots and pans, rolls of wire mesh, colourful fabrics, bags of oranges and bananas, chairs, and anything else. On the countertop large glass jars of multicoloured candy competed with a kaleidoscope of beads in other glass jars. Behind the counter on a tray next to the till were freshly baked *samoosas*, a sort of vegetable pie. The place smelled of spices, musty fabric, flour, and grease mixed with the smoke from the log fire outside for the ever present *pap potjie*, a three-legged black pot filled with porridge. Springbok Radio blared from under the counter. It was a happy blend of Indian and African culture.

"Springbok Radio here in the *bundu* [veld]. Can you believe it?" I laughed, rummaging through the fabric and beads, digging my hand into one jar after another. "Did you ever listen to 'The Creeeeeaking Door'?" I asked Pieter dramatically in a spooky voice. "Michelle and I used to think we were so brave listening to the program late at night when everyone was sleeping, but let me tell you, we were *poep* [shit] scared. Every time we heard the door creak on the radio we would dive under the bed with the cushions covering our ears. Eight years old and we thought the bogeyman was coming through the front door. Then we remembered the *thokolosi* under the bed and just screamed and screamed."

"No, we never listened to that program because it was in English," answered Pieter. He followed me around the store as I talked and seemed to be more interested in me than in anything the store had to offer.

"Ooh, look at these lucky packet rings. I used to fight with my sister to get the ring in the Christmas pudding. So what did you listen to when you were young?" I continued. I slipped one ring after the other on each finger and thrust my hands in front of me.

"Um, we listened to boxing and Afrikaans programs like '*Die Man van Staal*' [The Man of Steel]." Pieter answered.

"What's that all about? Is it some kind of superman program? *Die Man van Staal*—it sounds weird. Which ring do you like?" I waggled my fingers under his nose.

"Ja," said Pieter, "he was this superhero who always got the bad guys. He could wipe out a whole gang in a second." Suddenly he said as he flexed the muscles in his arms, "*Ek is* [I am] *Die Man van Staal!* When you and Michelle were still playing with dolls, I was helping out at the circus when it came to town. I watched Willeman van die Kalahari, a famous Afrikaans wrestler, who used to lift cars with his chest. He was strong, like this." He gave me a huge bear hug.

"Ow, ow, you are squeezing me," I giggled as Pieter buried his face in my neck. "Willeman van die Kalahari!" I repeated laughing. "What kind of guy would call himself Willeman van die Kalahari?

And what did you do in a circus? I never thought the circus would go to such a small *dorp* [town]."

"I was an usher, I showed people to their seats," Pieter answered. "I got to see the circus free and earn pocket money so I could have enough money to buy you a ring, like this one." He grabbed my left middle finger on which I had a red and white stone lucky packet ring. "See, with this ring we are now formally *gekuis*," he announced as he slipped all the other rings off my fingers and put the red and white one on my right hand, second finger.

"What's *gekuis*?" I asked, never having heard the word in my life.

"*Gekuis* is when a guy and girl formally go out."

"Oh, you mean like going steady?" I said, suddenly half serious.

"Ja. Like going steady. You are my chick now!"

Then Pieter kissed me gently in the middle of that colourful Transkei store.

The world stopped for that magic moment in time, then the stars guiding my path altered their course. That ring, all of a dime's worth of coloured glass, caught the rays of the sun and flashed.

The lion let out a powerful roar.

CHAPTER FOURTEEN

1974: A coup in Mozambique by leftist military fighters forces Lisbon to finally throw in the towel and abandon all her colonies in Africa: Mozambique, Angola, and Guinea. Fourteen years of conflict have taken their toll. The ripple effect is seismic. Overnight almost half a million Portuguese citizens flee, either back to their homeland or further south to South Africa. Homes, land, businesses, and possessions are simply abandoned as they board planes, ships, and trains to get out of the conflict areas. The result is an immediate shift on the political chessboard. Russia, in the midst of the Cold War, seizes the opportunity to try to gain control of Africa and its mineral riches. Sympathetic guerrilla fighters and liberation movements, who suddenly find themselves moving into abandoned political offices, businesses, and homes, welcome the attention with open arms. Fidel Castro immediately deploys three ships and one thousand troops to Angola. In an instant, white-ruled South Africa and Rhodesia become vulnerable.

P ieter's English was rapidly improving while my Afrikaans continued to be *vrot* [bad], *vrotter* or *vrotest*, depending on who was listening.

"How would you like to come with me to the *sokkie* on Saturday night?"

"What's a *sokkie?*" I asked while my heart did flips over the words "Saturday night." At least it was only my voice he heard over the phone.

"Looks like I will have to teach you some Afrikaans," Pieter laughed. "A *sokkie* is a party that is held on campus at either a girls' or a boys' hostel. My cousin plays in the band so you will have a chance to meet him." After agreeing on a time to meet, I leapfrogged up the stairs to my bedroom and emptied my entire cupboard onto the bed.

"Don't worry Sara, I will pack everything back again," I said quickly as Sara walked in with my freshly laundered clothes. "I am going to a party with Pieter on Saturday night and I don't know what to wear!"

"Does the madam know?" she asked, knowing full well the madam didn't.

"I am just telling mommy that we are going out with a whole group of girls and boys so that she does not have to ask any details. So don't say anything to Jane or any of the other maids. In any case, mommy is going out on Saturday to the opening of *Swan Lake*, it has a party afterward. Pieter said he will drop me off at eleven, so everything should work out fine."

"Madam is still not going to like you kissing an Afrikaans boy. There will be lots of trouble," Sara said while I tried on one shirt after another.

"It will be fine, Sara, stop worrying." But I knew she would worry. After all, she was like a second mother to me.

*   *   *

"So, tell me about your cousin. When did he start playing in a band?" I asked Pieter as I climbed out of his yellow truck. The throbbing sound of *House of the Rising Sun* mixed with laughter under the starry African night. I wore tight jeans, pale blue blouse with three-quarter sleeves, a dash of Revlon's *Charlie*, and nervous excitement. Some older girls were chatting animatedly in Afrikaans.

I am so out of my league here, I thought, holding Pieter's hand. I don't even understand what they are saying. We worked our way through the crowd and Pieter pointed out his cousin with the rest of the band members.

"Are you cradle snatching now, *Neef* [Cousin]?" asked Pieter's cousin, looking me up and down.

"Ruchel, this is my cousin whose name is also Pieter but we call him Pietie. *Oppas wat jy se, ek sal jou bliksem* [Careful what you say, I will kill you]," Pieter said, only half joking. Pietie sounded English and had a good command of the language. Shorter, small brown eyes, a round face, with receding blond hair on a wide forehead, Pietie favored his mother's side in looks.

"What have the architectural *windgats* [show offs] decided to build for the Rag Parade?" asked Pietie. He kept looking at me.

"Something more creative than what you guys in accounting can ever hope to dream up," answered Pieter.

We turned to see a stunning, shapely, dark haired girl saunter up to Pieter and give him a hug, while looking at me curiously out of the corner of her eye.

"*Elsie wil weet hoekom jy haar nie bel nie* [Elsie wants to know why you don't phone her]," she said for the world to hear.

Embarrassed, Pieter turned to me and mumbled, "*Ekskuus* [sorry], Gerda is my sister. Gerda, I would like you to meet Ruchel. She is English."

"Hello." Gerda looked me up and down

"And very young and cute," chipped in Pietie.

"Shut up, Pietie!"

Gerda pulled Pieter aside and spoke in Afrikaans, hands waving in all directions.

"Doesn't look like she likes me," I said to Pietie.

"It is not that she does not like you," said Pietie. "She is mad at Pieter. Her best friend used to go out with him, now she has to tell her that he has fallen in love with a *rooinek* [a derogatory term for the English]. She knows Elsie is going to be heartbroken."

Later on the dance floor Pieter explained it had been over with Elsie the night he kissed me by the river but he hadn't had the courage to tell her. He'd been avoiding her since returning to University.

I tossed and turned in bed that night. My intuition told me that Pieter was genuine in his explanation. But it did make me wonder. Then my heart said, oh screw it.

* * *

Rag Week was a huge tradition at the universities in South Africa, culminating in a parade of marching bands and colourful floats through the center of town. Monies raised were given to different charities in the townships. In Bloemfontein, it was the highlight of the year, starting with university students bursting into school classrooms and begging school children to buy the *Rag Mag*, a student magazine filled with editorials, rude jokes, and pictures of the Rag Queen and her two princesses.

"Psst, Ruchel! Miss First Year has the same last name as your boyfriend," whispered Linda as she scanned the *Rag Mag* hidden on her lap.

"What? Slide it over here, let me see!" I whispered back.

"That's Pieter's sister Gerda! I met her last Saturday. She is very beautiful!"

"Ruchel, what are you doing?" Sister Mary shouted. She got up from her desk and started to come toward me.

"Nothing, Sister. I thought I caught my sock on the edge of the chair," I replied. I surreptitiously handed the magazine back to Linda.

"Well, get on with your work immediately—and that applies to all you girls," threatened Sister Mary.

Pieter was excited about his sister when he phoned that Friday.

"My mother was over the moon when she heard. We're building the float for the Rag Queen and her princesses. Gerda will sit on this huge velvet chair. I can't remember how many hours I have been sober this entire week. Conrad keeps on bringing this *poeswyn* [cheap wine] and before we are ready to pound in one more nail or stuff one more wire mesh hole with *donnerse* [bloody] papier maché, we have to drink at least two jugs. You should have seen Deon trying to climb on the flatbed to put this huge giraffe head on the body we built the night before."

"Why? Was he too drunk?" I asked, wishing I was there.

Pieter laughed. "No, well, maybe a little. We had Beethoven blaring through these speakers rigged onto the telephone poles—I am talking midnight here—and Deon started to swing the giraffe's head like he was conducting some Viennese orchestra. Left, right, up, down. I swear, he looked like a baby elephant imitating a fairy. Then just as the music reached a crescendo," Pieter laughed harder, "he finally got to the truck and swung his leg up. Only the idiot missed the truck and collapsed, giraffe and all, on the floor while the music played on. Conrad and I were choking from laughing but Deon just stood up and tried again until he finally got onto that stupid truck. Oh man."

"So what happened then? Did you finish building the float?"

"No. Anton and I and a couple of other guys, we decided in our drunken state to screw building any further and streak past the girl's dorm."

"Streak!" I said, horrified. "You mean run naked? Did anyone see you?"

"Nah," Pieter said smugly. "We all had our underpants over our heads. It was so late that all the dorms were lights out by that time. Pity, it would have been nice to know some girls would have had pleasant dreams that night!"

"Yeah right, you're just lucky you weren't caught!" I said, sounding surprisingly like Mother. "So, are you going to ride on the float tomorrow?" I said, quickly changing the subject in case I slipped further into Mother mode.

"No," Pieter answered. "Pietie helped me build this huge *catty* [catapult] on the back of my truck at four this morning with some tire tubes he fetched from our uncle's garage. We rigged it so that we could fire bags of flour into the crowd. Tomorrow, you can meet me on campus before the race and help fill plastic bags of flour. It'll be fun."

I said goodnight and went upstairs, my head spinning.

Early the next morning, Gussie dropped me off at the rugby field. The place had been transformed into a carnival with brightly coloured floats jostling for position like thoroughbreds at the start of the Derby. Students who managed to survive the night's intoxication made last-minute adjustments to their floats. I searched for Pieter and his yellow truck. In the distance I saw Gerda sitting regally in her velvet chair high above the crowd. White satin and red roses enveloped her. Finally, at the back of the long line, I spotted what looked like a yellow truck.

"Oh my heavens!" I exclaimed as I came near.

Perched perpendicular to each other at the back of the truck were two wooden logs secured by rope. A half-circle brace made from two rubber tubes was attached to the end of one log so that it roughly resembled a huge *catty*.

"How are you going to shoot the flour bags into the air? You will have to stand a mile back as you stretch this thing," I asked.

"Pietie and I have already practiced. You should see how far these bags of flour fly," Pieter said. He smiled and gave me a kiss.

"All you have to do is sit at the back of the truck and fill the plastic bags with flour."

Pietie walked up to the truck, beer in hand. "Are you two lovebirds ready?" he asked smiling. "We have to beat the Reitz Hostel guys on the float in front of us. Bloody copycats! They decided to pinch our idea and throw bags of flour from the top of their float as well, stupid idiots."

"Aagh! We will be much better and more powerful," Pieter readied the *catty* for the first shot. Suddenly the start gun went off and Pietie scrambled into the front of the truck and started the engine.

"Okay, just pass me one bag when I stretch this rubber band," shouted Pieter. As we moved slowly down the road, the bag sailed into the air and burst against a tree, showering the crowd along the street with white dust. That was followed by a bag of flour from the Reitz Hostel float in front of us. It also caught a tree branch and ripped apart, and a crowd of white ghosts underneath scattered in all directions. I handed another bag of flour to Pieter. The bag shot forward in a low arc and careened off Deon's giraffe head, bending it to one side and making it look like one dead giraffe.

By now I was laughing so much my sides hurt. I was just getting ready to help Pieter load the next bag when the sirens started blaring. The next thing I knew I was staring into the very red face of a policeman.

"*Wat de donner dink julle doen julle* [What the hell do you think you are doing]?" he bellowed as he and his fellow officers surrounded the float and truck with their motorcycles. "Who is responsible for this?" he added, in case none of us understood Afrikaans. A black policeman in the meantime was trying to calm the crowd using Sotho, broken English, and Afrikaans.

"She's not with us, officer. *Sy is net 'n Engelse skool kind* [She is just an English school girl]," I heard Pieter saying as he pushed me into the crowd before they could herd me into the group of accused. Standing beside a floured ghost, I watched apprehensively as Pieter and group, together with the truck and float, were escorted to the police station.

Later that week, Pieter told me how he had royally confused the police as to who was actually responsible for the flour shower. In the end they let him and his friends leave with a stern warning.

* * *

The next week I was back on the phone with Pieter.

"You can't be serious!" I exclaimed

"I am," Pieter said. "Someone gave the president of the university our names as the guys who had streaked past the girls' dorm. Now we are the scapegoats for the spate of streaking that has been happening on campus. We know of others but they are so *ingekruip* [in bed] with the faculty that no one will ever rut on them."

"But that's unfair!"

"I know," said Pieter. "We were targeted because we are architecture students. Someone who knew what we did that night reported us. I think I know who it is but it doesn't matter now. The five of us were called into the president's office this morning. We are expelled for a year. My father is going to kill me!"

The thought of not seeing Pieter again was devastating. It felt like the end of my world.

Days went by without a word from Pieter. Then I bumped into his cousin, Pietie, at the FVB Center.

"Pieter's father had a huge fit, naturally," Pietie said. "For an Afrikaner to have his son expelled from university for streaking is a huge shame on the family. Pieter has gone to work for an architectural firm in Johannesburg so it's going to be a while before he'll phone you. His pride is hurt right now."

As the days passed without a phone call, my neurosis started to rear its ugly head again. Maybe I was just a passing fancy, a summer romance? All those big city girls with their big city attitudes would surely divert his attention from me.

Tears rolled onto the pillow each night as I argued with myself over and over again whether he really loved me. In my mind those arguments reached epic proportions.

The season reflected my mood. The bright sunflowers of autumn closed their eyes in defeat as fall gave way to the biting winds of winter. Black women wearing thick woolen blankets wrapped tightly around them walked the icy roads to the townships. A pall of smoke seemed to hover over everything. I sought solace in my friends.

Ineka's house became the central meeting place. Occasionally Conrad and his friends would join us to watch *The Avengers* on a home movie screen after eating a home-cooked dinner of *nasi goreng.* Conrad sometimes brought his 'flavor of the week,' which I duly reported to Michelle. She still carried a torch for him. Soon it was July, and I was turning sweet sixteen.

"We must invite Ian and some of the other nice boys at St. Andrews," Mother announced during lunch one day. "I think we should set a tent up in the garden. George, you will have to ask that delightful saleslady at the Johannesburg showroom to set aside one of her modern dresses for Ruchel."

Over my dead body! I still cringe when I see the colour orange.

"Ma, can't I just have a small dinner party like Liz had on the farm?"

"But my Ruchie," interrupted Father before Mother could continue, "don't you want Mommy to make a lovely big party for you? I will get you a pretty dress in Johannesburg. You will look like a princess on that night."

Now I was almost in tears. I knew my parents wanted the best for me and it was not that I wasn't grateful. It was just that something inside of me felt trapped and was fighting to get out.

Evelyn came in to clear the dishes. "*Hauw,* Pulani! What's the matter?"

"I don't understand her, Evelyn," Mother sighed. "I want her to have a big party and all she wants is a small dinner. What kind of sixteenth birthday is that? I never battle like this with Jenny or Wayne."

"*Hauw!* We make a nice dinner then, Madam. I will make all of Pulani's favorite dishes. Roast lamb, peas, some roast potatoes, and I will ask the old Madam to make apple pie. It will be like one of Madam's dinner parties with lots of flowers and candles. Why don't you ask Miss Michelle to come and visit, Pulani?"

"I agree with Evelyn," Father answered as he dabbed the corners of his mouth with a starched napkin. "Have whatever party you feel like, my Ruchie, and if you want your friend here just let Mommy arrange it." He smiled as he bent down to kiss me on the head before walking out of the dining room.

"When I turn sixteen, I want a huge party with a band and a tent and a huge cake!" interjected Jenny.

Right before the big day, Mother fetched Michelle from the airport.

"Everyone from Liz's party said they are coming," I said excitedly as the two of us sat on my bed. "Everyone except bloody Pieter. I have not heard from him since he left town, can you believe it?"

"Agh, forget him," said Michelle between mouthfuls of cookies we had sneaked up from the kitchen.

"Don't make crumbs, Pulani!" Sara reprimanded me as she walked into the room. "Madam says you are not allowed to eat in your bedroom!"

"Let's go and sit on top of the hill," said Michelle. "Grab the cookies."

We ran out the kitchen door and climbed the fence that separated civilization from the wild. Skirting loose rocks, thorn bushes, and deer droppings we made it to the top.

We sat on the rocky outcrops surveying the world around us. Below, we could see old Stephen pruning the roses along the driveway while Wayne and Jonas kicked a soccer ball around. The sweet sharp smell of the dry African veld seeped into our noses. A gentle warm breeze brushed passed us as a deer ambled by, followed by another. At that moment, sitting with my best friend, I did not want to be anywhere else in the world.

Too soon, my birthday arrived.

Jenny and Wayne were banished to friends' homes for sleepovers. Old Stephen placed lanterns in the garden. They gave off a magical light in the cold night air.

Alex, who was still the most perfect blond Greek god I had ever seen, arrived with Conrad and Johan.

"It is just another year and a half before I join you on campus in Cape Town," I giggled as Alex handed me a bunch of white roses.

"You will love it there, Ruchel," he smiled. "Not at all conservative and boring like this town. The politics are so liberal. Everyone there is genuinely concerned about the inequality of the blacks!"

Sara moved through the small crowd, handing out glasses of champagne.

"Did you know," Alex said, picking up a glass from Sara's tray, "that the Indians were not allowed to stay in the Free State for longer than twenty-four hours? So, imagine, if they drove from Durban to

Cape Town through the Free State, they would have had to drive right through with only stops for gas or food. How crazy is that? And we are living right in the middle of it!"

"It's so depressing," replied Conrad. "I hear it all from my uncle. Coloureds were arrested in Cape Town because they used a 'whites only' exit at the train station. Four white mayors boycotted a church service because the mayor and his wife from Soweto were going to attend. It is all so ridiculously petty!"

"If things don't improve, I might go to America after I complete my degree," said Alex.

"Didn't their president, what's his name, Nixon, just resign because of some scandal?" asked Ineka.

"Yes," replied Alex. "They might have a corrupt president but at least they got rid of their stupid segregation laws in the sixties. More than a decade later and we are still stuck in some ridiculous time warp. We must be the only country left that does not have TV."

"Don't forget our lovely censorship department," interjected Michelle. She and Conrad joined the conversation.

"I know," I said. "You can't believe all the books written by South African authors that are for sale in London but are banned here."

"Well, at least in Cape Town, you're more informed," said Alex. "But enough politics! Let's toast the birthday girl!"

Halfway through the evening, Sara tapped me on the shoulder.

"I think Boss Pieter is on the phone for you," she whispered.

"Sounds like you are having a party," Pieter said.

"Yes, and I would have invited you if I knew where to call. How are you?"

"Having a great time, can't speak for long since I'm on a pay phone. I'll call you again."

Having a great time? Talk about having a sobering effect.

"What does he want me to do?" I anguished later in the bedroom to Michelle, kicking off my shoes. "He disappeared from the face of the earth. He broke my heart! Then out of the blue, he says hello as if I had spoken to him yesterday! And then I hear the stupid coins dropping into the phone box and he says he will phone me again and that's it!"

"He wants you to sit around like some *kloosterkoek* [nun] waiting for his call," replied my sage friend. "I suppose when he heard there was a party going on, he thought you had found another boyfriend and moved on."

"Tonight was such fun. I could be myself and talk to everyone without worrying what I looked like or said. Bloody hell, what should I do now?"

"Just have some fun, Ruchel." Michelle sighed. "We'll both be in Cape Town at university soon and who knows who we'll meet there."

She was right. I had just turned sweet sixteen and there was a whole world out there.

CHAPTER FIFTEEN

———————

1975: A meeting to address the Rhodesian situation is convened in a railway carriage parked in the middle of the bridge that spans Victoria Falls. Present at this symbolic "no-man's land" conference is President Kaunda of Zambia, Prime Minister Vorster of South Africa, and Prime Minister Ian Smith of Rhodesia. Smith is forced to attend after Vorster threatens to limit supplies of South African fuel and ammunition to Rhodesia. Before the meeting Smith is persuaded to accept a ceasefire and free the captured insurgents and return them to Zambia. In turn, Vorster withdraws the South African police from Rhodesia, and Kaunda delivers the dissident leaders to the meeting. But the talks prove to be nothing but talk. The dissident leaders present demands outside of the agreement and four South African police are killed immediately after the ceasefire. Vorster misreads the fervor of Smith and his white electorate's desire to remain in power. In turn, Kaunda misreads the dissident leader Sithole who heads the Zanu delegation at the meeting. Sithole, in reality, is losing power to Robert Mugabe, who should have been at the meeting but refused to attend. Five years later Robert Mugabe beats Smith in a landslide victory in Rhodesia's first free election. The Union Jack is lowered and Rhodesia is renamed Zimbabwe as it celebrates its independence.

T he sticky sweet aroma of freshly made donuts, *pannekoek* (pancakes), and pink cotton candy wafted through the outdoor swim stadium. Uniformed school children giggled and whispered behind the food vendors.

"Charlene, let's see if we can get our team to out shout the Eunice School girls!"

We were cheerleaders for our school's swim team, and we were anything but ladylike. Sexy and loud was more like it. We urged our ladylike audience to reach new heights of uncouth swaying, dancing, clapping, and shouting.

"*Ai zika zumba, zumba, zumba. Ai zika zumba, zumba zay* [Hold him down, you Zulu warrior. Hold him down, you Zulu chief]!" The Eunice girls on the bleachers next to us screamed and chewed gum as they responded to their cheerleader's war cries. Placards, coloured streamers, and balloons shook after each cheer.

"*Daar in die ou Kalahari*... [There in the old Kalahari...]," began the Grey College boys, who were thumbing their noses at the St. Andrews School boys, themselves trying valiantly to outshout the overwhelming number of Grey boys next to them.

"*Oh when the saints*"—clap, clap —"*oh when the saints*"— clap, clap —"*oh when the saints go marching in*," sang the St. Andrews cheerleader in his bowler hat and blue-and-white striped pants held up by suspenders.

"Hey, *souties!*"—a derogatory term for English people —shouted the stout Grey cheerleader who also played defense for the rugby team. "*Julle klink soos 'n klomp moffies* [You sound like a bunch of gays]!" Then they sang tauntingly, "*Oh when the saints*...," in a high-pitched Dutch accent, sashaying their hips girlishly.

"Hey, Ruchel," one of the girls shouted from the bleachers. "There's a guy who says he knows you and wants to talk to you. He's kinda cute. Says he'll wait under the stairs behind us when you're done."

"What?" I shouted back but the girl had already joined in with Charlene, who had started the African-English rendition of *A Wimba Weh, Ohi'mbube, ohi'mbube.*

"I'll be back just now!" I shouted to Charlene, hopping off the platform. I walked around the back of the bleachers to the area where the St. Michael's girls were sitting.

"Hmm, you are looking quite good tonight," said a familiar voice. Was I hallucinating? I turned and saw emerging from the dark none other than Pieter himself. He'd seen my whole screaming performance. From where he was standing you could clearly see Charlene through all the hanging feet.

"What are you doing here? Why didn't you phone? How did you know I was here?"

"I have my sources."

I approached him cautiously, not sure where we had left off and where we would start again. Pieter smiled at me as his fingers crept up my neck and through my hair. Muscular arms weaved across my back. Instant shortness of breath. So much for acting nonchalant.

"It's so good to see you again," Pieter said. "Have you been a good girl while I was in Johannesburg?"

I pulled away before my emotions got the better of me. "Wait for me, the meet is nearly over. Back here in a half hour?"

I raced back to Charlene, who paused in mid song to ask what was wrong when she saw the look on my face.

"Pieter is back in town," is all I said.

The cheerleaders screamed. The crowd screamed. But nothing could drown out the clamor in my brain. After disappearing for a year with just a few phone calls and a Christmas card, Pieter appeared as if only a day had passed. It was so good to see him. So unbelievably good. I wanted to bury myself in his arms and never emerge alone again.

*   *   *

Every moment not assigned to school or family obligation was spent with Pieter. We had Camembert cheese and wine picnics on the banks of the Mazelspoort Dam, university *sokkies*, long walks on the small hills that skirted town, pizza every Saturday afternoon, glasses of *Tassies* [a cheap South African wine] shared with fellow liberal Afrikaans architecture students. All were five or six years older than me. At sixteen, I was caught up in a life that was going faster than perhaps I should have gone.

Where was Mother in all this? In a whirl of soirees, art exhibitions, theater, and IZWE meetings that distributed antiapartheid literature. One day I overheard her telling friends over a cup of tea that she was very much against the war in Angola.

"There is no way I am going to allow my son to fight some stupid war in Angola," she said. "If this government cannot get their politics and house in order, then I do not see why I have to sacrifice my son for their twisted ideals."

"Why are we fighting a war in Angola?" I asked Pieter the next day as we lay stretched out on a picnic blanket on the bank of the Mazelspoort dam. Tall dry grass whispered in the summer breeze while black beetles and large brown ants competed for the last bread crumbs that had fallen to the dusty red earth.

"That is not an easy question to answer. Much of what we were told when I was doing maneuvers in the Swakopmund Desert in South West Africa [now Namibia] was top secret. All I can tell you is that South Africa is supposed to help make sure the Russians don't control Angola—it's a uranium-rich country. As I'm a lieutenant, the army can call me up at any time to fight the commies on the border."

"But you've finished your compulsory army and you're studying now! They can't call you up."

"Oh, yes they can. I still have a series of three-week camps to complete. They can call me up whenever they want, tomorrow even! So in the event of my leaving for the border tomorrow morning, I am now going to hold you in my arms and kiss you all over for the rest of the day!" He buried his face in my neck and kissed my ear.

"Stop!" I giggled. "It's ticklish!"

"Hmm, then I have to find new places to kiss." Pieter smiled mischievously as he put down his glass of Nederburg Pinotage and slowly unbuttoned the top of my blouse. Suddenly my bra was loose and I shivered with desire. What the hell. I did not want to stop.

I could smell his cologne as he moved down my neck, hovering around my breasts like a bee gathering pollen. I was drowning in an uncharted sea of passion. His smooth muscular chest, suddenly devoid of T-shirt, slid over my body.

"I really do love you," he whispered, threading his fingers through my hair and kissing me.

Could I please stay here? Please…

The hands of time moved slowly as the burning red sun smiled over the rippling water and bade the world good night.

Ohi'mbube, ohi'mbube… The lion sleeps tonight…

* * *

"I notice you have been spending a lot of time with that Afrikaans boy. I hope this phase passes soon," Mother remarked after Pieter dropped me off at the house one Saturday afternoon. On the way home Mother did not say a word about Pieter. Instead, she continued her ongoing lecture. Lectures were more frequent since Mother noticed I was spending more time out of the house.

"I hope you realize that you have to focus on your homework, Ruchel," she said, thus avoiding any reference to Pieter and the fact that he was Afrikaans. "This is your senior year and you need to make sure your grades are good. Your cousin Millicent went to finishing school in Switzerland. I spoke to Uncle Habib, and he agrees it is the best choice for you. Might even undo some of the bad habits you seem to have picked up from these friends of yours. I don't know why you do not mix more with the St. Michaels and St. Andrews girls and boys. Don't roll your eyes like that, and sit up straight!"

To Mother, everything went in phases. There was the bottle phase, birthday party phase, Barbie Doll phase, Michelle phase, clothes phase, and now boyfriend phase. Since Mother was intent on making sure we had the utmost fun in all phases of life she tended to allow a little leeway in the boyfriend phase, believing that it would quickly pass and that I would soon be shipped to some far-off country to enter my next programmed phase complete with fun, excitement, and, she hoped, marriage to a European aristocrat.

Grandma Gussie knew better. She now had her own two-bedroom apartment a few blocks away, and had gotten to know Pieter by talking to him at length when he visited her with me. He loved her cooking and was often invited to have a bit of *kibi* or *mamoul* that just happened to be in the fridge. Many times on the weekend when I spent the night at Gussie's, she would not only let me go out with Pieter at night but also let me sleep till late the next morning with not a sound from any maid. I drew great comfort from the quiet times I had with my grandmother.

At home, Evelyn was ruler when Mother and Father were out. She sounded more like Mother each day.

"Pulani!" she called from the downstairs phone one morning. "Boss Piet says he is coming to pick you up in an hour to go to Maseru. Does the madam know you are going across the border?"

"Mommy already left before I had a chance to tell her," I shouted from my bedroom. Sara was holding the hairdryer while I pulled and tugged at thick strands of hair. "Evie, just tell her we are going to meet Pam and Dudley for lunch and then we are going to see the *Rocky*

Horror Show and that we will be back at about eleven tonight. You know Dudley! He used to live on the same street as us."

Evelyn walked into my bedroom. I looked up at her.

"He was able to get tickets to the show and it's being performed in Maseru because they're not allowed to perform here in South Africa," I pleaded, making it an issue of national significance.

"Have you done all your homework?" she fired back.

"Yes, yes, yes," I sighed as I heard Pieter's new blue Citroen rolling up the driveway. It was a present from his father for his 21st birthday. "Got to go! Just tell Mommy I am with Dudley and Pam too, she likes them!" I ran downstairs and out the front door.

Maseru was the capital of Lesotho, a tiny landlocked country that bordered the Free State. Observing the interaction between whites and blacks in that vibrant little community, you would never think that apartheid existed just a few miles away. My group of friends often made the hour and a half journey to the casino in Maseru on Sundays, so it was really nothing new to Mother.

"Dudley and Pam are sleeping over at the hotel so we'll meet them there," said Pieter as I climbed into the car. "I have to get you back tonight."

"I know, I know. At least we get to see the show"

What a show it was, with the London cast and a sold-out crowd they earned the maximum number of curtain calls. At nine-thirty we were still dancing in the aisles doing the Time Warp again. "*Just a jump to the right, and a jump to the leh-h-h-heft…*"

But if we did not jump into the car by nine-forty at the latest there would be no way we could make the border before it closed at ten o'clock.

"Ruchel, now! We have to go," shouted Pieter over the singing and dancing.

"Just another minute!" I shouted back.

"Your mother will kill me if I don't get you back!" Pieter shouted. He grabbed my hand and pulled me through the crowd.

"We have ten minutes to get through the border. It takes ten minutes just to get there!" Pieter yelled as he maneuvered through the traffic and raced to the Lesotho border. Ten minutes later, give a second or two, we could see the lights ahead.

"Oh thank God, you are still open!" Pieter said to a surly black guard on the Maseru side of the border as we gave him our passports. "We have to hurry to make the South African border on the other side of the bridge, so please could you just stamp them quickly?"

But the guard was clearly relishing taking his time. "I have to check the trunk of your car," he said. "Please open it now." He leisurely walked to the back of the car.

"Shit, shit, shit!" muttered Pieter as he watched seconds tick by on his watch. "We have about thirty seconds to cross the bridge before they close on the other side."

The guard finally nodded his head and gave us a curt dismissal wave. We flew over the cast-iron bridge that spanned the Orange River—only to find the South African border in total darkness with all gates shut tighter than a maximum-security prison.

Pieter yelled a string of words in Afrikaans that needed no translation. "They closed early! Bloody government *dooses* [idiots]! We are so screwed!"

He spun the car around and raced back over the bridge to the surly guard at the Lesotho border. As we approached the border our worst nightmare unfolded. The guard had locked up the office and gates and was climbing into his van as we screeched to a halt on the other side of the locked fence.

"Let us out, the South African border is closed!" shouted Pieter to the guard.

"The border will open again at six in the morning." The guard laughed. "You will just have to wait."

He then put his van into reverse and sped away.

"Your mother is going to have a fit!"

"My mother is going to have a fit!"

"We can't even phone to say what has happened." Pieter looked up and down the bridge as if in the hope of finding some miraculous pay phone. "We'll have to sleep in the car. There's no way out of this mess until six tomorrow morning." More Afrikaans words.

This time I was truly in deep trouble. We were stuck between two borders on a bridge across the Orange River in the middle of the night. The only way out was to abandon the car, climb over the ten-foot-tall chain-link barbed wire fence, run through snake-infested grass to the river, swim fast enough to avoid predators lurking in the water, crawl up the steep embankment on the other side while dislodging and dodging scorpions under the rocks, cross through remote farms where an attack by a vicious pit bull was a distinct possibility, and finally get to a national road and walk all the way back to Bloemfontein because there would not be a single vehicle on the road after midnight. Curfews kept most people off the roads at this time of night. It would be desolate.

That I even considered the feasibility of such an attempt showed how panicked I was. Instead we slept in the car. I had dreamed of staying all night with Pieter but this was a nightmare. Six o'clock in the morning could not come fast enough. Pieter called Mother from the South African border. Her tirade over the phone was just a hint of the eruption to come.

"Go to your room immediately, Ruchel and change for school! I am terribly disappointed in you, Piet! I trusted you to look after her. You are never to see my daughter again. Is this what you call acting responsibly?" said Mother. Then she slammed the front door and marched upstairs to continue in my bedroom. Gussie arrived as Pieter was pulling out the driveway, and went immediately towards the shouting.

"Calm down Shirley," Gussie ordered. "The child is now safe, and she has certainly learned her lesson."

"Gussie!" I sobbed, running to her outstretched arms. This infuriated Mother even further.

Evelyn brought Mother a cup of tea, and joined in the admonishment. "Ai, Pulani! The Madam! *Ho hlakana hlolo.*" This is a Sotho saying that means 'to be so angry that you're confused in the head.'

"Madam even called the police. They left after boss Pieter's phone call this morning." Evelyn handed the tea to Mother. "Drink this Madam. It will calm your nerves. The old Madam will take Pulani to school. *Tlong ka tsela ena* [This is the way it is]!"

The phone rang.

"Mrs. Denny from the Arts Council, for you Madam," Evelyn announced. Once Mother left the room, I pleaded with Gussie to make Mother change her mind and let me continue seeing Pieter.

The cajoling and begging continued throughout the following weeks. Finally, with the help of Gussie, Pieter was called to the house for a talking-to about the rules. It was worse than the Spanish Inquisition but it got Pieter back.

Mother was not pleased. I think she secretly prayed for the year to end so that she could ship me away from Bloemfontein and out of the clutches of this—Afrikaner.

A knowing grin spread over the lion's face as he surveyed the world below him.

CHAPTER SIXTEEN

———————

1975: *Angola spins out of control. Independence is set for November 11 and the fight to become the ruling party heats up. The Marxist-led Movimento Popular de Libertacao de Angola (MPLA) are supplied with ammunition, training, and troops by Russia and Cuba who are eager to gain control of Angola's mineral wealth. The Frente Nacional de Liberatacao de Angola (FNLA) are covertly being supplied with ammunition by the U.S. Central Intelligence Agency (CIA). When the MPLA seizes the capital Luanda, the conspiracy is intensified. The US Congress sends arms and ammunition to the FNLA while Russia and Cuba increase their supply of troops and ammunition. South Africa is initially reluctant to become party to this conspiracy, fearing that it might hurt their efforts at détente with the other African nations, but eventually they step in to help the FNLA fight the MPLA. The deciding factor is their fear that Marxist rule in Angola would provide fertile training ground for SWAPO, whose target is Namibia. With the assumption that they have US support, the SA Defense Force leads a covert operation to crush the MPLA. The result is not as planned. The United States pulls its support while Cuba and Russia up theirs. Under US pressure, South Africa is forced to make a humiliating withdrawal. The soldiers have fought valiantly, have won all their battles, and have done more than expected of them but in the end it is all in vain. South Africa receives condemnation from the other African leaders after four captured South African soldiers are paraded at the Organization of African Unity (OAU) convention in Nigeria. At the convention, on 6 December, the key state Nigeria formally recognizes the MPLA as the ruling party.*

Michelle and I shared secrets and laughter that distance could not dim. I told her everything, up until now. I feel guilty because I can't bring myself to tell my best friend what inroads Pieter's hands were making.

"I'm sorry I haven't phoned you in a while, Mali. When I'm not at school, I'm with Pieter and then I don't think of anything else. How are you?"

The truth was that Pieter was seeing more of me naked with each new encounter. Mother would have died a thousand deaths if she had known what was happening. Filled with fear, but unable to stop. Just plenty of guilt and fear.

"So, how is the great love affair? Have you gone on the pill yet?" Michelle asked.

"Don't be crazy, I'm not going to have sex with him, my mother would kill me! But I will get to meet his parents," I said, quickly changing the subject.

"How did you pull that one off?"

"Pieter asked my parents if he could take me to Postmasburg to attend his high school reunion and meet his parents. My dad thought it was a nice idea. My mother was another story."

"I can believe that! Your mother probably thought the nails were being driven further into the coffin. What changed her mind?"

"Gussie and begging," I sighed. "But wait, let me tell you. It's a five-hour journey into the Northern Cape—and Pieter tells me it's like driving through the desert—actually, a few miles beyond his dorp is a place called Hotazel. Hot-az-el! Can you imagine?"

"And…?"

"So it's a small *dorp,* Pieter says it makes Bloemfontein look like a major metropolis. He says there's only one school in town, four churches, and one main street. His father built their home, it's on top of a hill. It sounds like his mother is very sweet. but I don't think his parents socialize very much."

"Oh, your mother would get on famously with his mother," teased Michelle.

"Well, no worry there. I doubt if my mother would ever even come to Postmasburg."

*   *   *

The minute I arrived at the Coetzee family home, I was welcomed with a cup of tea and a homemade *karringmelkbiskuit* (oven-dried buttermilk bread, like rusks or biscuits). Like our family, life in the

Coetzee household revolved around the kitchen and eating. In the background the radio rattled out the latest news in Afrikaans.

His mother, busy snipping the ends off string beans, kept conversation going by asking me lots of questions. Very plain looking, she wore her long black hair pulled back in a bun. She spoke to me in English and I replied in Afrikaans. My Afrikaans is *vrot,* but I wanted to make the effort.

"Kan ek jou help [Can I help you]?" I remembered Mother's instructions to be helpful and courteous. It was my first mistake, as Pieter would gently remind me later that evening. In the Afrikaans tradition, to address your elders as "you" or "your" showed great disrespect. What I should have said was *Kan ek Mevrou help?* (Can I help Madam?) Pieter's mother was too polite and too interested in hearing about my ballet and tap lessons to worry how I answered, but his father looked a little strangely at me.

I enjoyed speaking with Pieter's mother, but my Afrikaans sentences were getting so *vrot* that I eventually switched back to English.

I realized how far apart were the worlds of our mothers, Pieter's and mine. Hers was an Afrikaans world with its prejudice and preconceived ideas. Even though both our mothers were obsessed with cleanliness, his mother had difficulty retaining maids because of the way she had been indoctrinated to mistrust black people. She simply could not work with the blacks in town and preferred to do the housework herself. Pieter's mother was immersed in the lives of her children, especially the youngest one, who had been born with Down's syndrome a year earlier.

In our home, Evelyn, Sara, and all of our household staff, were an integral part of our family. Mother trusted them, depended on them, and cared about them. The staff gave Mother the freedom to host elaborate soirees, to leave the home whenever she wanted, to expand her horizons, and try to change what she could in the world.

My second mistake was trying to make my bed the next morning. Pieter tried to show me how to fold the sheets but I made a hopeless mess of it. It was my first attempt ever at making a bed.

The predominantly Afrikaans *dorp* was too small to interest any major grocery or clothing store. In the local supermarket, *biltong* and *koeksisters* (deep-fried sweet bread) reigned supreme. "How did you ever survive here?" I asked Pieter as we stepped over discarded paper bags and empty cans in the middle of the sidewalk. A layer of dry red dust from the surrounding dirt roads and iron-ore mines covered every nook and cranny of the single-story buildings. Coloured and black people wandered aimlessly from bottle store to corner café with vinegar-soaked fish and chips wrapped in newspaper.

"Well, we all just hung out together at friends' houses, played rugby, or watched movies," replied Pieter. As we walked eyebrows were raised at the sight of this *snaakse Engelse meisie* (strange English girl) he had wrapped around his arm. Down the main street he introduced me to his ex-girlfriend's mother, who owned the local *apteek* (pharmacy).

"Looks like she was rather surprised to see me with you," I said as we stepped back onto the hot pavement. "You still have not answered my question. Why are you not still going out with this Elsie if you were so into each other? How do you say 'going steady, *gekuis?*"

"Her parents thought we were getting too serious at a young age, so they sent Elsie to boarding school in Bloemfontein. The following year I was called into the army, as you know, in Bloemfontein. Then I ran into her at an annual gala. She was glad to see me, but she was seeing another guy. I got so angry I just left. Then I saw you in the Cool Cat. You cast your spell on me and that was it, *klaar* [finished]. And now I am not going to let you out of my sight."

*   *   *

"So you weren't born in Postmasburg?" I asked as we traveled through the dusty veld to the place where Pieter spent many of his childhood afternoons.

"No, I was born in Welkom," he replied. "My father was working as a foreman on a large construction site."

"Isn't that where they have lots of big goldmines?"

"Ja. Welkom is bigger, more like Bloemfontein."

"So how come your parents landed up in the middle of the *bundu?*"

"After my father had a few too many drinks with the boys, one too many times, my mother got so mad that she just piled us into her car and drove all the way back to my grandmother's house in Olifantshoek."

"You mean your mother just left without telling your father? He must have been furious!"

"Not as furious as my mother, who suddenly had to figure out how to feed and clothe the four of us. Those years we did not have a lot of money."

"And your grandmother…?"

"Ja, my grandmother was not amused. What I remember was having some fun times there. She had this big backyard with about 300 chickens running around inside a huge pen with a henhouse."

"300 chickens!?"

"She sold them to the market, provided the whole town with chickens, eggs, fresh milk…We helped her. She taught us how to catch them and chop their heads off."

"How could you chop a chicken's head off—eeeuw—that is so cruel!"

"How do you think we had roast chicken?" Pieter laughed. "I also helped my uncle cut up a sheep."

"I could never eat a sheep that I chopped up. I would have nightmares forever after that!"

"Ruchel, how do you think people on farms eat? They don't have shops around the corner like in Bloemfontein." Pieter sighed patiently. "You should have tasted my grandmother's *pannekoek*. She made the best *pannekoek* and *souskluitjies*."

"I'm afraid to find out what that is."

"Pancakes, and dumplings!" Peter laughed.

"So what happened to your dad?"

"One day I was kicking my ball around in the yard and I saw my father walking down the road. He asked me where my mom was and the next thing I saw was them kissing and talking. Not long after, we moved into an old blue house down the road. My father took a job in Olifantshoek, about an hour and a half from here. After my brother Hendrik was born we moved to Postmasburg. By that time I was thirteen, and my father started his own company, Henco Construction. It was tough in the beginning. I remember my mother patching our school clothes over and over again because money was always tight."

His was a world so very different from mine.

"Then my father became very successful, put all six children through University. We were known as the clever kids in town. We were clever, because my mother was so clever. She was the only person in the whole of South Africa that year to receive two honor medals, as the smartest person in matric [senior year]."

"Very clever!"

"Here we are! See the big water hole below? That was our swimming pool."

As we climbed out of his father's truck into the searing dry heat of the endless veld, I tried to make sense of what I had just learned. I squeezed his hand as we walked to the rock ledge.

Beneath us ran a tunnel of water. "If you drop a bottle in this hole here," said Pieter, "it will travel all the way under ground and emerge someplace else"

"Are you serious?

"That's what my father said. Eventually it will surface miles and miles away at *De Oog* in Kuruman."

"Did you try it?"

"Never thought of trying it, I didn't know how to get to the other side." He giggled like a little boy. "I should take you there. Also to Witsands—the different layers of coloured sand roar like a lion when it shifts under your feet."

"You are joking, right? Sand that roars?"

"It's true!" He smiled as he leaned over and roared softly in my neck. "When small planes fly over this area, their engines are known to stall because of the strong magnetic power."

"I don't believe you!" But Pieter was right. It was an unusual area, as I eventually witnessed. You *could* hear the sand roar when you walked on it.

We were working our way through a box of chocolates his mother had given me. I was taking a small bite of each then handing the rest to Pieter to finish off. It was the bum, of course, ready to grow to unimaginable size. All around us we heard the crickets and birds carrying on like frenzied teenagers at a disco club. Dry thorn bushes rolled hesitantly over tall cracked grass. The rock we sat on was a fraction cooler thanks to a huge *kameeldoringboom* tree that lent us its shade.

"You worked for your father during the vacations?"

"He taught me construction. I used to stay with him on the job sites, since I was twelve. That's how I learnt not only to target shoot with the *windbuks*, but also how to drive. By the time I was fourteen, he used to send my brother and me to Kimberley to pick up supplies for the job."

"You mean you drove a truck to Kimberley by yourself at fourteen?"

"Sure." Pieter smiled as he rubbed my shoulders. "Not only did I drive to Kimberley without a license but my brother and I also had to figure out how to load a huge cement-mixing machine onto the truck. We finally got some blacks to help us push it up two planks. It was a hell of a job but that was typical of my father. He would just instruct us to do something and we had to come up with the solution."

"You poor baby," I teased as I pressed the muscles on his arm. "At least it made you strong and big enough to tackle those oxen on the rugby field. No wonder they made you captain of the team. You were the strongest ox in town!" I giggled.

"The strongest ox who is now going to grab you and pin you down with no escape."

"Ouch, ouch, the grass is prickly." I continued giggling as my shirt sailed into the wind.

"Mmmm, this ox is now going to start grazing. He is a hungry ox!"

Slowly his hands inched closer to forbidden territory. A nervous tingle rushed through my veins. Pieter's head was cradled in my neck as he gently kissed me. His body was pressing tightly on my breasts, leaving me no space to breathe.

"Don't stop" I whispered.

CHAPTER SEVENTEEN

1976: For the South African government, the invasion into Angola turns out to be a political failure. The MPLA is recognized not only by the OAU but is also formally admitted to the United Nations. Vorster's program of détente is severely derailed, especially now that SWAPO has gained a friendly base in Angola to move into Namibia. White South Africans view this "border war" with much suspicion back home. The English newspapers, severely hampered by the government's heavy hand, try through innuendo to report what is happening in Angola based on reports they are receiving from their counterparts overseas, but the full picture is never obtained. Instead, rumors of communist infiltration and SWAPO invasion are circulated by right-wing Afrikaner organizations, fanning the fear of the white electorate that they will have their businesses, land, and possessions taken away from them.

There is something to be said for a man who can dance well, or at least enjoys dancing, even more for a man who permits the mystery of music to course through his body.

Pieter was such a man.

Electricity enveloped us as Pieter snaked his body around mine on the dance floor. On the night of the Matric Dance, teachers watched disapprovingly from the side of the hall, although I knew deep down their bodies spoke otherwise. Above us, balloons and streamers hung in disarray while the town's local band belted out their rendition of *Yellow Brick Road.*

"Great dress, Ruchel," mouthed Charlene as she sailed past on the arms of a St. Andrews boy she had found at the last minute. I smiled in return. For once, Mother had succeeded in hitting the jackpot of teenage approval. After scouring the stores of Bloemfontein for The Dress, Mother promised that she would personally find something in Johannesburg.

"*Hauw*, Pulani" exclaimed Evelyn when she saw me slip into The Dress in my bedroom. "*U ea kae* [Where are you going]?"

"*Ho tsola leoto* [To dance], Evie! I am going to the Matric Dance with Pieter. How do you like my dress?"

"*Tcho*, very nice, very nice," she sang while clapping her hands and swaying her hips to an imaginary tune.

Very nice was an understatement. I was shocked when Mother unfurled the dress from the tissue wrapping. After the orange horror and its subsequent cousins, here came a pale green silk halter-neck ballgown with a low back. I could not believe it.

"Oh, my heavens, I love it, ma. Thank you so much!" I cried. I studied the dress in front of the mirror, twisting and turning, to see how it flowed over the bum. "Gussie says I can borrow her crystal necklace, which will go perfectly. Oh, thank you, thank you!" I smiled as I hugged Mother.

"Now, remember to walk with your shoulders back and stomach in and do not talk with your mouth full," Mother said while inspecting the cleanliness of my room. "Dale's mother says that she is having the girls and boys at her house before the dance, which is very sweet of her. Make sure you do not laugh too loud. And offer to help. Now look at all this dust! Evelyn!" Mother called.

She turned back to me as she left the room. "Ruchel, take the dress off before you make it all sweaty under the arms. I am glad it fits, I was a bit worried. Make sure you show Evelyn where the maid missed cleaning under your bed. I am late for the Arts Council Meeting."

The night of the dance I was a princess in a fairy tale. On my body was a drop-dead gorgeous dress and on my arm was a drop-dead gorgeous man and if I had died at that moment, I would have died happy. But that night a mystical magic carpet hurtled the princess straight into a cyclone of desire.

We were like two oceans crashing together, swirling and foaming, their boundaries breaking and merging.

"No, don't go there…Yes…Wait…What do you mean?.. Naked…Hang on…Bum…Not beautiful…Yes beautiful…Falling off…Gentle…Are you nuts?..Love you, too…Yes…Nothing gentle here…Oh God…What?..Double, double, toil and trouble…Teach me…Not ready to be taught…Enjoy…How?..Relax…Too tense!.. Hold me…Falling…Falling…Falling…Ow that hurts!"

"Wait…Relax…Trying…What muscle?..Didn't know it existed down there…Slower…Hold what?..You must be joking…Relax… Can't…Too nervous…Don't want to look…Hold me…Falling… Sorry!..Slowly…Gently…Still sore…Love you, too…Careful… Ouch…Careful, careful…Love you…

Oh look, it's a pink balloon. A pink balloon filled with guilt floating up, up, and away. Don't let it get away. It's yours now, Pieter. Hold tight. There's a strong wind coming. Hold the string tightly. Bring it down. Gently. You own it now.

* * *

"Ruchel," Mother called from the bottom of the stairs one morning. "I have just spoken to Bruce and he has managed to secure you a single room in Baxter Hall. This is a huge favor, I want you to write a thank-you letter immediately. You have no idea how I have dreaded the thought of you sharing a room with someone you do not know, even if she is a student like yourself." Mother was off on one of her tangents.

"Besides," she continued, "who knows how clean this person will be? A single dorm room is so much better. You can be very grateful that Bruce happens to sit on the board at the University of Cape Town. I must phone the florist to send them a nice bouquet." With that said, Mother walked down the passage to pick up the phone.

"You have to get a transfer to the University of Cape Town's architectural department," I told Pieter as I sat crosslegged on his rumpled bed doing homework. Pieter was at work on his drawing board, surrounded by a dozen layers of butcher paper and a transparent architectural paper, depicting the various stages of a building. Below the drawing board was a model of the building in wood and cardboard with trees that were painstakingly cut by yours truly with a sharp blade. As if I had no homework to do myself. On the far side of the drawing board, Pieter and his housemates had constructed a wooden partition so that Pieter's bedroom would not look like an extension of the dining room. In his infinite affinity for all things strange and different, Pieter had cut out a hole just big enough to crawl through to enter his hallowed chamber. Don't think I didn't ask what prompted this Alice in Wonderland door.

"The people who enter my room have to bow down," he explained.

"Over my dead body."

"Naked dead body!"

Hold that string steady now, Pieter. Careful.

According to Mother I was, of course, supposed to be celibate until I was married to some unknown chinless wonder, aka European aristocrat. The emphasis during the boyfriend phase was to have *Fun*.

Well, when did anything ever go according to plan? My hormones had already decided to be in charge of my body. Pieter, with his sultry eyes and his enormous muscular torso, God, the man was a sexual magnet.

Which brings me to why the heavenly stars threw up their hands in utter despair before storming out of the room.

"I told you that we should see the doctor about you going on the pill," Pieter said.

"Are you crazy? My Mother knows everyone in town and they would immediately report back to her. I can just imagine the conversation. 'Oh, Mrs. Louis, is your daughter not rather young to be going on the pill? She came to see me the other day with this Afrikaans boyfriend of hers.' She would faint on the spot, but not before shipping me off to outer Siberia."

"What about when we go on our tour around South Africa after you graduate?" Pieter gently pushed. "Your mom agreed to allow you to travel with me. Surely she knows we would naturally have sex?"

"She agreed for me to travel with you around South Africa for the vacation because I convinced her that we would be sleeping in separate rooms and that we would be visiting your sister in the Northern Transvaal and your parents in Postmasburg. When it looked like she was not totally convinced, I added that this would be the only opportunity I would get to see the whole country without her having to show me each and every town. I told her that you would be taking me to Kruger National Park, Swaziland, the Transkei, the Cango Caves, the wine farms, etcetera. She said okay after I rattled off the twentieth place and said that I must act like a lady at all times and to thank your parents for giving you and me the opportunity to do such a tour."

"You shouldn't have lied to her. Your parents should know that we're staying together in a tent. Otherwise, how else would we be able to see all those places with the small amount of money my parents gave me?"

"Okay, then I would never have been allowed to go. And besides, I was not lying, I was just not giving all the details. We will be staying in separate bedrooms at your parent's and sister's house. When we visit Michelle in Margate, I will be staying with her in her room. So what does it matter if I didn't mention the other times when we'll be sleeping in your tent. The less said the better."

"You need to go to a doctor…"

"I don't want to go to a doctor. No way! Can't you find some other method? No one will even look at you strangely if you ask for birth control methods."

The relief that came with each period was indescribable and also made me think I was invincible.

"What do you mean you are not going on the pill, are you out of your mind?" argued Michelle on the phone the day before we were due to leave on The Trip. "What makes you think those over-the-counter foamy things are going to work? Who is feeding you this shit?"

"Pieter asked the chemist [pharmacist]. They must know what they are talking about," I countered.

"Listen, my dad has a chemist. I am going to phone and ask him what he thinks!"

"Are you nuts?" I panicked. "He will phone your mom, she will phone my mom. Forget it. Besides chemists are the same everywhere. Pieter says he knows what he is doing, we should be fine."

"Oh, great!"

"Stop stressing. We can chat when we get to your house."

The Trip…

There are not enough trees in this world to make enough paper to fully describe the mind-blowing, mind-numbing experiences I was to have over the next six weeks on The Trip. It was a journey to the center of the earth, with all the good, the bad, and the ugly imaginable.

I will tell you the good first.

The good was what dreams are made of. Pieter whisked me away to far-off lands. A drum beat echoing across the African landscape carried us from Bloemfontein to Tsaneen in the northern Transvaal, across the Kruger National Park, and then right around the coast line of South Africa to just below South West Africa (now Namibia) before crossing inland again to Postmasburg and home. Six whole weeks of passion under trees and starry nights, on rocks and on beaches, under campsite showers and under waterfalls—with Red Jerepigo, that sweet wine, as a sometime friend. Red Jerepigo. *Rooi Here-pik-my,* in Afrikaans. 'God's biting me', in English.

How could I ever forget the time we were naked on that huge rock in the remote part of the park near God's Window. We could hear the waterfall a few meters away as the river flowed around us. It was so peaceful, so delicious, what with the wine, the Camembert, the French bread, the birds, the love. A hazy afternoon. Warm bodies. I remember. We were putting our clothes back on when that Afrikaans warden shouted from the top of the ridge telling us that the park was closing in ten minutes. I always wondered how long he had stood there watching.

There was the time we were in Swaziland and we decided to sell beaded necklaces in the market. We strung them together at night and tried to sell them in the morning. Wasn't it after all that rain? Seven days of rain that managed to wash away all the labels on the tinned food so that we didn't know if we'd be eating canned peaches or canned sausage for supper. But our beads were nice and we exchanged them for soapstone carvings the locals made on the side of the street.

Then, there was the time when the lion came right to our tent on the other side of the fence at Kruger National Park. It was frightening but exciting. I wondered what he smelled that made him come so close. Probably the Red Jerepigo.

And I still can't remember how we managed to get from one wine farm to another in Stellenbosch after tasting all that wine. The farmers themselves came to pour us glass after glass while we just giggled and sipped, and giggled and sipped.

Then there was the time I was driving and that wild deer ran into the road. It was dark and you know I don't have good eyesight. I remember crying after I ran into it. I couldn't stop shaking. Pieter was holding me so tight that he didn't even see the truck coming from the opposite side of the road. It stopped, picked up the deer, and drove off again. Pieter said we could have got a butcher to slaughter it and make some *lekker biltong.* But if you thought I was ever going to pick up a deer I had just run over, you were crazy. It was bad enough that I had dented his father's truck.

That was just a minor blip on the tour, Pieter said. What about all the cities we saw, the countryside, and the people we met. It was such fun even when we ran out of money in Cape Town. I had to phone my mother in Postmasburg to send us a little more. Maybe we should do something like that again, Pieter said. We could rent a motor home and stay in sophisticated campsites. It wouldn't be like those campsites where we stayed that had all those primitive cold-water showers, but it would be fun.

What?

Go camping again? Pieter will have to wait for Hell to freeze over.

Now let's talk about the bad.

After the first week I think my brain just ceased to function. Shell shocked. *Bosbefok*, as he would say. Doesn't he remember me screaming when I went into that bathroom where there were spiders and insects all around the toilet seat? Spiderwebs in every corner and snakes that nearly crawled into our sleeping bag at night? I think I only slept properly when I was drunk.

And then it rained. Seven whole days and seven whole nights. It seemed like forty days and forty nights. Rain everywhere. Rain that just poured and poured. Rain that rusted tins of food and the rusty tins turned everything else in the trailer red brown. Rain that rusted the ball bearings of my father's trailer that he let us borrow to carry all the tinned food Gussie had given us for The Trip. We left the trailer to die a slow death at the top of that mountain in Swaziland.

The rain just wouldn't go away. We slept in wet clothes. How else could we get to the toilet except in the rain? Moses had it better in the desert. Or did he? And the dust? Oh, and the sand. In our eyes, our clothes, our food. Between the rain and the dust, it was a *"bliksemse"* war zone. That's what it was.

And at the end, a bomb just fell out of the sky. *Boom!* By the time we reached Cape Town, I had missed my period. That was the ugly part.

"Maybe it's from all the stress on this tour," I reasoned innocently to Pieter. We sat on the edge of the wharf in a small coastal town, watching the seals dive in and out of the water. Seagulls swooped ominously overhead, screeching loudly. I thought of Hitchcock and his birds, twisting and swirling through my panic.

"Have you ever missed your period before?" Pieter ventured hesitantly.

"Once when I was not eating and trying to lose weight. The doctor said that it sometimes happens. This other friend of mine who had a severe case of anorexia didn't have her period for three months. Her mother found out and took her to the hospital. So maybe it's nothing."

My breasts did feel a little strange but I figured it was because I didn't have my period. The idea of pregnancy was so remote to my seventeen-year-old mind. It couldn't happen to me. Couldn't, shouldn't, wouldn't. The tour went on.

When we arrived at his parent's home in Postmasburg, the sky continued to drop bomb after bomb. Pieter opened a letter from the University of Cape Town regretfully informing him that there were no openings at the School of Architecture. In fact, there was a waiting list.

"What are we going to do?" I asked. It didn't help that my breasts were now having trouble staying within their thirty-four A homes.

"Maybe you should forget about going to Cape Town and study with me in Bloemfontein. Whatever happens, pregnant or not, we will still be together."

If being pregnant was the atomic bomb, Armageddon was around the corner.

For as long as I could remember, I had wanted to go to Baxter Hall, Cape Town. It was the Holy Grail of all universities, where my princess life could resume its happy course. This little six-week detour outside the palace gates was just that. A detour. Beyond every spider-infested toilet, rusted can, and soggy blanket there was this light at the end of the tunnel. Pieter featured in this dream world but not in Bloemfontein. It was too late to turn back. I had become his Galatea.

*   *   *

"You know, Bruce is going to be highly disappointed, Ruchel," Mother continued as she tried desperately to change my mind.

"He went to all the trouble to secure you your own room and now you tell me you want to stay at home and study at *this* university. I cannot understand you. Why must you listen to everything this Afrikaans boy tells you? Don't you realize what a huge mistake you are making?"

Mother was trying all angles but it was no use. I was ensnared in a way she had no way of knowing.

"I know, Mali. As much as I hate the thought of going to this dutchman university, at least I will be with Pieter." Even Michelle was not convinced of my decision. I could not confide in anyone, even my best friend. Over the phone only half the truth was spoken and my being pregnant was not even remotely discussed.

"Well, at least you get to do what you want," replied Michelle. "My father is only paying for me to go to the University of Port Elizabeth where he lives, so I am not going to Cape Town, either."

I had just missed my second period and the time bomb was ticking loud and clear.

Tick. Tick. Tick.

* * *

"Welcome to the University of the Orange Free State. For those of you who are English, lectures will be given in Afrikaans, but your textbooks will be in English. Any other notes given out by your professors will be in Afrikaans. For those of you who require translators please see me after this meeting. All psychology students will be required to take standard courses for the first year. Those choosing industrial psychology as a major will have to see Professor Swart in Room 402 this afternoon. He will explain the criminology and statistical courses to you in more detail. The rest of the social science courses will be held in this building. Thank you and we hope you enjoy your time with us."

Barbara, a Lebanese girl from Eunice, was the only face I recognized in a sea of fresh faces. I waved back at her from the top of the room. *"Wat is jou naam* [What is your name]?" asked a smiling gum-chewing brunette bombshell next to me. Her nails were immaculately painted in wild hot red and large gold hoop earrings dangled from her ear lobes. She was SO excited to be assigned to Madelief. All the girls in that hostel were SO fabulous and there was SO a party tonight. Did I want to come? The boys from the Reitz Hostel were SO going to be there and she knew two awesome rugby players who said that they were SO going to bring the whole team.

Imagine!

She was from a small farm outside Kimberley and just itching for this stupid lecture to end so she could finish painting her toe nails. I felt so old.

*   *   *

"Men at some time are masters of their fates: The fault, dear Brutus, is not in our stars, But in ourselves, that we are underlings." —— *Shakespeare*

The Ides of March had come.

"What are we going to do?" I cried as Pieter held me tightly in his arms. "I am so dead. Even if we wanted an abortion we couldn't do it because abortions are illegal in this country."

"If you want an abortion, my friend Danie knows someone at Baragwanath Hospital in Johannesburg who can do it," Pieter ventured. "Although it's a hospital for blacks, there are white doctors there and Danie says there are a few girls from the university who have already gone there. I really don't want you to have an abortion. You know I will marry you tomorrow."

"I don't know what I want," I wailed. "I know I don't want to be in this situation. I see the students next to me in class, happy, plotting their next night out and what they are going to wear. I see them laughing with not a care in the world and I hate them. I hate their freedom and their carefree life. Oh God, my mother is going to die!"

"Well, come with me to Postmasburg this weekend. My father needs me to draw some plans for a garage. If nothing happens by this weekend, we can then decide to go to Johannesburg or not."

I was drowning in an ocean of guilt and shame. I could see no glimmer of hope. I had reached the edge of the abyss and the only way out was down. We went to Postmasburg.

"Pieter, can I speak to you for a moment?" called his mom from the kitchen door.

I watched him walk with a heavy heart around the pool and across the brick patio.

Maybe I should just disappear, I thought. Then no one would have to walk with such a heavy heart. I wouldn't be such a burden, such a pariah, such a Scarlet Woman. Maybe if I stepped into the pool and never surfaced again. An accidental drowning. What a shame. Poor girl. She was always such a happy child.

I buried my head in my arms.

"They know, my mom suspected it. She wants to help us," Pieter said as he gently lifted my head off my lap. "I had a long talk with my father and he says we have to get married immediately. It's the right thing to do in God's eyes. He does not want to hear about any abortion. I love you and I want to marry you. If you're so scared about telling your parents, then my parents said they will come with us to speak to them."

"Noooo!" I shook my head violently, rivulets of tears streaking down my face. "No. They can't tell my parents. I have to tell them myself. I have to tell them myself. Oh God, I don't know how I am going to tell them. I feel so ashamed."

"I'll be there with you. Supporting you," Pieter offered. "We will do this together."

But I knew this would not be a together conversation. It would not even be a conversation. It would be a confession with no absolution. This would be my lonely road, so desolate that not even the vultures would come.

*   *   *

"Pulani not happy today?" Sara asked as she came into my room that morning to open the curtains. "Why Pulani so sad?"

"I have to talk to mommy, Sara, where is she?"

"She is downstairs in the kitchen with Evelyn. Something wrong?" Sara was concerned. I had not been my usual self for the past two months and she constantly probed to find out why. I think she already suspected but was waiting for me to confirm her suspicions.

I crawled out of bed, flung my robe on, and funeral marched down the passage. I reached the top of the stairs.

Mother opened the kitchen door below.

"What is the matter with you, Ruchel?" she demanded. "You are morose, you've gained weight, and you never smile anymore. What is wrong with you, for heaven's sake?"

Tears began to roll down my cheeks as I slowly descended the stairs.

"Don't tell me you are…" Mother stopped. Shock flashed across her face. Complete anguish quickly followed.

"Are you telling me…?" She could not complete her sentence. "Ruchel!" she shouted. "Tell me this is not true! Oh God!"

Evelyn ran out the kitchen door.

"Yes, Mother, I am pregnant and I am so sorry, so very sorry," I whispered as I crumpled to the floor.

CHAPTER EIGHTEEN

────────────

1976: June 16. Soweto erupts in violent anger as thousands of students take to the streets to protest the government's official attempt to make Afrikaans the medium of instruction in black secondary schools. Police move quickly into the area to quell the violence and to prevent it from erupting in other townships. Shots are fired, stones are thrown, vehicles are overturned, and buildings are set on fire as the angry mass runs through the streets. It is a protest never before seen in South Africa in the three decades of apartheid. Hundreds of protesters, many of them secondary school students, are killed by the government's security forces and thousands are injured. For the protestors, it is the final nail in the coffin after years of resentment at the government's "Bantu" education system that retards black education. To the more perceptive white electorate, it is the beginning of the end of South Africa as they know it.

The lion let out a thunderous roar from the top of the mountain. At his side stood the young lioness nervously swaying from side to side as she heard the jungle rumble below. *Ohi'mbube, ohi'mbube...*

Pieter and I married May 1, 1976.

"When I heard you were pregnant and about to get married, I said to Justin that there was no way I was missing this wedding," announced Susan as she walked into the guest bedroom of Uncle Habib's farm house.

Outside the door there was a flurry of activity. Six legs of lambs were roasting simultaneously in the old Aga ovens of the cavernous farm kitchen. Farm workers carried trestle tables into the large living room. A festive mood sailed through the air.

"Oh believe you me, Susie," said Michelle, rubbing her thumb over my cheeks to blend the pale blush. "I only got to know about the wedding four days ago after I finally got hold of Sara on the phone.

I couldn't reach this bloody woman for weeks. I thought she was kidnapped or attacked. But, no. Just too damn scared or embarrassed or both to phone any of her friends. I was on the next plane out and what do I find? A bloody zombie!"

"Mali, you would be a bloody zombie, too, if you had to go through what I had to," I said. "I don't know how I was dragged up to Johannesburg to fit on this hideous wedding dress. And this veil! It looks like a bucket sprouting foam. Oh God, I feel so fat and ugly!" Tears threatened to zigzag over the freshly blended blush on my face.

"What did your mother say when you told her you were pregnant?" asked Susan.

"I don't know what she said," I sniffed. I was shredding the tissue in my hand into tiny bits. "I don't know what has happened since that day. All I know is that this was supposed to be the happiest day of my life and I can't stop my heart from wanting to shrivel up in pain. It is all my fault. All the embarrassment, all the heartache, all the tears I have caused my family is my fault and I don't know how to make it better."

"Don't you dare start crying on me now!' admonished Michelle while trying to hold back her own tears. "Now look what you have done!"

All three of us were sobbing away.

"*Hauw*, Pulani!" shouted Evelyn as she stormed into the room with a tray of cucumber sandwiches and tea. "*Thula, thula. Mamelang iona* [Listen here]! Madam's nerves are very short today. *Ai, ai, ai!* If she sees you crying like this, she will get very upset. Ver-r-ry upset. *Shoh!* It has taken all my energy to calm the Madam these past six weeks. Eat some sandwiches, all of you. Eat now. Enough crying!"

I cannot remember the exact events that happened from the time Mother found out I was pregnant to the day of the wedding six weeks later. Call it amnesia. And for good reason. Shock rippled through our society. On our Richter scale it reached epic proportions, producing a tidal wave of hushed whispers behind white lace curtains. Michelle was right. I was just a zombie being pushed in all different directions by a hundred dos and don'ts. Sighs, tears, and guilt were monumental. The wedding dress was a tent. At five months pregnant, I had no other choice.

Mother and Father finally met Pieter's parents. How was that? Oh, Mother was cordial to say the least. The local Anglican minister from Ladybrand was invited by Uncle Habib to officiate the wedding in the small chapel next to the main house on his farm, and Aunty Babs' twelve-year-old twins were chosen to be page boys. The Judge, a family friend, was called upon to give a speech on behalf of the Louis family at the reception.

"And I would like to conclude," boomed the judge, "by saying that it has been a great privilege to speak here today. I wish the bride and groom many years of joy and happiness. Before I call upon the groom to say a few words, let us raise our glass in a toast. To the Louis family. To the Coetzee family."

On and on it went as I watched the roast leg of lamb congeal on the plate in front of me. Traveling around the room I could vaguely pick out Mother's friends on the right and the Coetzee siblings with their husbands or partners in the middle. My eyes rested on the table in the corner where sat our collective friends. There was Justin and Susan. Michelle and Conrad. I wondered if they were playing footsie under the table. Pam and Dudley were talking animatedly to Pieter's housemates and their girlfriends. Others, too, who blended together in a sea of guiltless pleasure.

Mother leaned over at the head table to catch my attention. Sit up, said her eyes. Then Jenny's head blocked her view as she reached for the champagne. I slowly turned my head. Father was having an intimate conversation with Pieter's mom—thank you, God.

By now Pieter was nearing the end of his speech. "I would like to thank my parents for everything they have done for me," he said. "And now to my beautiful bride." He put his hand gently on my shoulder. My eyes instantly returned to the congealed lamb as my pale blush turned dark red. "When I first met her, I found a soft gentle rose bud. A rose bud that has slowly begun to open into the most lovely woman I have ever laid my eyes on. I thank God for delivering to me someone so precious. Her eyes make me want to climb the highest mountain and pound my chest in triumph. Her smile brings instant sunshine into any darkened room. I love you more than all the stars in the sky. I love you now and forever more. To my beautiful wife."

I cried as I turned to kiss him.

The room broke into a round of applause as Mother dabbed the sides of her eyes with her tissue. Gussie's look told Mother that she did not want a repeat performance of the copious tears she had witnessed in the church. They are in love, Shirley. Be happy. Enough now!

Hush, my darling, Don't fear, my darling, The lion sleeps tonight…

*   *   *

The day after the wedding Pieter and I moved back to our respective bedrooms at each of our houses. Why? Because none of the half decent Mother-approved one-bedroom ground floor apartments was available. Strings were eventually pulled and within three months we moved into a Mother-approved one-bedroom ground floor apartment near the center of town.

"After your exams for your first semester you will have to take a break from University and pick up the final semester of your first year next year, in August," lectured Mother. She hovered over the one maid to make sure she was scrubbing the apartment's bathroom raw. "I am not having any argument from you. You are to finish your degree, baby or no baby. I will see to it that your tuition is paid and I don't want to hear a thing from that husband of yours."

"Mom," I sighed, "you can't blame him from wanting to make it on his own. Just because he said that he doesn't want any money from you, and that he is going to pay back the 400 rand [$400] a month that his father is lending him until he graduates, does not mean he is ungrateful. At least it shows that he wants to be successful."

"Stubborn is what I call it!" said Mother. "Besides, how does he expect you to live? In squalor until he becomes successful?"

"Mom," I sighed for the hundredth time that day and the millionth time that week, "we are not living in squalor. This flat is very clean and nice and we will buy something for the lounge as soon as Piet finds the furniture he likes. He hates all this Hartman and Keppler stuff. He is studying to be an architect and you know they have their own ideas. Just be glad that he agreed to have my Hartman and Keppler bedroom suite in the flat." Hartman and Keppler was an exclusive store in Johannesburg. Their furniture filled Mother's house.

"Glad!" retorted Mother. "He should be glad that you have such decent furniture and that you come from such a decent home! Marie, make sure you scrub those bathroom handles, especially the door handles. God knows who touched these doors. This place needs to be scrubbed from top to bottom."

Mother was now into on one of her major lectures.

"Tell me, Ruchel. Do you have any idea what it entails to have a baby? Well, do you?"

"Mom," I replied, "I have been reading Dr. Spock. Besides, millions of babies are born every day. Babies are even born in the middle of the bush here in Africa. Surely it can't be that difficult?"

"Heaven help us!" Mother sighed. "Ruchel, you listen to me carefully now. The first thing we are going to do is enroll you in a Cordon Bleu course so that you can learn how to cook for the baby."

"Mom, the baby does not need Cordon Bleu cooking!"

"Do not give me any cheek, Ruchel. This has been a huge shock to my body and I don't need you to make it worse. This embarrassment would never have happened if you ever bothered to listen to me. You know, I always wanted the best for you and look what you did? You betrayed my trust, you—"

"Okay, okay. I am listening!"

"Then listen good because I am tired of repeating myself. Tell that husband of yours to take speech lessons with Mrs. Fox. His accent is too awful for words and he cannot continue to wear those tight short pants. Everything sticks out, it makes him look so common. You also have to tell him to stand up when a person greets him. It is rude not to stand up. Oh, I don't know anymore." Mother sighed. "The list just goes on and on. You will have to teach him some culture if he wants to become successful and be accepted in society."

"What do you mean I have to take speech lessons with Mrs. Fox?" said Pieter when he returned from class that afternoon. "And what's wrong with my shorts? You are my wife now and I don't need your mother telling me what to wear or how to speak. And you have to tell her to stop bringing all this stuff into the flat. Why do we need four buckets?"

"One is for the kitchen, one is for the bathroom, and two are for the babies nappies," I replied, as instructed.

"That's ridiculous! We don't need four buckets. Give your Mother two back."

Look how the once carefree lioness retreats to her lonely patch under the baobab tree.

*   *   *

My eighteenth birthday was a nonevent, unless you think "The Art of Stuffing a Mushroom" is of any significance. Mother got her way with Cordon Bleu classes and three buckets. Pieter took a few speech lessons with Mrs. Fox before calling it quits after two months and he continued to wear tight short pants in Mother's presence.

The harsh winter that settled over the town that year reflected my somber state of mind. The strain of trying to take one day at a time weighed heavily on my shoulders as I continued to play referee between Mother and Pieter.

"Yes, I would love to be godmother," said Michelle over the phone one afternoon. "What did the doctor say?"

"He said we should expect the baby at the beginning of September, so plan on coming down," I replied as I rested my swollen ankles on the bed. I looked and felt huge. "I asked Justin to be godfather and he said it would be his honor. He and Susan are very much an item, you know. I think they will get married one day."

"So how are your mother and Pieter getting on?"

"You ask? My mom still thinks I am too young and too useless to know anything about cleaning a house or having a baby, and Pieter thinks I am now old enough to think for myself and should not be listening to everything my mother tells me to do. The problem is, they are both very strong-willed Leos who want me to behave their way.

The other day, I tried to make Chicken Kiev. Total disaster. So I phoned Gussie in tears and she brought over a cooked meal just as Pieter was pulling up the driveway. Of course he had a fit because I wasted all that food and money and asked then Gussie to bring over some food. My mother then heard about the Kiev disaster during one of her arguments with Pieter and also had a fit because I should not have been standing over the stove for hours in my condition and should have just had a simple salad and scrambled eggs. What was she thinking, taking me to those stupid Cordon *Blah* classes if I was supposed to be eating scrambled eggs and salad? Besides, eggs give me major heartburn right now. Ugh! I can't wait for this pregnancy to be over. I feel like a beached whale!"

August drew painfully to a close. Looking back I don't think I fully comprehended the enormity of it all. I spent the final weeks of pregnancy writing thank-you notes for the bucket loads of gifts I received at the huge baby shower Mother had organized. Someone there asked how my breathing classes were coming along. What breathing classes? That's a laugh. Any physical or mental preparation for the upcoming birth was buried under the strain of just getting by each day. Pieter was far better prepared.

*   *   *

September came around and I was staring vacantly at myself in the mirror one evening. Wrong move. My breasts looked like hanging watermelons and my bum rivaled my stomach in breadth and width. Does he still love me? How can he? Oh God, would I ever get my body back again?

"What are you doing, Ruchel?" asked Pieter from the dining room where he was making last-minute changes to a model he was building for an upcoming project.

"Nothing," I said. "I think I'll go to bed. I'm tired."

"Okay, I'll join you soon. Just finishing up here," he said without looking up.

Midnight rolled around and I found myself waddling in the dark to the bathroom. I had barely gone five steps from the bedroom door when the floodgates opened.

Whoosh!

Water everywhere—between my legs, on the floor, in my slippers, everywhere. Slimy sticky water pouring out of me like the Victoria Falls. I screamed blue murder.

"What is happening? Help me! Mommy, help!"

Pieter woke and jumped out of bed as if responding to an emergency fire drill.

"What's wrong?" he screamed as he ran toward the bathroom. "What's the mat—*aaaargh!*" His foot hit the slimy water puddle and he slid straight into the bathroom door. *Boom!* He hit his head on the door knob. Just like that. Immobile.

My hysteria rose several decibels. I had no idea what was happening and thought I was about to die a slow and horrible death. Punishment for all the sorrow and shame I had caused everyone.

"We have to get you to the hospital immediately," Pieter shouted over my hysteria as he came out of his daze. "I'll phone your mom from the hospital. I think your water has broken."

How the hell did he know that?

I heard Mother from way down the passage as I was being wheeled into the operating room. Never was I so glad to hear her voice. Moments later she swept into the room like a hurricane.

"Have the nurses washed their hands?" she demanded. "Where is my doctor? Where is Ebby? Piet, go and get some rest at home. Husbands are not allowed here in the operating room. Nurse, make sure she does not catch a chill. Let someone fetch additional blankets. Hello, Ebby, dear. Now Ruchel, you listen to what Uncle Ebby tells you, do you hear me?"

The pains were coming fast and furious, dagger jolts through the stomach at increasingly shorter intervals.

"I don't want to listen!" I cried as another jolt shot through my abdomen. "I don't want to push! Mommy, please make the pain go away!" My hysteria did not abate. It only increased in volume.

"Push!" shouted the nurse.

"Listen to the nurse and push, Ruchel!" shouted Mother. "This baby will not come if you do not push!"

"I can't push anymore!" I cried. "Too tired. It's no use!"

"Listen to me Ruchel!" Mother commanded, thinking that Dr. Ebby would have to resort to cutting my stomach open. Not good to have scars all over one's stomach. Looks hideous when wearing a bikini on the beach. "You listen to me! You are going to push hard. I don't want to hear any more excuses, otherwise I am going to get very mad. Very, very mad. Do you hear me?"

I don't know what was more painful, pushing or the thought of Mother becoming very very mad. I pushed and pushed. Then I took a deep breath and pushed some more. Pushed until suddenly, an incredible relief. No more pressure. No more pain. No more hysteria. Just calm.

"It's a girl, Shirley!" exclaimed Dr Ebby, "a beautiful blond little girl."

"Look at all the hair!" said one nurse.

"And the blue eyes" said another. "A gift from God. *Ho sa le ngoese.* All is well."

"With what name shall she be blessed?" said Dr. Ebby.

CHAPTER NINETEEN

1977: The Black Consciousness activist Steven Biko is a charismatic and well-respected visionary who commands attention and is in a position to play a powerful role in the future of a new South Africa. The government thinks otherwise. They see a man who is troublesome and who poses a threat to the stability of South Africa and its citizens. Biko dies of head injuries at the hands of the secret police in a prison cell in Port Elizabeth. It is said that Biko was interrogated to death while being held under Section 6 of the Terrorism Act. The outside world responds to his death with horror.

Michelle spoke to me over the floral display surrounding my bed. I was a week in the hospital and had hardly seen my daughter. Bandages were wrapped around my breasts to dry them out.

"So what's it feel like to be a mother?"

"I have no idea," I said. "The nurses bring my daughter only during the daytime for feeding and then whisk her away again. Then my mom arrives with more instructions and to top it all, my breasts ache no matter how I shift these stupid bandages. My mom says it is better to bottle feed so I am just going with the flow."

"How is Pieter on all this?"

"Oh, he is all over his daughter and can't stop kissing her. For that I must say I am so grateful because I was scared he might panic and leave us both but no, he can't stop telling me how much he loves me and our baby girl. He is, however, going on and on about finalizing her name so he can register her birth. He is panicking about missing some government deadline."

"So what did you decide?"

"Well, after much discussion and compromising I chose her first name and Pieter chose her second name. Nicole Bianca. What do you think?"

"I like it. Sounds French. What does your mother think?"

"I don't know what she thinks right now. She's panicking about what happens when I have to go home with the baby."

Mother had every right to panic.

I myself was in a panic.

What happens when the baby cries? Do I feed her, burp her, change her? How do you fold the nappy again? Forgot. When is the milk at room temperature? What is room temperature, anyway? Does she sleep on her side, her back, or her stomach? Will she suffocate if she sleeps on her stomach? What if she chokes?

It was overwhelming and Mother could sense it. Instructions were written on the fridge: Sterilize the bottles three times before use. Wash your hands before touching the baby. Pieter received instructions: Make sure Ruchel does not drop the baby. Help her hold the baby when bathing her. Gussie received instructions: Check on Ruchel to see that she is feeding the child properly. Knit more booties, the baby's feet should not get cold. My new maid, Veronica, was issued instructions: See that the madam boils the bottles three times. Wash the nappies every day and sterilize them. I was drowning in instructions.

*　　*　　*

Somehow, likely by divine intervention, I coped with those first six months without being admitted to a mental institution. Nicole, bless her, was a model baby who slept through the night from three months on. I believe she sensed her mother's minimum qualifications in motherhood and just decided to get on with the job of growing up as quickly as possible. Of course, in her favor was my unconditional and fiercely protective love. We were in this together and somehow we were both going to get through these first few months of battle.

Battle?

On one side of the field was Mother with her team: Father, various aunts, and more importantly, the ever sage-social friends. On the other side of the field was Pieter, Sara and his often silent but clearly present family. Refereeing the struggle was Gussie, with help from Evelyn. What a struggle it was. It was a battle of great lions on my playing field littered with guilt, ignorance, and immaturity. I was the football tossed back and forth, a football more in the air than on the ground.

One major battle was fought over the question of religion and the almighty place of worship. The Louis family belonged to the Anglican church on the hill, with its imposing bell tower. The Coetzee family belonged to the NGK church, which stood for everything that was *volk en vaderland* (people and the Fatherland). Mother won the first round and Nicole was baptized in the church of the bell tower. Round two was a tie when the question of schooling later arose. The result was private English school and NGK church.

But even wars have lulls between the battles, good days filled with the love and shared moments that brought us together in the first place.

By the time I had begun my second year at university we had moved into a rented three-bedroom house up the road from Mother. The move was not without the obligatory cleansing from not only Veronica but also the whole team from 10 Sowden Street. All dirt was exorcised and after two days the house was declared fit for habitation. Never mind that the house had seemed fit for habitation the first day we saw it.

"It is so much better here, Mali," I said over the phone one afternoon while Gussie was out taking Nicole and her standard black poodle, Liefie, for a walk. "Pieter now has a study with his drawing board and mountain of books and Nicole has her own room. We decorated her room with clown curtains and a clown bedspread. Found the fabric in town and my mother had her sewing lady put it together. Looks nice and at least both Pieter and my mother like it, so that's a relief."

"So do you like it?"

Ah, the ever sharp Michelle.

"It makes no difference what I like. Just having both of them agree on something is enough. At this point I feel qualified to negotiate a peace settlement between Israel and Palestine."

"So how are your classes?"

"Not so bad as I thought. I'm actually getting the hang of Afrikaans now and don't need the services of this stupid translation guy my mother found through some friend of hers. He was fat and sweaty and kept hovering over me like a fly. Yech! I now listen to the lectures in Afrikaans and then write my notes in English. Aren't some of your classes in Afrikaans as well, in Port Elizabeth?"

"A few," said Michelle. "But I don't get to practice it at home with an Afrikaans husband like you do."

"Oh, believe you me. I don't practice Afrikaans at home. Are you kidding me? We speak English at home and even when we visit his parents, Pieter speaks English to me and Afrikaans to them, even if I am perfectly fine speaking Afrikaans. Actually, half perfectly fine."

"And your cooking?"

"I can make pizza and lasagne if that means anything," I said. I thought of Gussie patiently showing me how to knead the dough from outside in before letting it stand in a bowl with a damp cloth over it to rise.

"Wow, I am impressed!" said Michelle, only half joking.

"Okay, Gussie helps. But I'm sure I'll be confident enough to go totally solo someday. Of course, my mother still has Evelyn cook the evening meal for us. Every day at five in the afternoon, her car pulls up and she toots the horn while the maid runs down the pathway with two plates of food on a tray."

"I am sure Pieter just loves that," she said, sarcasm creeping in.

"He's starting to get irritated with all this tooting, so yeah, another battle looming." I tried thinking of how to gently break it to Mother that at some point I would have to start cooking the evening meal myself if I was ever going to call myself a wife but it was something I was not ready to confront yet. "Otherwise things are getting better and we do go out at night while Veronica looks after the baby. Which is fun. We attend a lot of art exhibitions, music recitals at the university, and parties at his friends' apartments. They're a crazy bunch. You can't believe the raucous parties we have and my husband is right up front there with the best of them. Next time you come down, you can come with us."

Those early days were to set a pattern of how our marriage would move forward. To Pieter, it didn't matter that we didn't have much furniture. A thick slab of wood mounted on two trellises was perfectly fine for a dining room table and what's wrong with bean cushions on the floor? There was a great divide that loomed over us, largely in the area of home decor.

Whatever I had thought I liked was now squashed. If you were an architect or learning to be an architect, you had to have modern thinking. If you married an architect, that modern thinking did not include Laura Ashley and Louis IV furnishings. Throw that thinking out immediately. That is bad thinking. Cleanse that thinking from your brain no matter how much you believe you like something. Modern thinking from now on. Chrome and glass. Blue cutlery. Yellow tables. Red chairs.

Those bloody red school chairs.

They weren't red when we bought them at a downtown auction. They were old brown slatted fold-up chairs that had carried many bums through countless decades. Old fashioned yet modern in design. But they were the wrong colour. Wrong, wrong, wrong. Can't have brown in the house. Not modern thinking.

"So you bought these old school chairs for a song and then what?" asked Michelle.

"Well, I liked them as they were. They had this antique natural look and would have fit perfectly with an old oak table I had in mind but no, Pieter had to paint them. Had to paint them immediately." I sighed thinking of that day.

"So how bad do they look?"

"Oh they don't look bad. They actually go well with the yellow table in the kitchen and the rest of them we use outside for parties. It was the process that made me want to kill him that day."

"Why?"

"Well, tell me how you would have reacted. I was in the kitchen diligently working on my cooking skills."

"What cooking skills?"

"Shuddup! I can at least make the dough for pizza myself now. So here I was in the kitchen with flour up to my eyeballs when I suddenly realized that I hadn't heard a word from either Pieter or Nicole for at least a half hour. Which was a bit strange, mind you, both are very noisy creatures. I called out their names. Not a sound. I looked all over the house and in the garden until I finally heard this noise coming from the garage. Kind of like a hissing noise."

"That's weird. What was it?"

"A bloody spray paint can!" I said. "Pieter got a bee in his bonnet to paint all twelve chairs that same day and so he lined them up execution style along the garage wall and just sprayed. Sprayed and sprayed until there was no more paint in the can. I swear, Mali, I literally saw red. Red in Nicole's hair, red on her hands, and red on the new dress my mother had bought her. Red on the old white Volvo my mother had given us. Red on the lawnmower and tools scattered on the floor. Red on the garage door. Even red where it was supposed to be, on those stupid old school chairs. For a second I just stood there in disbelief."

"I would have made him stay and scrub every speck off everything, other than the chairs."

"Well, when I eventually found my voice I asked why he hadn't bothered to take the chairs outside. Before I could even finish my sentence he just shrugged his shoulders and said if I wanted to clean the paint off the other things, I could go ahead. So we have red chairs, red spots on the back of the car, and speckled tools."

Why didn't I argue back? Not sure. Perhaps I found it difficult to step with confidence into the role of wife and mother. Perhaps it was immaturity? Maybe it was the fear of starting an argument.

Maybe Mother and Pieter sensed my lack of confidence. Frightened by contemplating the disastrous consequences that might ensue, they both stepped up their respective levels of leadership. Okay, leadership laced with bossiness. But you can only follow one leader at a time. Since the bond of love was strong with both leaders, I found it difficult to nurture any confidence in myself.

Not all winds of change were ill winds. The deep and passionate love Pieter and I had for each other often calmed those ill winds as we sailed into our life's uncharted waters. We were young and daring.

In the jungle, the mighty jungle, The lion sleeps tonight...

"Ruchel" Mother called one morning on the phone. "Judge Bowers has graciously invited your brother and me up to South West Africa for a week. He is now the administrator general there and he wants to introduce me to a General who is coming from America. I want you to make sure that you look after Nicole and if she wants more *dummies* [pacifiers] just drive over to Aunty Tamara's chemist. She loves to choose them herself and knows her way around the shop so don't go anywhere else."

It must be noted here that while Pieter and I attended class, Mother, Gussie, Evelyn, and the troops passed our blue-eyed daughter from one arm to another. By her first birthday she was already a princess in the making and she did not disappoint. Thick blond curls cascaded down her rosy chubby cheeks as she confidently posed for the camera in either the traditional apron outfit draped with beads or in one of the dresses Mother bought in the stores of Johannesburg. Nothing shy there. By her second birthday, which was of course held in all its glory at Mother's house, the die was cast. The word "best" became the most overused word ever. Best cake, best party dress, best toys, best tricycle, best food. Nothing but the best was good enough for Mother's granddaughter. So if Mother left town on an extended trip, it was imperative that I clearly understood that second best did not apply.

Was I inclined to take shortcuts? Of course! There was no way I was going to ride across town to seek a particular dummy for Nicole when a perfectly good one lay stuck between the car seats, just waiting to be rescued and sterilized. Did she ever go to bed without bathing? Of course! Why wake her up after a long day at a friend's house just to bathe her and then let her go to sleep again. Did we ever tell Mother? Of course not! But this love and attention, sprinkled with her parent's youth and immaturity, is what molded our daughter into a caring and confident child. Her parents were basically her two older playmates while her grandparents, great-grandmother, Evelyn, and Veronica became her adoring caregivers.

Those were bonds so tightly woven that by the time Pieter graduated at the end of 1978, the winds of change began to stir again.

"We can't stay in Bloemfontein," Pieter announced after finishing his final thesis. "It won't work with your mother being so involved in our lives. I mean, don't get me wrong, I appreciate all that your parents have done for us, but you can't be their child forever. And you know your mother gets her way with you all the time. You have to start making your own decisions and learn how to run the household without all the interference. The only way this will happen is if we leave town."

"Leave town?" I stammered. "I still have one more year of university to complete my degree!"

"Well, you can finish it through correspondence. I've just received a letter of acceptance to work at a firm in Kimberley next year and I have made up my mind. I'm going to take it."

Take it? How was I going to cope on my own? No Gussie, no Mother, no Evelyn?

Leave Bloemfontein? That was more unthinkable than the thought of trying to finish my degree through correspondence. Bloemfontein and the family were my umbilical cord. To think of severing that in the throes of early motherhood, wifehood, studenthood, cookinghood, and all the other hoods was simply too daunting. Just the other day Nicole had been sitting in the back seat of the Volvo when I took a sharp turn and she slid right out of the car and onto the road. She had only a few scratches but I became hysterical. I panicked big time. So much so that I lied when facing the inquisition from both Pieter and Mother, saying she fell while playing outside. Neither of course believed me. And now I was to be left to my own devices?

"What do you mean you are moving to Kimberley?" demanded Mother as she stormed into our house. "Piet, you promised me that you would stay in Bloemfontein until Ruchel finished university. Why do you have to move now to Kimberley? I'm sure you can find a job here in Bloemfontein. I will make a few calls."

The heated discussion between my husband and Mother continued back and forth until I finally blurted out that it did not matter about university, that I was now a wife and mother and if my husband wanted to go to Kimberley, that was his choice and I had no option but to follow. That made Mother even madder.

Finally, after weeks of traumatic negotiations and compromise, it was agreed that, as Kimberley was only two hours away, I would catch the train to Bloemfontein on Tuesday afternoons with Nicole and attend classes both day and night before returning to Kimberley on Thursdays. The train did not run to Kimberley on Thursdays so Mother agreed to drive us back that day. It was the only solution she would accept, knowing I would never finish my degree through correspondence. Mother insisted on seeing to it that her daughter became a woman on her own with a college education. It was a selfless gift that I really fully appreciated only many years later. The umbilical cord might have been partially torn that day but it was never ever completely severed.

And so, with my tears flowing copiously, Pieter and I watched the receding lights of Bloemfontein fade slowly behind Naval Hill as we drove away.

We had altered course.

CHAPTER TWENTY

1979: *By the time Vorster resigns amid an "Info Scandal" in which he secretly used taxpayer money to fund efforts to improve South Africa's image abroad, the mood of the white electorate has become fear for their safety and possessions. Vorster's successor, Defense Minister P. W. Botha, sees himself as a man with no patience for weaklings, a man of strength, a man who after his election said "we will not bend our knees before Marxism or revolution." Botha sees the events on the border as an attempt by the Russians to install Marxist governments in Rhodesia and South Africa. He is also concerned with the safety of the white electorate should he bow to the Western powers' call for democracy. Botha begins to formulate his strategy to counterattack this "total onslaught." He merges the military, police, and intelligent services into the National Security Management System, known as the State Security Council (SSC), and names himself chair. Decisions at the SSC are sometimes taken without the knowledge of the Cabinet.*

What can I say about Kimberley? It has a big hole in the middle. A manmade crater so deep that if you dug any further you would reach China.

Kimberley was a dry and dusty place that gave new meaning to "one horse town." It was the first place in the world to have a gallop-through pub. You could gallop up to the window on your trusty horse, order a drink, and gallop off into the sunset.

A lot of drinking had been done in that town. Lots of drinking because digging that big hole with only a bucket and a spade under the African sun made a man very thirsty. And if you did not see anything glimmer in your pan as the river water washed through your sieve, then you doubled up on your drinking. That, or you kicked your neighbor—who was encroaching on your stake—down the hole. But if you did find something glittering, you stopped drinking and built yourself a nice two-story Edwardian mansion complete with *broekie* lace, slapbang in the heart of Main Street.

There were only a few of those Edwardian mansions left by the time Pieter and I arrived there in January of 1979.

"Considering all the diamonds that were found in this town, I'm surprised Kimberley didn't turn out to be a metropolitan city, like Johannesburg," I said, as one small mining house after another whizzed past the window. "It's as if we've stepped into a time warp."

"I wouldn't be a bit surprised if we saw Barney Barnato swaggering out of the colonial Kimberley Club with a beer in hand," said Pieter.

"Who is Barney Barnato?" asked our ever inquisitive and talkative daughter from the back seat of the car.

"Barney Barnato was a man from London who came to Kimberley about a hundred years ago," I said. I turned and smiled at the curly blond head bobbing left and right to an imaginary tune. If you are born in South Africa you are born with tunes in your head. Silent, soulful beats.

"Ja, this *rooinek* loved boxing and even started his own boxing school," added Pieter, who was consulting the street map on the dashboard. "Didn't think *rooineks* were capable of boxing. We always *donnered* [hit] them at school."

"So tell me again why was he so famous?" I said to Pieter.

"Barney Barnato," he explained, "was a diamond broker who started a firm called Barnato Brothers in the late 1800s with his brother. They began buying up diamond mining claims and a couple of years later formed the powerful Barnato Diamond Mining Company."

"But I thought De Beers was the main diamond mining company in those years?"

"Barnato's company was major competition for De Beers at the time. Cecil John Rhodes, another bloody *rooinek*, started the De Beers mining company. He and Barnato were constantly fighting to control the industry. Rhodes eventually won by convincing Barnato to join him. Together the two companies became De Beers Consolidated Mines. End of competition."

"I am sure Barnato was bullied into the deal," I commented.

"Most probably. Rhodes made Barnato a life governor, but he left Kimberley soon after to go north to the gold mines of Johannesburg. Eventually he started his own bank there. He was a shrewd guy, but he could not have been a very happy person because he jumped overboard on his way back to England and drowned."

By now we were skirting the Big Hole on the old Bultfontein Road.

"Look, Nicky, there is the Big Hole. Mommy will show you once we have moved into the house."

"What's a big hole, ma?" she asked as she tried to see where we were pointing.

"Kimberley is famous for the Big Hole. It used to be a small hill belonging to the two De Beer brothers. It was full of diamonds," I replied.

"Ja, these *rooineks verneuked* [cheated] the Afrikaners who, by the way, were there first," Pieter chipped in.

I ignored the jibe and continued. "You see, my darling, someone first found this huge diamond in a place near here, called Hopetown. Once the secret was out that a diamond had been found, the whole world wanted to see if they could also find diamonds. So everyone rushed over here as if it were the grand opening of a big store. People were pushing and shoving each other to find these diamonds. It was a very wild town those years."

We finally arrived at our first rented house in Kimberley. It was a block from the railway line that ran through town. Each time we forgot to close the doors and windows we would find speckles of black soot on the furniture. Dirt seeped through our air.

Poor sweet docile Veronica, a sister of one of Mother's maids, lasted two weeks before hightailing it back to Bloemfontein. Mother of course was livid, and descended on Kimberley with two maids in tow to scout the township for someone decent, kind, and clean—Mother's stipulations. Dirt was not an option.

It was here that Martha came into our lives. Martha, with her smiling round face, pug nose, and Evelyn personality. Martha, with her dancing eyes, eager laugh, and crisply starched uniform. Martha the Griqua [a tribe from the Cape] who was to become part of our extended family—and who would need to be taught the art of cleanliness, the art of housekeeping, the art of washing a toilet, and the art of everything else that involved a bucket of water and soap. Evil dirt would be arrested.

"Now, Martha, my dear," explained Mother on her third day in Kimberley, "it is very important to use one cloth for the toilet seat and a separate cloth for the toilet bowl. When you have washed *first* the bath, *then* the washbasin, and *then* the toilet seat in that order, throw the bucket of water outside in the drain, put new soap and water in and proceed to wash the inside of the toilet bowl with your other cloth. Once you have done that, throw that water out, then wash the bucket out properly before using it for the other bathroom, do you understand?"

"Yes, Madam."

"Ruchel!" Mother turned to see if I was taking in these instructions so I could see to it that they were carried out in future. "Make sure you use this bucket for only the bathrooms and the floors. Do you hear me? Do not let your husband wash the car or anything else with this bucket.

"Nicky has a separate bucket for her bedroom," she continued. "Each day her room and her toys have to be wiped down. You have to make sure this is done every day. No grandchild of mine is going to sleep in filth. And make sure you keep those windows shut. I don't know why the both of you had to choose a house that is so close to the railway line. All that black soot is unhealthy for her little lungs. Martha!"

Mother turned once more to Martha, who was vigorously wringing water out of a cloth while antiseptic fumes wafted over us.

"The *kleinmies* [small madam] is very busy studying and is always forgetting things. I want you to make sure you remember my instructions. I have written them down and will paste them on the kitchen wall. Always wear your yellow plastic gloves and phone me if you need anything."

"Ma, if she needs anything she can let me know and I will get it for her!" I said.

"Ruchel, you don't have much money and the money you get from your husband has to buy proper food for Nicole. Do not feed her chips from the take-away places here. They're all filthy. Honestly, I am going to have nightmares worrying how you are going to cope here!"

I had two months to settle in the house before beginning the weekly trip to Bloemfontein to finish my studies. Pieter began working at a local architect's firm in town and came home each night with additional work from the office. The firm was owned and operated by a young Afrikaans architect whose wife sold Tupperware and nonstick pans at house parties.

I must say that the transition from Bloemfontein to Kimberley was not as traumatic as I thought it would be, except for the dirt that suddenly confronted me from all angles. I felt invigorated being in a house I knew would demand most of my attention without any outside help. For the first time neither Mother nor Gussie nor the rest of the clan would be there to help out at every given second. This was home-alone time.

Pieter seized the opportunity to mold me into the good little wife I should become. He bought me a sewing machine.

Being the eager to please pupil, I went out the very next day and purchased three Vogue patterns from the local store: one skirt pattern, one waistcoat pattern, and one smock dress pattern for Nicole. I was very ambitious.

I then bought the fabric (nothing even resembling what was suggested on the covers of the patterns) and heaped everything in the living room.

What did I know about sewing? Nothing. But if Pieter's boss' wife sewed all her own and her children's' clothes, I should also be able to sew with the best of them. Right? Right! All wives can sew their own clothes. All wives!

All except Mother, who was not considered an ordinary wife.

I spent the next night figuring out how to work the idiot sewing machine. Now, I don't have the best sight in the world. My left eye is almost useless because of a jagged cornea, so my right eye does all the work. Still, there I was squinting my one good eye, trying to thread the cotton in and around various parts of the machine before threading it through the eye of the needle. Even on the rare occasions when I was drunk, things never doubled this much.

"Piet, you have to thread this cotton through the needle for me. I can't get it through the hole," I called to him in the next room.

"Ruchel, my mother and all my sisters find this so easy to do. I can't be threading the needle or the machine for you every time you want to sew." Pieter sighed as he came through to the living room for the third time that night.

Good wives don't throw sewing machines at their husbands who expect them to sew.

Every morning for the next month, while Nicole was at play school and Pieter at work, Martha helped me thread the cotton through the machine each time it snapped. I did manage, with her very patient help, to finish the skirt and waistcoat for myself and the smock dress for Nicole. At the rate I was going, I would be wearing one outfit per month, day in and day out.

"See how easy that was?" said Pieter as Nicole and I paraded before him in our homemade outfits. "That's very nice. Next time though, you should be more careful about how you finish it off. Your hem looks a little skewed."

Good wives don't throw sewing machines at their husbands.

Mother, when she eventually saw us getting off the train in Bloemfontein in our homemade outfits, said I looked like the local washerwoman.

"What are you thinking, Ruchel?" she exclaimed as Nicole ran to her. "If you have no money for clothes, I will send you some. Come, my little darling. Gansi has lots of toys waiting for you at home. You look ridiculous, Ruchel!"

The next day Martha inherited the sewing machine.

But the good wife must persevere in her endeavors. She must continue to help her husband in all his attempts to succeed. Bad wives waste their husband's money. Good wives learn to be frugal if they want to afford their own house. Frugal.

Coming from a family in which the subject of money was rarely discussed, this was a little hard to swallow at first. Of course, Mother still bought all our daughter's clothes and toys and even loaded the car up with gourmet food every time we traveled back to Kimberley on Thursdays. But now that I was married, I had to think twice before buying anything.

So, when the sugar-blond wife of Piet's boss suggested that I should also sell nonstick pans at parties, I jumped at the idea. Who wouldn't want to make extra cash in her spare time and win that trip of a lifetime or that pink Cadillac? There were women who were top sellers in their field and were already millionaires. The boss' wife was not a millionaire but that was not the point. My million Rand would help buy us an Edwardian mansion on Main Street and a new dress every now and then.

The set of nonstick pots arrived the following week.

Pans and pots of all shapes and sizes with new black Teflon coating. Never before seen in the *platteland* (rural areas)! Once I showed these *tannies* (an Afrikaans word for women) how pancakes or fish sticks could be made without butter, they would be ordering pans by the dozens. All I had to do was take homemade pancake mixture, some frozen fish sticks, one hotplate, and the set of pots and plastic utensils to their homes and I would become a millionaire overnight. Easy!

So what if I still had to study to complete my degree, cook every night, read to Nicole, bathe Nicole, feed Nicole, dress Nicole, take Nicole to school, pick Nicole up from school, pick up my husband's clothes from the floor—that was not the point. I was going to have an Edwardian mansion on Main Street with a pink Cadillac in the driveway and a new dress every other month. Yes!

So did I sell pots? Of course! At parties that were held at night in and around Kimberley. At parties on farms that were held at night and in the day on the way to Postmasburg when I spent the weekend with my in-laws. At parties given by my arm-twisted friends.

Was I becoming a millionaire? Of course not! I would have had to sell pots morning, noon, and night, all day every day, before even reaching a tenth of that target.

Did I tell Mother? Of course not! Too much to explain and I was not in the mood for the heavy lecture.

So what did I learn from the exercise? That I could sell ice to an Eskimo.

Now, during my traveling pots-and-pans road show through the *platteland* I stumbled upon Afrikaner cooking. What a taste sensation! Meat mixed with raisins, apples, and curry. Spiced coriander sausages. Puddings soaked in brandy. Custard milk tarts—each and every one made lovingly by the very patient Afrikaans wives in their overworked kitchens.

Good wives must bake delicious cakes and cook very tasty food. Bad wives burn or dry out the food.

My life that year followed two distinct paths. From Tuesdays to Thursdays, I was "psychology student", attending classes and generally learning what supposedly makes people tick. From Fridays to Mondays, I was "good wife student" learning the art of being housewife, mother, hostess, cook, and seller of pots and pans. Neither path crossed until examination time, when major studying had to be done. The idea of opening a university book in Kimberley never crossed my mind.

Four months later we decided to move to a bigger rental house. Pieter was by now making a good impression at the office by working like a slave. He never crawled into bed before midnight. One night, after I had returned from another pot and pan party, the phone rang an hour after we had both fallen asleep. It was 2:00 AM. No one phones you at 2:00 AM unless something major has happened and by major, I mean tragic.

Pieter picked up the receiver. "Oh God, no," he blurted out.

"What happened, what happened?"

"Nico died this morning," he said before switching to Afrikaans on the phone.

"Can't be," I said. "He's only twenty one!"

Nico. Pieter's handsome, mischievous younger brother. At eighteen he also got a girl pregnant, married her, and had two daughters. Nico was driving his truck late at night over farm roads outside Postmasburg when a deer jumped in front of him. He did not wear his seat belt, and fell out of the car as it flipped over. Nico, the father of two little girls who would never know him. Nico. May he rest in peace.

Pieter and I returned to Kimberley after the funeral and moved to a house away from the railway line on the other side of town. Life looked a little fragile as we pondered the sense of it all. Pieter's parents were devastated and his father began spending more time on his building sites.

Pieter coped by burying himself in work. He began taking on private work. Store owners who needed a small alteration, a wealthy coloured woman who wanted to build her own mansion just outside the town, a farmer who decided to build a brand new homestead further up the hill on a ten thousand-hectare farm. All needed him after hours to discuss where bathrooms and bedrooms should be placed. All kept him busy enough and allowed his broken heart to heal.

* * *

Pieter began to gain a reputation for being the "go to" architect for private alterations and small jobs. New duties were constantly added to my list.

Good wives are always ready to fill any role with competence and vigor. Bad wives moan and sulk.

Things were looking up. I was starting to field calls, deliver plans to the city, and serve as hostess when people came late at night to discuss their plans.

One Saturday morning while Nicky was at home with Martha, Pieter and I traveled to the farmer's ten thousand-hectare farm outside Kimberley to see how the building was progressing.

"*Die huis kom mooi aan* [the house is coming on nicely]," commented Pieter to the farmer as we all walked over wooden planks and dry cement blocks. The half-finished farmhouse looked decidedly bare. For miles around dust flew up as the wind gently whistled through the *kameeldoringbooms* (trees). The veld could have been categorized a desert if it were not for the bushes and short trees scattered around like polka dots.

It was a searing day and the portly farmer battled to climb the stairs. "*Bliksem! Dis donners warm vandag* [Damn! It's bloody hot today]!" He panted as he paused to wipe the sweat that ran in rivulets down his forehead. "Let's go back home," the farmer continued, now in English for my benefit, even though I understood everything he said. "Your wife must be very thirsty."

"Oh, don't worry," said Pieter. "She is used to walking all over the sites with me. Let's look at the plans again to see where it is you want to change that wall."

Pieter and the farmer made their way back to the truck while I dawdled behind. By the time I reached the truck, plans were spread out on the hood of the truck and the two of them were hovering over them.

"Someone is calling," I announced as a faint sound pierced the cricket-filled air.

"Shh, Ruchel, can't you see we are talking here?" said Pieter. "Just stand quietly until we are done here!"

Good wives do not interrupt their husband's meetings. I know, I know. But the faint cry for help was getting closer and closer. I couldn't just ignore it!

"*Baas*, come quickly! Help!" We saw a black man running toward us. His checkered shirt was hanging loosely over torn baggy pants. "Help!" he screamed, waving his arms.

"*Wat's fout* [What's the matter]?" demanded the farmer. It was one of his workers. My eyes said I told you so to Pieter.

"*My vrou* [My wife]!" shouted the man. "She have baby, *Baas*!"

"What, where?" asked the farmer.

"In the bushes over there." The man pointed to a spot behind him. "Please help me, *Baas*!"

We followed behind the man as he ran in the direction he had pointed. About a half mile away we found his very pregnant wife crouching under the shade of a tree. Her round face was contorted with pain. She avoided any eye contact and was making those pushing noises I half remembered during my ordeal in the labor room.

"I think she is going to give birth any minute" I said. The farmer and Pieter stood there like confused statues while the husband ran around us begging for help.

"Listen, you two!" I shouted. "Go back to the truck and fetch the hot water from the tea flask. There is no time to take her to the hospital, it's on the other side of town. Hurry! She is about to give birth! Now!"

So what if I was only twenty and not a doctor. So what if we were in the middle of the bush with no hospital in sight. Had I not given birth to my own baby?

I grabbed the blanket tied around the woman's waist and spread it on the ground.

"Lie down," I gently said to her.

"*Thula, thula!* Sit behind your wife and hold her head," I instructed. No one had held my head when I gave birth but I figured that was the only way to get the husband to stop circling like some frenzied jackal. She was clearly in a state of shock and even younger than I.

I played doctor.

"Okay!" I smiled as reassuringly as possible while pulling her panties off. "Bend your knees, that's right, now push! Push again. Again. You, hold your wife's head, don't look here. Wipe her tears with your shirt. Push. Look the baby's head is coming through." Oh hell, the head is going back again. The baby is going to suffocate. Please, God, make her push. "Push! That's right. Push hard. The head must come out. Look! The head is coming out! Push! That's right. Just one more push. Oh look, it's a girl!"

The baby slid through the mother's legs as I held her wet little head. We made it! We made it! Hallelujah!

Wait! Wasn't there something about the umbilical cord? Oh bloody hell! Aren't you supposed to cut the umbilical cord so that the baby can breathe on its own or something like that?

"Give me your knife!" I demanded of the husband as I gently lay the baby, still tied to the mother, on the blanket. "Give me your knife!"

"Whaaaaah! No madam! No!" screamed the husband. He dropped his wife's head on the blanket and jumped up. "Madam not kill my baby! Madam not kill my baby!" he screamed as he started running toward the farmer's house.

I ran after him, leaving the poor wife and her baby on the blanket, afterbirth pouring out.

"Whaaaah! Madam not kill my baby!" the husband kept screaming while holding his head with his hands. I grabbed him by the shirt.

"I am not going to kill your baby, you bloody idiot!" I screamed back. "I want to save your baby! Give me your knife!"

With much reluctance he handed over a pocketknife and, with drooped shoulders and more begging to not kill his baby, followed me back to his wife.

By now there was afterbirth all over the baby and the blanket, and I was panicking that the baby had drowned. Panting to get my breath, I lifted the baby onto my lap and started to slice through the umbilical cord with the pocket knife. Blood and afterbirth were all over my legs and arms. I had no clue what I was doing. All I knew was that you had to hear the baby cry and this baby was not crying, just wriggling. At least she was alive. Please God, I promise to be good. Please let this little baby live.

Just as I cut through the umbilical cord, Pieter and the farmer arrived in the truck as if on cue. "What took you so long?" I demanded as I swung the baby upside down to see if she would cry. The mother sat upright and, clearly embarrassed, tried to cover herself with her skirt. "We have to get them to the hospital I can't get the ba—"

"Whah!" choked the baby as she tried to draw some air.

"Oh look! The baby is crying! She is going to live!"

Now I was crying. Crying with the baby and the mother and the father as I helped them get onto the back of the truck. The baby was going to live. She was going to live. I had saved a life! Thank you, Lord.

A few weeks later, the farmer told me that the baby was healthy and fine and that the husband was very happy.

"What's her name?" I asked.

He smiled. "Pulani."

* * *

"The madam will be blessed for a long time," replied Martha as she ironed the shirt. "Madam did the right thing!"

"I promised God I would be good if the baby lived, Martha, so maybe I should tell the boss that the dress I bought for my birthday cost sixty rand instead of twenty rand."

"Ai, no, Madam!" replied Martha. "*Baas* will just get mad and God will not judge you on that. Besides, *Baas* told me that he and *Baas* Trevor are going hunting on Friday. He asked me if I can cook the meat."

"What do you mean, hunting?"

"Mommy, come look," called Nicky from the bedroom. "I painted a picture for you."

"I am coming, my darling. Mommy just has to phone Daddy quickly. I will be there in a minute."

"What do you mean you are going hunting with Trevor on Friday?" I asked Pieter over the phone. "My twenty-first birthday party is on Saturday, did you forget?"

"No, of course not," replied Pieter a little too jovially. "Trevor and I will be back early Saturday morning. I am bringing a *springbok* [deer] home. Martha says she can cook the meat for the party, and Trevor's wife, Lorraine, is going to make the sauces. Henk and Marietjie said they will bring the *pap* and *chakka laka* [a tomato and onion mixture], and I ordered twenty pounds of *boerewors* [sausage] from the butcher. This is going to be a *lekker Boere braai* [lovely Afrikaner barbecue]. About fifty people said they are coming already. Oh, and the secretary at work offered to make your birthday cake so all you have to do is make a few salads and your lemon meringue pie. Stop panicking, it's all taken care of."

Good wives believe their husbands' promises. Bad wives are suspicious.

What a lovely gesture! I mean, how nice of Lorraine to offer to make all the sauces. They were such special friends, always inviting us to their huge double-story home with its Barney Barnato original staircase and huge swimming pool. And how sweet of Henk and Marietjie, the newlyweds we met at the annual Architect's Dinner at the snooty Kimberley Club. Henk worked for another architectural firm in town, and shy Marietjie exceeded all expectations in the good wife department. Then there were Charles and Retha. They drove all the way from their Brahmin cattle farm in Douglas, on the other side of Postmasburg. Suave Charles, Pieter's army buddy. Such nice people!

Lorraine brought the sauces early that Saturday morning. Marietjie also came early to help. It was rather worrying that Pieter and Trevor had not arrived back from the farm but surely they would arrive any minute. After all, they knew that the *springbok* still had to be skinned, cut, soaked in vinegar for an hour, and then pressure cooked for another two hours before it could be eaten. It was only 10:00 AM and others weren't due to arrive until 7:00 PM. Pieter would be here any minute now. No need to panic.

By noon, Martha was muttering under her breath as she chopped and diced potatoes with the vigor of a galley cook.

At 3:00 PM Pieter and Trevor dragged the *springbok* dripping with blood across the kitchen floor. "We skinned it at the farm!" Pieter announced triumphantly. "Don't worry, Martha, we kept the insides and the skin for you like you wanted." Then he plonked the carcass on the lovely clean kitchen table. "It's in the black bag at the back of the truck. Still don't know why you think that if you wear some of the skin around your wrist it'll ward off evil spirits. Bring me the knives!"

By the time we ate the food, the guests were too drunk to notice whether it was game or pork.

Good wives never shout or scream in frustration or anger. Good wives only sigh quietly.

And thus I placed my foot firmly on the first rung of the good wife ladder. It was a ladder I climbed not only with much sighing but also with much learning, compromising, laughing, and occasionally, battling.

At the end of the year I graduated with surprisingly high marks at university. Don't ask how, because the only time I seriously studied was two weeks before the exams. That studying included a final cram in the car on the way to Bloemfontein with one hand on the wheel and both eyes on the book that lay on the passenger seat.

Kimberley proved to be a warm and friendly place. It was a place that enabled Pieter and me to work out our cultural differences and meet somewhat half way. Actually it was more skewed to Pieter's side but I didn't mind because, despite some rough seas, the calm waters were wonderful. Our love for each other was stronger than the day we met. And our love for our daughter was even stronger. Our childlike approach to life that bordered on the crazy was what made us the couple most likely to succeed.

We were not afraid of work and constantly discussed our next move on the chess board of life: If we bought that piece of land in the center of town, we could possibly afford to build the house; Pieter would design the house and we would owner-build with me supervising the daily building operations. Together we plotted and planned our future. We had it all mapped out. I even planned my next pregnancy and was pregnant within a month of going off the pill. The pieces on our chess board were perfectly positioned.

Pieter was called into the office at the end of March of the following year and told that he was fired. Fired? Yes, fired because his boss had found out about all the private jobs Pieter was doing at night, had heard how popular Pieter was becoming with the local farmers and businessmen looking to do alterations or build new houses, and was not happy. But being popular could not guarantee Pieter another job in a town that was too small for an architect to make a living doing just alterations and new homes.

There was a long discussion that night. What would be our next move on the chess board? Did we want to stay in Kimberley? Did we want to go to the coast, where Pieter had always dreamed of sailing, or to a big city like Johannesburg, where many of his college friends were thriving? The coast won hands down a month later when he received a letter of appointment to an architectural firm in Durban.

The lion had made his decision. It was time to conquer a new jungle. The lioness nodded.

"Durban!" Mother cried in horror when she heard what had happened. "That's where all the cockroaches are! What's wrong with Piet's job in Kimberley? If he is not happy there, why do you not move back to Bloemfontein?" Mother was on an increasingly limited need-to-know basis. "And what is going to happen to Martha? Durban is so far away. Six hours from Bloemfontein. This is dreadful. And you are pregnant again. This is a disaster. You are never going to cope by yourself!"

Kimberley was not such a disaster for Mother because it was only two hours away and that meant she could hop in the car if she detected the slightest nuance in the voice of Nicole or Martha or me. Durban was no hop in the car and drive over. Mother knew that and knew too that the umbilical cord would be severely stretched. Pieter knew it as well.

As for me, I was still trying to figure out who I was and what I wanted to achieve in life. Was it all about being the perfect wife, perfect mother, perfect daughter, perfect hostess, and perfect everything else that either Mother or Pieter expected? Or was it something else? Because I was trying to achieve perfection in all the aforementioned there was little time to reflect on myself, so like driftwood in the ocean, I went with the tide. Durban was where the tide flowed.

Mother shed extra tears that day.

And so, amidst dire warnings to avoid the Cuban Hat on the beachfront with its filthy hamburgers and cockroach-infested milkshakes, we bid Kimberley and all our family and friends a sad goodbye. The only small consolation to Mother was that Martha agreed to move with us. Martha might have been trained by Mother but she had never gone outside the borders of Kimberley or the world of the Griquas. Now she was moving with us to the world occupied by the mighty Zulu nation. She would face, along with us, the new culture of the people living in the province of Natal.

The lion led the way toward the receding glow on the distant horizon.

CHAPTER TWENTY-ONE

1981: Reagan is inaugurated as the thirty-ninth president of the United States. Unlike his predecessor who held a more detached position regarding Africa, Reagan sees the value of South Africa's minerals and sea route and promises to promote a policy of "constructive engagement." He appoints the former head of African Studies at Georgetown University, Chester Crocker, to be his assistant Secretary of State for African Affairs. Crocker's task is to prevent Russia from advancing further south in Africa and to implement the withdrawal of Cubans from Angola. Crocker seeks to find a solution in which everyone will come out feeling a winner.

This is different from the demands imposed by the Carter administration forcing South Africa to surrender unconditionally. Crocker's political enemies view his negotiations with the South African government as a deterrent to the African liberation movement in the region. He, however, sees it differently. He sees serious global implications if Russia takes control of the valuable minerals and seaports of southern Africa. The United Nations has already proposed a straight transfer of power to SWAPO in Namibia. The South African government is opposed to this and continues sending its military deep into Angola to fight the Russian- and Cuban-backed MPLA, who are aiding SWAPO in their attempt to take over Namibia.

Crocker eventually negotiates a deal that will prove somewhat acceptable to the South African government. The United States will endorse the MPLA in Angola if Cuba withdraws from Angola and South Africa withdraws from Namibia simultaneously. It takes several more years of back and forth before Castro finally pulls his troops from Angola, claiming victory on the way, and South Africa withdraws from Namibia. In 1989 Namibia obtains independence through a free and fair election, the South African flag is lowered, and SWAPO leader Sam Nujoma becomes Namibia's first president.

I had no idea what to expect in Durban other than childhood memories of perfect sand castles, pink candy floss, dripping ice cream cones and boogey boarding in the warm Indian Ocean.

Oh, and rickshaws! I used to love rickshaw rides with the big Zulu in a beaded headdress. He looked so important and brave and jumped so high in the air as he tilted the rickshaw back. I remember how Jenny and I would hold on for dear life while the Zulu kicked his legs in the air and let out a war cry. Mommy would shout at him not to go so high but we just pleaded more, more.

That was then. When Gussie packed freshly made Lebanese food in a cooler for us. When Daddy stopped at a roadside picnic table in the middle of nowhere. When we smelled the salty sea air long before we were there. When my only worry in the world was how fat my bum really looked in the new bikini.

Now was different. Now I was going to live there. Live with the Zulus.

I learned in school that the Zulus were a large tribe, much larger than the Sotho tribe. I learned that years ago, their chief, Dingaan, chopped some Afrikaners into bits and pieces and then more bits and pieces while they were still gasping for air. Dale said her brother told her that the Zulu witchdoctors liked to use a fresh beating heart with other bones and leaves in their black *potjies* for their *muti* (medicine). I wondered if there were still witchdoctors in Durban. Evelyn said there were, when I phoned to say goodbye. Evelyn also said that the Zulu men were lazy and made their wives work in the fields while they sat at home drinking *majuba* (homemade beer).

Father said there are lots of sharks in the sea and that I mustn't let Nicky swim too far out. Gussie said she would send some homemade apricot tarts in the mail every month. Piet's mom said she would send some homemade jam and *karringmelkbiskuit* with Pieter when he comes to visit. Mother said she was packing a year's supply of Raid in the van with our furniture and that I had to use all the cans.

Mother's friend Aunty Linda said that Durban had many more British residents than Bloemfontein or Kimberley. She also said that you had to put your children's names down at the good schools when they were born.

Pieter said she was talking rubbish and that the government schools were just as good as the private English schools. Mother said I must make sure to go and see the good private school and put Nicole's name down immediately. Pieter said that he was not paying for any private school. Mother said she would send me the money. Pieter said if she goes to an English school then all his children must go to the Afrikaans church. Mother said, the Anglican Church.

We stopped at Ladysmith to pick up some *biltong* from a butcher. *Biltong* and *droe wors* (dried sausage)—real *Boere kos* (Afrikaner food). Martha and Nicky wanted *Nic Naks*, cheese puffs that made their fingers orange by the time we left the town.

"Do you know how to get to the house?" asked Pieter. We were approaching Durban, weaving through the mountains of Natal.

"I have a map here," I replied. "They said it shouldn't be too difficult as their house is on the main road that leads down the hill and into the center of town. The owner's wife gave me directions. She sounds very nice. They have a daughter about four years older than Nicky."

"When we arrive, don't spend hours chatting. Just because we are going to rent the top half of their house doesn't mean I want them coming to visit every day, do you hear?" said Pieter.

"Well, you have to be nice to people!" I said. "You can't just say 'Hello, can I have the key?' and then leave."

"I am warning you, Ruchel. I don't want to have to talk to these English people every day, so if you want to chat with the wife, do it when I'm at work."

Fine.

The English people referred to were the aloof descendants of early British settlers. Very different from the English-speaking Europeans with whom we socialized in Bloemfontein and Kimberley.

The English in Durban were no different from their counterparts in England. Everything revolved around a country club, and the Durban Country Club was the litmus test of your social standing. If you were a member you reached the higher echelons of society. Once you were in, other "musts" followed.

Must have your children attend the top private English schools. No exceptions. Must belong to the downtown Durban Men's Club. Only white Anglo-Saxon men allowed; women must enter through the garage at the back of the building. Must own a box or suite at the

Greyville Race Course for the Durban July, which is South Africa's answer to Ascot. Must have...

Of course, I had no clue that all this was in store. I had just graduated from university after giving birth to one child and helping deliver another in the bush. I had just learned how to cook typical Afrikaans dishes like *bobotie* (meat loaf), *sousboontjies* (beans in sauce), and *pap*. Okay, Martha made the *pap*. I had just learned that the sky would not fall down if you didn't use the full set of cutlery at the table or if you ate with your plate on your lap or if you used a kitchen knife that had been used to pry open something in the engine of a car. I had just learned that peace was quickly restored in the house if you didn't argue back.

All this learning, but nothing to prepare me.

"*Hauw, Hauw!* Madam!" exclaimed Martha in horror as the car veered down the steep *kloofnek* (mountain pass) dotted with Tudor-style mansions hidden by gigantic green banana leaves and palm trees. "*Hauw*, Madam, what is that over there?"

"That's the sea, Martha, a big ocean," I said.

I tried to explain as best I could what surely looked like the end of the earth to Martha. Martha had never seen the sea. The only large quantity of water she had ever seen was at the bottom of the Big Hole in Kimberley and it signified danger, drowning, and death.

"*Hauw, Baas*, don't go so fast!" Martha yelped, clutching Nicky in a life or death grip. "We will fall into the water." Her face was contorted with fear, her eyes were closed, and her forehead was pouring sweat.

"Martha," laughed Pieter. "That's the sea, you can swim in it, don't be silly!"

"Don't worry, Martha," I said. "The sea is very far away and when we have unpacked I will drive slowly toward it so you can see it up close. The water tastes like salt and there are small waves that wash up to the sand."

"We'll take you swimming Martha, you'll love it," said Pieter.

"I want to swim in the sea!" demanded Nicky, taking her cue from her father. "I want to swim in the sea!" She would not stop.

Our arrival at the rented house could not have been more dramatic. The two prim and proper English people with their prim and proper daughter Danielle were in the garden when we pulled up to their prim and proper house. What poured out of the car was anything but prim and proper.

"Good afternoon, so lovely to meet you," I said in a somewhat normal voice as Pieter (in his Mother-despised tight shorts and tight T-shirt) tried to placate his screaming daughter.

"Her father promised she could swim in the sea," I said apologetically. "Look, Nicky, here is a little friend for you!" Nicole calmed down once she eyed Danielle, who was clearly several years older than she.

Just then the moving van pulled up to the curb.

"Okay, Ruchel," announced Pieter after saying the bare minimum to the owners of the house, "we don't have all day to unpack. Start carrying some of the small boxes." He then turned to the owners. "It was such a pleasure meeting you and thank you, but we can manage on our own."

Of course the husband had to go and ask Pieter to please make sure that we all walked quietly in the apartment upstairs because noise traveled quickly through the wooden floors. That sent Pieter right over the wall.

"Bloody English *dooses*! The sooner we move into our own house the better!" he mumbled under his breath as he lifted a box from the van. "I can just see it. This won't be the last. It will be, 'Don't do this, don't say that!' I don't know what you thought when you said we must rent this place. I just agreed to keep the peace with your mother because her friend found the place and God forbid we upset her friend. Make sure I don't see them in my portion of the house!"

Fine.

Pieter would never be happy until he had his own house, a house where he could drag a dead *springbok* through the kitchen door and carve it on the table, blood dripping everywhere. I could just imagine the faces of the owners if they saw Pieter carrying a dead animal on his shoulder after a weekend of hunting.

"They would throw the *baas* into the sea," giggled Martha as we sat unpacking boxes while Pieter went to work. "*Baas* likes to make much noise. The Madam downstairs does not like a lot of noise. She said I must make sure Nicole does not jump up and down as she can hear the jumping."

I began plotting how to get our own house. What sent me over the edge was Martha's room at the back of the house. Behind the very elaborate Victorian house we rented was what looked like a tool shed. Instead, it was the servant's quarters. Jail would have been a more appropriate term. It was a small dark room with one small window at the top. The bathroom made me gag: The door opened to a hole in the floor with a shower head attached to the back wall and a cracked wash basin on the side wall.

I had grown up in a place where not only did we sleep in comfort but so too did the household staff. I could not fathom why anyone would spend millions building a mansion and then build something like that at the bottom of the garden. Mother had warned me about the servant's rooms in the old houses in Durban but I thought she was exaggerating. This was no exaggeration. It was inexcusable.

"I am afraid that is what we have here. All these old houses on the Berea were built in this fashion," the wife explained when I made a beeline to her front door.

"If your maid is not satisfied she could always sleep in the township, like our maid, and catch a bus in the morning."

"I don't mind it, Madam," said Martha after I stormed back upstairs. "It's better than going to find a place in the township. Besides they are not my people there and I am frightened of the Zulus."

"Piet! As soon as this baby is born we must look for a house of our own!" I announced after we had moved everything into the top floor.

"I am not buying someone else's home," Pieter replied. "We are going to build our own house and that's final. If you're in a hurry to have your own home then you better go and find a cheap piece of land and not think of sending your daughter to all these expensive schools."

Fine, I thought. Say what you want, but I will achieve both. I was so determined that I immediately began with the subject of school.

After speaking to the wife downstairs (of course when Pieter was at work) I established that the best school was where her daughter was enrolled: Durban Girls' College.

Durban Girls' College was a block from the house we rented. It was an all-denominational English private school presided over by a Scottish headmistress with a very strong accent. The girls wore a green dress with white cuffs on short sleeves, regulation short white socks, black shoes, and a white Panama hat with the school's badge sewn onto the green and white band. It was almost one hundred years old and regarded as one of the most prestigious girls' schools in South Africa. It was what I wanted for my daughter.

Call it blind determination, call it naivety, call it stupidity, call it what you like but whether we had the money or not, Nicole was going to Durban Girl's College. End of story.

A week after moving in, I toured the school. I was met by the school secretary who armed me with enough literature to occupy me for a week, on everything from dress code, history, rules and regulations, to academic requirements and application forms. The air was thick with competition and old colonial tradition. She gently reminded me that they already had a long list of applicants for the year my daughter was due to enroll and that the sooner I put her name down the better.

*   *   *

"Ruchel!" boomed Mother the instant she obtained our new telephone number from Pieter at the office. "Why have you not phoned to give me your new number? Why do I have to find it out from your husband?"

"Ma," I sighed, "the phone was only installed yesterday. I've been trying to find a pre-primary school for Nicole. The one that the girl downstairs attends is full with a waiting list."

"What do you mean full? I will make a few phone calls!"

"Ma, I have sorted it out. The headmistress referred me to the Jewish pre-primary school opposite the road and they phoned me this morning to say they had a cancellation. I immediately went over and began filling out the forms. It is a lovely school called Kadimah and it reminds me of my old nursery school."

"Just make sure you put her name down at Durban Girls' College. Both Juliet and Linda say that that is the best girl's school in Durban. Now let me talk to my little darling."

Ears perked up and whiskers twitched as a faint roar from the lion's old stomping grounds came sailing across the dry African veld.

The very next weekend we were invited to Pieter's boss' house for dinner.

"Now both he and his wife are very upper Afrikaans," Pieter reminded me as we drove to their home in La Lucia, an exclusive area on the north coast of Durban. It was about twenty minutes from town.

"What do you mean, upper Afrikaans"

"They are part of the wealthy and snooty Afrikaners here in Natal and they are very traditional. So don't talk about English this and English that."

Fine.

We pulled up to the driveway of the Cape Dutch home that was not too far from where Harry Oppenheimer, of De Beers fame, had built his sprawling holiday home. Cape Dutch was a style of architecture favored by Afrikaners, especially in the Cape. Many homes and wine farms sported the traditional gables and yellow wood floors that were so typical of their forefathers' homes.

"*Goeie-naand* [Good evening]," I said as a petite blond woman opened the door. Inside the house was all yellow wood, Persian carpets, and Afrikaner chic.

I learned a few things that evening while sipping Boschendal Pinotage.

I learned that the upper Afrikaner was as snooty as the snootiest Englishman. I learned that tradition was passed down from generation to generation and that it was the Afrikaners who ran the town and not the English. I learned that the *Kajuitraad* was one of the first clubs Pieter had to enroll in.

"The *Kajuitraad*," continued his boss as the maid cleared the roast beef and potatoes from the table, "is a group of Afrikaners who get together once a month to network, talk business, and promote the Afrikaans culture. We always include the reading of a poem or a verse by a respected Afrikaans poet. Last month it was Breytenbach. You can come to the next meeting, Pieter, and I will introduce you to everyone. It will be good for the firm for you to start networking."

"Sometimes they have functions that include the wives," added the wife for my benefit. "It will be nice for you to meet other wives, if you haven't already met them at church."

"Oh, we haven't had the opportunity of going to church yet," said Pieter before I could embarrass him by saying that we hadn't settled the matter of Afrikaans church versus English private school.

Good wives don't embarrass their husbands in front of their bosses, friends, or family.

"The *Kajuitraad* is also much easier to get into. I belong to the *Broederbond* as well, but membership there is very tight," continued the boss. "Anyway, the church you should attend is the one on the hill in Umhlanga, which is right next to La Lucia. It is the NGK. They have a lot of young new families who are members."

"I help with the tea on Sundays," added the wife. "Ruchel, let me know when you join so I can introduce you to our Dominee." The Dominee was the preacher.

I couldn't wait to get back in the car.

"What does he mean that the *Broederbond* is very tight to get into?" I asked. "It sounded like you would have a snowball's hope of becoming a member there."

"That's because I'm married to you," said Pieter. "The *Broederbond* is for the pure Afrikaners and I am married to a *rooinek*."

"Oh, that's ridiculous! Just because I'm English they will never accept you? Ridiculous!"

But was it so ridiculous? The English had their club, the Jews had theirs, what was wrong with the Afrikaners having theirs?

"Ridiculous!" I muttered again. "We should all be able to belong to each other's clubs. That way, we learn from the traditions of others."

"Well, I have decided to join the NGK. I don't care what your mother says," continued Pieter. "My children must learn their father's culture."

"Well," I replied, "then the children are definitely going to the English private schools!"

"I am not paying for some stupid private school," snapped Pieter, "and you will not accept money from your mother to pay for those schools either!"

Fine.

I would figure out a way.

Pieter had no idea what he was doing when he tried to stop me from doing what I had set my heart on. His resistance only made me more motivated, as if I was unconsciously responding to a dare.

But before I go into that, let me give you a slice of our rapidly developing social life.

Both Pieter and I were social animals. We loved to have friends over and they loved to have us and as a result we quickly got to experience quite a few communities in town.

A good deal of time was spent with the Jewish community because of the school our daughter attended. The mothers would get together after school while children played, the fathers would talk to each other at the school events. It was how I found out about enrolling Nicole in ballet lessons when she was only four. Our daughter also learned to swim from her friends at school after fighting swimming lessons for months on end in Kimberley. One day she called out to me while I was sipping tea with one of the mothers and said, "Look, Ma, watch me swim!" Just like that. No lessons, no guidance, and there she was, swimming the length of the friend's pool.

Then there was the group of friends Pieter met at the *Kajuitraad*. He joined the very next weekend and immediately met a group of young Afrikaans professionals. There were the two engineers, Jan and Johan, the property developer, Thinus, and the quantity surveyor, Albert. Real *manne*! Their wives and I socialized on the occasion.

"They are all very different, Mali," I said over the phone to my very best friend who, thank God, had moved to Durban a year ealier to work for Unilever. Just to have her in the same town again was a relief greater than I could have imagined. "I can't see them socializing with each other. But then again, I suppose if I invited them all to a huge party they would all get along just fine."

"No, they wouldn't. They would huddle in their own little groups," said my wise dear friend.

"Well, I think that's weird. Why do you think they all like us then?"

"Because you guys are crazy," replied Michelle. "I mean, that husband of yours is a party animal and you are just like your mother. A socialite to the core!"

"Rubbish! I am not like my mother... maybe a little..? Mali, I can't wait to have our own house so we can have *braais* in the backyard. I would invite them all to the party."

* * *

Our own house.

But if I wanted our own house, Pieter said I had to find a cheap piece of land so that he could design a house to his specifications. Pieter said he was not going to live in someone else's house. No way. Pieter said he was an architect and architects lived in their own houses.

Fine.

"You are doing what!" demanded Pieter one night.

"I said," I replied patiently, "I am going to work as a real estate agent so that I can find a piece of land to build our house on."

"But you are four months' pregnant. Who is going to go and see houses with a pregnant woman? Where did you come up with such an idea?"

"I answered an ad in the newspaper. This couple who is starting a new real estate agency said I could work there."

"But you don't even have a real estate license, you don't even know how to sell houses!" argued Pieter.

"They said I can study at night and if I sell anything before I get the license, then the owner will draw up the contracts. They said I looked very energetic and had lots of enthusiasm."

"I don't care what they said," replied Pieter. "What about Nicole? I don't think this is a good idea!"

"Rubbish!" I replied. "Nicky is at school in the mornings and I can still fetch her at noon. Martha can look after her in the afternoons. Besides, real estate agents work on their own time and they are always the first to find the good deals. My grandfather and father said that you should always buy the cheapest property in the most expensive area. Those properties would always increase in value no matter what."

"Your grandfather had lots of money so he was in a position to think like that. I am going to phone your mother and tell her that you are not looking after your daughter properly," Pieter said in a last-ditch attempt to win the argument.

After I calmly persuaded him to see my point of view, he finally relented on condition that I was to be at home no later than 5:00 PM to make supper and that I was not to go to any person's house at night.

Fine.

I found the piece of land within two months of selling one apartment and one house.

"So what do you think?" I asked Pieter the Saturday after finding the land.

"It's three times more than what we were going to pay in Kimberley," was his response as he climbed out of the car, "and look how steep the land is. It is going to be expensive to build here, you are wasting my time."

"But look," I quickly said before he climbed back into the car. "Look, it has two entrances, one where we are parked now and one at the bottom of the hill. Maybe we can subdivide the land and sell the bottom half to pay for the top half."

"Ruchel," he sighed, "why are you looking in one of the most expensive areas? Just because my boss lives in this area, now you want to buy here on the other side of the highway high up on the hill just so that you can say we live in La Lucia. We can't afford it—let's go!"

"Wait! This land will be far more valuable once we build the house on it and we will be able to increase our investment far quicker than if we build in a start-up area. Besides, this land is a bargain at 18,000 rand. Maybe we can subdivide and get our portion free?" I was not getting off the subject of subdivision because I knew that was my only glimmer of a chance to prevent Pieter from getting back into the car.

I also had an uncanny sense for real estate that was definitely a throwback from my grandfather. I knew a bargain when I saw it. The site offered sweeping views of the shoreline. You could hear the waves crashing on a quiet night. We could build a small house and add on as our economic situation improved. It would be our own home. Martha would have her own proper room and bathroom as well.

It did not take Pieter long to mull it over in his head and realize for himself that this land was truly a bargain. That he could possibly sell a portion and get the land free was the clincher that made him sign on the dotted line. That his boss and friends said he was making the right decision only added to his motivation.

So we plunged into the water and began swimming furiously. We hit a rock. The land was three hundred square meters short if we wanted to subdivide it. That we discovered after we had signed the contract. No problem. We would swim around the rock. We saw that the neighbor to the left did not use the lower portion of his site, which also bordered on the street below. It was overgrown with weeds. We offered to buy this portion, thus relieving his headaches of paying extra property taxes and clearing the brush. Besides, a new swimming pool would look simply marvelous in his front yard. The deal was made and many months later, after we had already begun to build on the site, the land was finally subdivided and the lower portion sold. We had made good on the gamble. We obtained our land free.

It was nearly Christmas. I still showed real estate when there was a need, until one frightened client politely told me that he did not think I should be driving a car showing him houses so late in my pregnancy. He refused to get into the car. So I quit. End of real estate job. Mission accomplished.

"You bought a piece of land where?" Mother inquired in her most shocked tone ever. "You are eight and a half months pregnant and you and your husband bought a piece of land? What's wrong with buying a small house?"

"Ma, we don't have enough money to buy a house and besides Piet wants to build his own house. Architects like their own houses," I replied over the phone.

"You have no idea what it is like to build a house. You will have two small children! Children need a calm stable environment as they develop. That's how you grew up. You already sound exhausted. You have lost all sense! Can't you see how difficult just looking after two children is going to be? I feel as if I am speaking to a wall right now. When the baby is born I am coming right up."

A couple of weeks later Pieter and I were watching *Dallas* on TV. *Dallas* was everyone's favorite show on Tuesday nights. We had bought our first television set in Kimberley when the government introduced television to South Africa. From that day forth anyone lucky enough to own a TV set sat glued to the box from the time the programs started at 6:00 PM until they ended at midnight with the national anthem.

I felt the first cramp.

"Oww!" I exclaimed suddenly, "Oww! I better walk over to my doctor and see what he thinks. Thank heavens he lives across the street."

I had been through one birth and helped with another—why interrupt the program? I even told the doctor, who was surprised to see me that night before New Year's Eve, that if he wanted to finish watching *Dallas* I did not mind. He said we could watch it together. Pieter was horrified when I phoned him as the credits were rolling to come to fetch me to take me to the hospital.

The cramps came fast and furious on the way to the hospital and the pain was no less than with the first child. "Hurry and shave her!" ordered the nurse as I was wheeled into the labor room. Colourful Christmas decorations flashed green and red between each pain piercing my body.

"Don't leave me!" I cried out to Pieter as he ran behind the nurses pushing the wheeled bed.

"Ma!" I screamed. "Ma, where are you?" But Mother was many miles away in Bloemfontein. I was once again reduced to a three-year-old child as I desperately willed Mother to appear.

"Push, Ruchel!" encouraged Pieter in the delivery room, all colour drained from his face. This was deja vu all over again. How quickly we forget the pain, the searing excruciating pain that threatens to tear your body open. The exhaustion of trying to push when all you want to do is pass out. The orders and instructions of loved ones in your ear when all you want to do is slap them.

"It's a boy!"

A boy. I have a boy? Oh thank you, Lord. Thank you. A boy and a girl. Now I don't have to have more children. I have one of each. Thank you, thank you, Lord.

Pieter was over the moon. A son to go hunting. A son to go fishing. A son to play touch rugby on the beach. A son to continue the tradition of the Afrikaner name, Coetzee. Hendrik Pieter Coetzee after his grandfather. No. He can't have two Afrikaans names—let's call him Hendrik Peter. I wanted Andrew or Nicholas but tradition won the day. We compromised by calling him Peter even though he was registered Hendrik Peter.

Peter came into our lives with a thick head of hair and big dark blue eyes. It was love at first sight all over again. That time I insisted on breast feeding, which was to last nine months. He was the baby who would be mothered by the three most important women in his life: his mother, his sister, and Martha. The baby who could do no wrong. The little brother who was carefully tucked into his bed each night by his adoring sister. The little man who Martha insisted carrying on her back wrapped snugly in a blanket as she went about her housework.

Mother flew up, hugged her new grandson, whisked her granddaughter off to the stores, dispensed instructions to Martha that rivaled in volume to *War and Peace*, and said I looked too dreadful for words.

"When the baby is six months old, you are to bring the children and Martha to Bloemfontein," she announced. "Nicky will be on school vacation so you can spend three weeks with us. I will not accept any argument from your husband. That's final! You have no colour in your cheeks and you look exhausted! I am horrified!"

Before Pieter could voice an opinion, Mother was back on the plane to Bloemfontein.

The lion's heart skipped a beat as he contemplated the perils of the jungle that lay before him.

CHAPTER TWENTY-TWO

1982: The Afrikaners in South Africa have come a long way since the Boer War at the turn of the century. No longer second-class citizens under British rule, the Afrikaners have risen to become a very powerful group both politically and economically. Major insurance and banking institutions are headed up by Afrikaners. Their presence in the government and educational sectors is all encompassing. Their greatest fears are not only being forced to live under black rule but also that their very culture and language will suffer a slow death.

The South African government seeks to stem this tide through the concept of separate governments for whites, coloureds, and Indians, with limited influence by the latter two groups. The blacks are excluded from this "segregation" plan and instead will be represented by their independent homelands. A referendum is submitted to the white voters. The reaction among all groups in South Africa is varied. The ANC and PAC reject the plan outright. The right-wing Afrikaners not only reject the plan in outrage but many also walk away from the National Party to form the Conservative Party under former National Party Minister Dr Andries Treurnicht. The Conservative Party will oppose any reforms that the National Party puts forward. Many coloureds and Indians also oppose the proposal as unacceptable.

The referendum is passed by a small margin, with the English and moderate Afrikaners voting yes in 1983 and a small minority of coloureds and Indians voting yes in their election a year later. Outraged, the ANC and PAC continue their political and armed resistance. The MK (a branch of the ANC) explodes a number of limpet mines at the nuclear power station at Koeberg near Cape Town, causing widespread damage. In retaliation, the South African Defense Force (SADF) attacks twelve houses and flats in Maseru, the capital of Lesotho, where it is presumed the ANC insurgents are hiding. Women and children are among the forty killed.

The violence in South Africa was escalating. Rumors about unreported incidents were flaring up around the country. We could no longer ignore it and think it was all just a bad rumor from people who were justifying why they were leaving the country.

Martha reported that some of her friends in the townships were becoming increasingly alarmed at the escalated fighting among the Zulus and Xhosas.

"Why would they be fighting?" I asked, confused. I truly had no broad picture, no concept.

"My friend Jane says that the Zulus are fighting with the Xhosas because they say that their chief is more important than Mandela."

I had no idea who this Mandela person was that everyone was asking to free. No such information was ever released by the government or media at the time.

Besides, I thought, the Zulus were a proud nation. They were not going to be told what to do by some other tribe, so I assumed they most probably were just squabbling among themselves. Right?

They were just squabbling because Zulu men and woman were far more outspoken than their Sotho counterparts. Right, Martha?

Right, Madam.

But Martha's Zulu friends knew a whole lot more than Martha did about politics, Mandela, and violence. A whole lot more than the limited, censored information I received that led me to believe that this would all blow over in a few weeks. After all, other countries experienced outbreaks of violence and not everyone was running around the streets packing a gun. Right?

Many of our friends kept guns in their houses and I always thought they were totally ridiculous. Who would they shoot? Burglars? Most burglars burgled houses when the owners were not there or else it was an inside job. Guns were dangerous and could be found by one of my children or a playmate. I did not think it was a smart idea to buy a gun for protection.

Pieter thought otherwise. He bought a gun. I thought he was being ridiculous and refused to let him take it out to show me. I did not have any reason to think my life was in any danger. Pieter said that he was hearing rumors that some blacks were becoming very dangerous and he was not going to take any chances.

Fine.

Now I did listen to what Martha was saying and to what Pieter was fearing but I don't think I really understood the gravity of the violence that was erupting all over the country. Whispered rumors usually surf fleetingly through your brain and rarely linger unless your eyes see for themselves.

I also had learned to "live in the moment." It was easier for me mentally, especially when ill winds threatened to sap my energy. By living in the moment I was able to snatch bursts of energy free of the burdens that usually accompany the "what ifs" in life.

Soon it would be time for me to visit my family in Bloemfontein. I began to look forward to taking the children and Martha with me and to being spoiled by everyone. I could already taste the food and smell the cold Bloemfontein air.

"Before you leave to go to your mother," Pieter announced the week I was due to depart, "we have been invited to spend a weekend with Jan, Albert, and everyone at Sani Pass. On Sunday you can leave directly from the resort to Bloemfontein and I will catch a lift home with Albert."

Sani Pass was a beautiful mountain resort in the Drakensburg Mountains where people from Natal went to unwind from the stresses of urban life. It was a place where you could breathe fresh mountain air, go horseback riding, play tennis, and eat scones with clotted cream on the big wide *stoep* (porch) overlooking the mountains.

This last-minute prospect of a back-to-back boost of energy sent me skipping through the air. A weekend with friends and two weeks with family… aaah. Heaven could not taste sweeter.

I was already drawing in some of that relaxed energy by the time we pulled up to the resort. Our thatched *rondavel* was set among a string of other one-bedroom *rondavels* overlooking the large pool and tennis courts below.

"Hey, Louise, I'll meet you on the patio for tea in about an hour," I called out from my *rondavel*. "Just give me a few minutes to unpack."

"Take your time," replied Albert's petite wife smiling. "I have to first find where I packed my husband's tennis shoes. I hope I didn't leave them at home."

"Tell him he better be prepared because Jan and I are going to *moer* [kill] them on the courts just now," Pieter shouted over my shoulder as he kicked his shoes off. He was pacing the room, waiting for me to retrieve his shorts from the suitcase.

"I want to go and jump on the trampoline!" declared Nicky.

"Just give me a moment while I sort your father out, my sweetheart," I said, handing the baby over to Martha standing in the doorway.

"Come with me and your brother," Martha said to Nicole. "I'll take you to the trampolines."

"Oh, thank you, Martha," I whispered to Martha out of earshot of Pieter. "You know how the *baas* gets when he wants something *now*."

"When we finish the game we are all going to meet in the pub for a *dop* [drink] before dinner," Pieter announced. He was testing the strings on his racket.

"Okay, okay, I'll be in the children's dining room then, so don't be too long as you still have to bathe and change before dinner. Tonight is formal night. There is dancing to a live band after dinner. That's what the program says."

"Agh, I hate formal. Come fetch me in the pub. Hey, *boetie* [brother], wait up!"

How the lion loves to preen among his friends. Look how they circle each other knowingly under the midday sun.

All the husbands had met at the *Kajuitraad* and were into male bonding long before the wives even knew each other. It did not take us long to catch up.

These Afrikaans wives were the epitome of the good wife. They were quiet spoken, ran well-organized homes, and made sure their husbands were thoroughly de-stressed before returning to work the next day. They sought the best private music lessons and the best Afrikaans schools for their children. They clustered together to talk in hushed tones about children, maids, recipes, and church while their husbands strutted about like peacocks. Their children hardly ever carried on like hooligans, and at barbecues they always served their husbands a plate of food together with their own.

Much of my early education in the good wife department came from these brave and unselfish women. Although Pieter would have loved for me to graduate summa cum laude, I only really managed a respectable "B" when all was said and done. I think that the small part of me—about ten percent—that I stubbornly clung to as my own individuality contributed to my lower grade.

That ten percent was to surface many years later with much pent-up drive and energy.

"You were so hilarious last night, Ruchel," said Louise. She laughed. "I didn't think you had the guts to do it."

"It was all Thinus' fault," I replied. We were lounging on the pool deck chairs watching the children play in the water. "He started it."

"Ja, but when he dared you to climb out the dining room window instead of walking through the door with the rest of us, I thought no way!"

"Ja, Pieter thought no way as well but it was midnight and I am sure the two glasses of wine contributed to my totally misjudging the ledge and falling flat on my face in the flower bed. Poor Thinus was laughing so much he could hardly help dig me out." I giggled before remembering the horrified look on Pieter's face. "Maybe I should try harder to behave and not act like a kid," I continued more soberly.

"Oh, as if those guys ever behave themselves," replied Louise. "Besides, you are such fun to be around. We only wish we had some of your energy and spunk."

It was that ten percent. That same ten percent that contributed to Pieter's and Mother's beliefs that I would never mature into a capable adult. Ever!

"Ruchel!" Pieter said as he handed the gun to me in the parking lot of the resort that Sunday. "I only agreed for you to visit your parents with the children if you took a gun with you in the car. You heard what Albert said this weekend. The roads are not as safe as they used to be. There seems to be an increase in violence."

"That's ridiculous!" I argued. "All I am going to do is drive to Bloemfontein with Martha and the children. I have not heard of any violence on the roads. I don't even know how to use a gun."

"Then I will not get a lift home with Albert and I will get into this car and we can all drive back to Durban immediately," Pieter said. Final authority.

"Okay, okay, I will take the gun," I replied, "but I can assure you that it won't be used so you don't even have to show me what to do."

"Just aim and pull the trigger if you get into trouble, the gun is loaded. Don't let the children near it, not for a second." Pieter sighed the sigh of a very patient parent as he put the gun into the glove compartment of the car.

I could not be like the other Afrikaans wives and just accept what my husband said. No. I had to protest. I was willing to fetch an extra plate of food for him and spoil him rotten but in certain ways I was very difficult to change, especially if it involved the children in any shape or form. Take, for instance, education. It would have taken torture in the darkest and cruelest chamber to make me change my mind about good private schools.

"Nicky, say goodbye to Daddy. Martha, let the baby sit on your lap until he falls asleep. Bye everyone, see you in two weeks." I waved everyone goodbye. It was a five-hour journey from the mountain resort and I estimated that I should arrive in Bloemfontein by 6:00 PM the latest.

"Ruchel, drive slowly and keep your eyes on the road. Only stop for petrol, do you hear me!" Pieter yelled as I rolled the window up and hit the dirt road.

"Look at all the dust, Mommy. I can't see Daddy anymore!" yelled Nicky from the back.

"That's okay, soon we will be on the main highway. Gansi is waiting for you at her house with lots of presents. Sit down nicely next to Martha and your brother."

Nicky began twirling the animal skin bracelet on Martha's arm round and round. "I'm three and a half, Martha!!" she blurted out while holding three fingers and a half bent finger up in the air.

Cars whizzed by as we passed small town after small town. Mountains and corn fields, farm houses and stretches of open spaces all sped past in a comforting African silence.

Wait! What was that? Could it be? Yes!

"Look! Someone has built a snowman! Over there, in the valley below!"

A snowman? South Africa only received snow on the highest mountain peaks. It was a rare occurrence to see snow in the fields, never mind a snowman. But my eyes were not deceiving me as we came closer to a lone snowman standing in a farmer's field.

"Look, Nicky, Martha, a snowman!" I called out to the back.

"Where? Where's the snowman?" My daughter craned her neck to see out each window.

"There, at the bottom of the hill, can you see it? There, Nicky, over there," pointed Martha as she too craned her neck to see this phenomenon.

"I want to touch the snowman, I want to touch the snowman!" demanded the little voice from the back seat.

"Okay, okay, I will stop for you to look at the snowman. Mommy also wants to see the snowman." I slowed the car and pulled off to the side.

It was indeed strange to see as there was hardly any snow on the ground, more like specks of ice, but in the field behind the fence stood a perfectly formed snowman with what looked like two small ears on the side of his head.

"Okay, stand here by the fence and I will take a photo of you with the snowman," I said as I helped my daughter climb out of the car. Pieter's warning was ringing in my ears but this was a rare occurrence, bloody hell.

"I want to touch the snowman, I want to touch the snowman!" clamored Nicky as she tried to climb over the barbed wire fence separating us and the snowman a few meters away.

"Martha, just wait in the car with the baby, I am going to help her over the fence so that she can touch the snowman. Nicky, wait! You will cut yourself! Mommy will help you."

I helped Nicky over the fence then climbed over it myself. She ran to touch the snowman.

"All right, stand still, mommy wants to take a photo of you next to the snowman, stand still!" I instructed.

A chill wind rattled my bones. Strange. I lifted the camera to press the button.

What was that? That rustle in the wind. That chill up my spine. I turned to look where Martha and Peter were sitting patiently in the car.

Nothing. A bucolic African landscape.

But listen to that rustle. Don't you hear the spirits awakening? Don't you hear them twisting and twirling in the air? Don't you, don't you?

"Okay, give mommy a big smile! That's my girl." Click. "Wait, another picture, my darling. I have to show daddy how big the snowman is."

I couldn't take the picture. My hands were shaking too much. I shook my head and steadied the camera again.

"Stop fidgeting, Nicky. Okay, stand still now."

Something was wrong. I could smell it. I could feel it. I could hear it. Who was behind me?

I spun around.

Nothing.

But something was out of sync.

An open truck with two black men in front and three at the back slowed down as it came down the mountain pass. Slowing down meant they were going to stop next to my car with Martha, the baby, and my handbag inside.

Oh God.

In the split second it took for me to assess the situation I realized that it would take too long for me to get Nicky and myself over the fence and run back to the car before the truck stopped completely.

"Wait here! Don't you move one inch, do you hear me!" I screamed at my daughter, who froze on the spot hearing a tone in my voice that was unknown and frightening to her. With a rush of adrenaline coursing through my veins I vaulted over the barbed wire fence and reached the passenger side of the car just as the truck came to a halt in front of me.

The three men sitting at the back glared at me as the driver opened his door.

"What do you want?" I demanded. I reached inside the glove compartment for the gun. "What do you want?" I repeated, thinking, oh God, Nicky is standing unprotected on the other side of the fence.

The driver walked toward me. A deliberate evil smile spread across his scarred face. Behind him was the most ragged group of troublemakers you could imagine. Nothing in their faces spoke of kindness or compassion. These were a very different group of blacks.

Alien people. Not the people I grew up with or came into contact with. Strangers from another country.

Confirming my suspicions, Martha whispered under her breath, "Madam, these people are evil, be careful, very careful."

"If you move one step further, I will shoot you!" I screamed, pointing the gun in his direction.

"You don't know how to shoot." He laughed as he turned to his friends and gestured for them to climb out of the truck.

"Take one more step and I will shoot, you bastard!" I screamed again. I raised the gun and took aim.

"Ha, ha, ha!" laughed the driver. "Sipho, go fetch the little girl by the snowman and then we will see how this lady shoots. Hurry up and lock her up in the truck."

The air around me went wild with my anger. Spirits swirled like ignited pinwheels.

By now, Martha was hysterical, which in turn made Peter hysterical, and both were crying. Poor Nicky still stood frozen next to the snowman, not knowing what to do. Never before had she seen her mother brandishing a gun at someone. Good girl, don't run to mommy, I prayed silently.

I pulled the trigger and fired a shot above the head of the man trying to climb over the fence.

"Ha, ha," laughed the driver as he took another step toward me. "You missed. *Maak gou* [hurry up], Sipho, *vat die kind* [grab the child]."

The next shot hit Sipho in the foot and he fell to the ground in agony.

"Take one more step you slimy stinking piece of rubbish and the next bullet is through your heart!"

The others stood frozen behind the driver. No white woman had ever become so crazy before their eyes. Maybe the witchdoctor had got hold of her? Maybe she was the devil?

The air was now screaming with madness.

I lifted the gun and took aim right at his heart.

The driver hesitated for a split second.

I took a step forward and fired another shot, missing his arm by an inch and striking the tail light of the truck. A look of horrified shock clouded his face.

"*Aieeee!*" screamed his cohorts as they took cover behind the truck. The driver assessed the situation.

"We will come looking for you," he threatened as he slowly retreated back to the truck. "We know what you look like and we will find you!"

"Go to hell, you bastards, leave! Leave now!!!" I screamed as I watched them drive away. "Go to hell!"

Just then another car approached, slowed down, and a white man asked if anything was the matter.

"I'm fine," I replied, shivering. Tears were streaming down my face. "Just please go. Please go!" Seeing the gun in my hand, the driver did not stay to argue and pressed his gas pedal again.

"Hurry, Nicky, run to mommy now!" I shouted after I put the gun back in the glove compartment and ran over to the fence. "Hurry, my darling!"

The air settled and was quiet as the spirits slowly calmed.

I gently lifted my now hysterical daughter into the car and passed her over to Martha, who had calmed down considerably after the truck pulled away.

"Come to Marti, my baby," she cooed to Nicky as she lifted her into the car, "there, there, let's sing your song. The song you liked to sing when you were a baby." Then she sang the Sotho version of *Frere Jacques*:

> *Tlong kaofela, tlong kaofela,*
> *Phakisang, phakisang,*
> *Tshepe e ya lla, tshepe e ya lla,*
> *Ting-Tong-Teng, Ting-Tong-Teng.*
>
> (Come all of you, come all of you,
> Hurry up, hurry up,
> The bell is ringing, the bell is ringing,
> Ding dong ding, ding dong ding.)

By the time I reached Bloemfontein I had calmed down considerably but Mother did not miss a thing. After demanding to know what had happened, she became hysterical herself and issued orders left, right, and center. The children were whisked away by

Evelyn, who knew exactly what to do with them in a Mother-frenzied situation. Rosie escorted Martha to her room to make her drink a strong cup of tea with ten teaspoons of sugar, and Mother ordered the doctor on the phone to come over immediately, then hung up and phoned Pieter.

It was so good to be back home in Bloemfontein. All the comforting sounds, smells, and sights instantly repaired aftershock effects. Father held me tightly in his arms and Gussie immediately brought over all my favorite food. I was once again their daughter and granddaughter to be spoiled as they saw fit.

But I knew that would never again be totally true. I had changed. With all the new experiences thrust into my life in such a short time, I had no option but to become a little braver. No longer was I the quiet and docile little girl they could protect within the palace gates. I knew I could not just get into my nice warm bed with its crisp sheets and think nothing bad was ever going to happen to me again. But I could pretend.

As long as Father, Mother, Gussie, Evelyn, and all the others were there to look after me and comfort me, I could close my eyes and pretend none of this had happened and I was once again a happy carefree child. But I knew that when I opened my eyes, that brief fantasy would be whisked away, so I tried to keep my eyes closed for as long as possible.

I soaked up the love during the rest of those two weeks like a sponge that had been left out to dry in the desert. I embraced the strength that once again flowed into my tired body and renewed the energy I thrived on. I thanked God for his protection, for the renewal and for the love and warmth of my precious and dear family.

And then I thanked God again for the renewed energy because I knew, I truly and instinctively knew, that I would need every ounce of my strength for what lay ahead: the building of 44 William Campbell Drive, La Lucia.

The lion roared.

CHAPTER TWENTY-THREE

1983: President Botha's new constitution is passed by 1.36 million white, Indian, and coloured voters; 691,000 vote against it, led by the ultra right wing Conservative Party. They believed the government was becoming too moderate. During a rally in Cape Town, another new party is formed to oppose the new constitution that year. It is called the United Democratic Front (UDF) and its members are of all races. The UDF is to become the country's largest internal political movement in decades. One member, Patrick "Terror" Lekota, tells the rally that "the laws will still be made in the white House. The so-called "Coloured" and Indian Houses will be there only to put a rubber stamp on the laws made by the bosses."

I t started off with a simple triangle. Not a square. Oh no. Architects do not draw plain square boxes. Please. A triangle. It must be a triangle.

But simple? Not simple at all. The larger portion of the triangle was a zigzag.

"Why are you drawing a zigzag there?" I asked as I peered over Pieter's shoulder one night after the children had gone to sleep.

"That's where the windows are, to see the ocean," he replied, leaning back to view the drawing.

"Why would you have zigzag windows? You won't see the ocean clearly."

"Ruchel," he sighed. "I can't help it if you can't read a plan properly. Just wait until I'm finished and then I'll explain. The windows will be double volume. You have to have them like this so that they can withstand any wind pressure."

"Why? How high do you expect to build this house? I thought we would start off small and add on later."

"Just leave me alone, I know what I'm doing," he said curtly. "This is going to be an incredible design, you'll see!"

I could see that this cake was now fully baked and no amount of argument could turn it back to a reasonable discussion. Was I frustrated? Of course. Could I win? Of course not! Did I try? Not really.

The house was to be an ode to Pieter Coetzee's architectural prowess, a six thousand square foot masterpiece that needed an explanation even for the local authorities.

"Ruchel!" Pieter called one afternoon after opening the mail. "I've been called up for a three-week camp again! It's so frustrating. I simply can't take all this time off."

"Why does the Army always call you up like this?" I asked. "You have already been twice while we were in Kimberley and now they want you again? Surely you could tell them you're now working and have a family to raise?"

"This is the last time I am going!" he announced to no one in particular. "I am going to write a letter to the general to tell him I have a family to support. This is ridiculous but since I can't get out of this one, it means that you'll have to hand the plans in and see that they get passed before I come back."

"What?" I said. "I don't know how to get plans passed. What if they ask me questions and I don't know the answers?"

"I've drawn everything they require and made five copies. Just hand it to them and tell them I'm in the Army, for heaven's sake. The more the plans are delayed, the more money it's going to cost us. So make sure you get them passed! Don't be such a baby, Ruchel."

A baby? Life until a few years ago had been simple, a gentle river flowing smoothly along in innocent joy. Flowing and exploring, unencumbered. Now the river was making sharp turns.

Again and again boulders blocked the river's smooth flow. The river had to adapt, had to become stronger, more fearless, smooth the sharp turns into curves, flow around the boulders. Otherwise it would be dammed up and cease to flow.

But it was hard. For so many years my only angst was the size of my bum. Now my behavior was being examined. How was I supposed to behave? More maturely? I thought I was mature. I had given birth to two children, delivered another child, fought off evil forces. So why did I feel so inadequate, so incapable of thinking when confronted with orders from Pieter or Mother? Why did I feel like such a baby still?

* * *

"So tell me, Mrs. Coetzee," said the chief town planner in Umhlanga, the borough for La Lucia. "We are having difficulty reading your husband's plan here. What does he mean, 'Martha's room'?"

"Oh, that is our maid's room and bathroom," I replied, shifting Peter from one hip to another, "and those are our children's rooms. See, it says Nicole and Peter. The circular shape between those two rooms is the bathroom."

"Yes...no...we have already figured that out," he sighed. "But you know, all plans are supposed to be indicated by bedroom one, bedroom two, etcetera. Architects should know that."

"Yes, my husband knows that, of course," I quickly said, praying that he would not throw the plans back at me. "He was working till late the night before he left for camp and I suppose he just left those names in when he was explaining it to me."

"And how does your husband intend building this project if we decide to pass it?" continued the town planner, beginning to melt under my sugary charm.

"Oh, my husband used to work on his father's construction sites, building schools, so he is very familiar with construction. He knows how to build this house and will assemble a team of workers to help him," I smiled so sweetly, so innocently. "You just have to pass it, please. Please?"

"Tell your husband to come in and see us when he returns, but we will pass it in the meantime." He smiled back, stamping the plans. "And tell him he has a very charming wife."

"Oh, you are so sweet, thank you, thank you!" And I was off before he could change his mind and before baby Peter started wriggling for milk. Heaving a breast out in front of the town planner was not a good idea.

Maybe I was not such a baby?

Pieter returned from his trip exhausted and sweaty. "Thank heavens for all my political connections! I don't have to go on anymore three-week camps. I am now done with the army unless South Africa goes to war. At least this trip gave me a chance to stop by at home because the camp was near Postmasburg. My mother sent you some *karringmelkbiskuit* and some of her homemade peach jam. You should learn to make *biskuit*, it can't be all that difficult. I hope you got those plans passed. I want to start building immediately."

"They want to see you," I replied. "They said they can't picture what the house will look like. They passed the plans."

"Good girl!" replied Pieter happily. "I can't help it if people can't recognize a creative design when they see one."

I just took my first baby step.

*   *   *

"I am going to need all the support I can get while we build this damn house, Mali. You have no idea how big it is," I said to Michelle on the phone. I finally comprehended the enormity of it all.

"What the hell did your husband draw?" she asked.

"You don't want to know, seriously. I mean, it took me forever to understand the plan and even the town planner still doesn't get it. Even after Pieter went over there and explained it to them."

"But you said they passed the plans," interrupted Michelle.

"Ja, because I literally begged them. This is going to be one *moerse* [bloody] big house."

"What does it look like?"

"Well, it's a basic double-story house, shaped like a triangle with zigzag windows in the front. On the top floor in one corner is the main bedroom, dressing room, and a round bathroom that juts out from the corner. On the opposite corner are three bedrooms, bathroom, and the study. In the middle is the entrance hall and balcony overlooking the downstairs lounge area. Double volume, you know? So if you walk in the front door you look straight out through the windows to the ocean and, you can also look down and see the lounges. Are you getting it?"

"Somewhat," replied Michelle. "How do you get downstairs?"

"Okay," I continued. "As you come in the front door, there is a circular wall and if you walk a little around it you will come to an opening, which is the stairs. These stairs go both up to the flat open roof and down to the bottom floor of the house. When you walk down the stairs you walk straight into a very large triangular main lounge, which you could see from the top balcony, and if you walked down three more steps to the right you would see the second lounge, dining room, kitchen, and then Martha's room. These are all under the three bedrooms and study at the top."

"Sounds like levels and levels, it will be gorgeous!" said Michelle.

"Everywhere, from different directions we'll see the views of the ocean and the mountains—yes, it is spectacular! Floor to ceiling glass all around."

"Pieter is a mad genius. Is there a pool?"

"Later—we'll add the decks and pool at the bottom. Piet wants to suspend the pool so that it's level with the lounge, and build a room underneath. I told him let's first tackle the main house before we do anything like garages and pools."

Another baby step.

Armed with a small loan and credit cards, we started to excavate the land. In South Africa, it was possible to build with labor that waited each morning on a certain designated corner in town. None were licensed in any shape or form and only a few were experienced. The rest relied on explanations and instructions from the person in charge of the building operation. They were called *tok* labor and in Durban they were mainly Zulus. Also, most houses in South Africa were built with brick and mortar both on the outside and inside walls. Wooden houses like those in the United States were not as common.

"Well, we've managed to clear most of the scrub and brush off the site," said Pieter as he collapsed exhausted into the chair one night. For the past week he'd left the house at 5:00 AM to pick up the *tok* labor and take them out to La Lucia. There he would give them instructions and show them what to do before returning to town to go to work. At the end of the day he would again drive out to the site to inspect the day's work, before taking the laborers back to the designated corner in town and returning home. After ruining at least three pairs of good pants, he began taking a change of work clothes in the car.

"I have to hire a Caterpillar to level a portion of the land. It's too hard for the workers to use shovels and picks," Pieter continued. "You will have to go out there tomorrow and check that they are doing it properly. Make sure they don't go too close to the neighbor that's higher up on the other side. His retaining wall looks a little suspect. I can see some cracks in the foundation."

Our site was on the downward portion of the hill; one house on the right was higher and the house on the left, where we bought the extra land, was much lower. There was another house slightly to the right fronting the street below. The neighbor who sold us the land was the one we remained in contact with, and the one who offered to let us use his phone when needed. Often Pieter would phone from work to the neighbor's maid to ask her to look over the fence and see that everything was okay. Cell phones didn't exist in those years.

"Madam, *Baas* is on the phone!" called Martha as I returned from dropping Nicole off at school the next day.

"Tell the *baas* I am on the way to the site now," I called back while changing Peter's nappy.

"Baas is in a hurry and wants to speak to you now!" Martha replied, sounding worried.

"Ruchel!" Pieter said urgently "The maid next door phoned, I'm leaving my meeting. Get over to the site NOW!"

"Martha! Come take care of Peter, something has happened at the site!"

The first thing I saw as I raced round the corner was the flashing blue light of a police car. Oh God, maybe a fight broke out and one of the workers died. I pulled over and sprang out the car fearing the worst. I was not far off.

What appeared before my eyes was a poor man's version of Victoria Falls. A gush of water was rapidly pushing sand into the neighbor's house below. The neighbor to the right with the suspect wall was standing on his property spewing anger. I could see his retaining wall slowly collapsing in front of him. The *tok* labor all had their hands on their heads, shaking them in disbelief and repeating "sorry Madam, sorry *Baas*," over and over again. Pieter arrived just as the police were walking toward me.

"*Wat die donner* [What the hell]?" Pieter shouted.

"One of your workers hit the main water pipe to La Lucia," announced the policeman as he turned to Pieter. The town planner brought up the rear with a drawing in his hand.

"I know, I know," said Pieter as he saw him approaching. "They were told not to dig so far into the hill. I showed them this morning where to stop digging. I even marked the area. "*Hoekom het julle so ver weggekruip* [How come you dug so far]?" he now demanded from one worker.

Suddenly the water ceased to flow, as if someone turned off a giant big tap. The devastation was indescribable.

The enclosed patio of the house below was covered in ten inches of red mud. The neighbor to the right, shouting at the top of his lungs that he was going to sue us, had a collapsed wall with his main house threatening to follow suit. And the whole of La Lucia was out of water.

Pieter charged forth in battle.

He first told the *tok* labor to immediately start digging the mud out of the house below.

"*Maak gou! Kry al die sand uit! Hamba! Hamba!* [Hurry up! Get all that sand out! Go! Go!]"

The *tok* labor raced down the hill with shovels in hand. Some slid down the mud in their haste to get to the house below, only too glad to escape the firing line. Pieter then turned to the town planner and policeman and promised them that this would not happen again, that he would pay for the damaged water pipe and for damages to the house below. He apologized profusely for the inconvenience caused to the residents of La Lucia. He also assured them that he would take care of the neighbor to the right. They seemed to be satisfied with his take-charge attitude, said accidents can happen, and returned to their cars shaking their heads and smiling.

The neighbor to the right was another story, however. He was still ranting as Pieter made his way over to him.

"I will take you to court and sue you for everything you own!" he screamed as Pieter walked toward him from below.

"And I will sue you for not building a proper retaining wall!" returned Pieter. "I have pictures showing how you used builder's rubble as a foundation before building your wall, and now your negligence has caused damage to my site!"

I was amazed at my husband's audacity and astuteness.

Back and forth it went, with each threatening to sue the other, but there was no way Pieter was going to back down or apologize. I had never seen him so angry.

The end result was the neighbor's acceptance of Pieter's proposal to build a proper retaining wall between the two properties. It would take Pieter two years to get round to completing it.

* * *

Before this point, I had attacked my obstacles almost in self-defense. They were really small moguls on a ski slope. What faced me now, however, looked more like a cavernous gorge. I had never confronted such a task before, and I was forced to dig deep to find hidden strength. An unfamiliar determination came to me.

"*Ja, Pa, nee, Pa* [Yes, Dad, no, Dad]," said Pieter over the phone to his father, begging him to send a couple of his bricklayers with a spare truck. "*Ses maande. Dis al! Dankie. Ja, ek sal Pa terrugbetaal.* [Six months. That's all! Thank you. Yes, I will pay you back, Dad.]"

"What did your father say?"

"He agreed to send his bricklayer, Karools, and another friend, in one of his trucks, to help me build the foundation and walls. All I need is to build to roof height. Should take no more than six months. Then they can go back to Postmasburg. Also, I've asked him to lend us some money until I get the loan through. We'll have to pay him back."

Karools and friend arrived the very next week in a yellow truck. They were two wiry Cape coloureds with minds of their own and talents not yet seen in Natal. During the day Karools oversaw the *tok* labor, issuing orders left, right, and center while laying brick upon brick.

"*Bring die donnerse water, jou luigat* [Bring the bloody water, you lazy arsehole]!" he screamed at a worker while brandishing his trowel in the air. "*Die cement word droog* [The cement is getting dry]!" Karools was now half naked, sweating under the midday sun as I stood on top of the site unloading bags of cement from the trunk of my car.

"Hello, Madam!" he shouted from below, his red hat lopsided on his head. "Did you bring ten bags?"

"No, my husband said I should bring six bags!" I shouted back at him, yelling like a fishwife. Mother would have been apoplectic to hear me.

"Phewww," he whistled through the gap in his mouth where two front teeth were missing. "I am nearly finished here and I *skiem* [gather] *baas* Piet wants to also help lay bricks after work. *Hy gaan sy moer strip* [He's going to lose his temper]."

"All right, all right, I'll go fetch more cement. But I have to first pick up my daughter from school." There had to be a better way to deliver supplies than this constant running back and forth.

By the time I had arrived with the fresh batch of cement, Pieter was already on the building site alongside Karools. "You bought the wrong damn nails!" he shouted as he saw me unloading the cement from the car. "I told you I needed the flat head nails. Can't you think?"

"You just said nails to me, you did not say flat head nails. I thought nails are nails!" I shouted back.

"You should know what I need. Think!" said Pieter angrily. "Go back and fetch some flat head nails from the hardware store. They are more expensive there, but I need them now!"

"Mommy, I want to go home!" whined Nicole, who was fidgeting with her brother's blanket.

"Whaaaah!" screamed Peter right on cue.

Was I frustrated? Of course! Did I throw the last bag of cement at him? Of course not, although it seemed like an excellent idea.

*   *   *

"Ruchel!" said Mother angrily on the phone one afternoon. "What is wrong with you? You sound exhausted. Let me speak to my granddaughter. She is the only one who will give me any truth here!"

Nicky," I called, holding the phone and sighing, "Gansi wants to speak with you!"

"Hello, Gansi," chirped Nicky. "I am fine, Gansi. Yes, I play with friends in the afternoon. Yes, Mommy takes me to the friends. Yes, Peter is crawling now. Yes, the floor is clean. No, Gansi, there is no food in the kitchen. Ma, Gansi wants to speak with you. Gansi says she is sending me some money."

"Why do you not have any food in the house?" demanded Mother after Nicole handed the phone to me. "Is that husband of yours not giving you any money?"

"Ma," I replied wearily, "there is food in the house and I do have money. Nicole just knows the drill now and says there is no food so that you can send her something. She's not stupid."

"I don't believe one word. My grandchild will tell me the truth and you sound dreadful. You most probably look dreadful as well. I told you that building a house is not easy, but you never listen. I am sending some money. See that you buy some food for the children!"

In truth, I was exhausted. Pieter was exhausted. The house was exhausting and there was no end in sight. But at the same time it was exhilarating. To see this work of art rising was all the motivation we needed to forget the exhaustion.

*   *   *

My brother Wayne came to visit.

"Don't tell Mommy," were the first words out of my mouth when I saw him drive up to the site. Nicole was running along the concrete edge of the first floor while Peter sat quietly playing in the sand.

It was the July vacation and Pieter had taken two weeks off from work to give the house a serious push forward. Wayne was on vacation from University and thought he would come and check out the scene. I'm sure Mother had issued plenty of instructions on each detail she wanted reported but I knew my brother would tell her that everything was just fine.

"Hello, *ou swaer* [old brother-in-law]!" shouted Pieter as he stopped to wipe the sweat off his brow. "I hope you are coming to help. You can't just stand there like some *donnerse rooinek*! Get your shorts on and come and pass me some bricks!"

"Sure!" laughed Wayne. "You bloody dutchmen need us English to show you how to build!"

"Aaaagh! Shut up and come show me what kind of man you are!"

To Wayne this was the ultimate adventure and he dove in head first. It didn't matter that he almost sliced one of his fingers off with a saw or that he nearly knocked himself unconscious bumping into one of the overhead beams. What mattered was that he was learning how to build, something he never got from a father who had trouble changing a light bulb.

"My younger brother Hendrik is also coming down to help," announced Pieter one night at dinner. "He's worked on my father's construction site so he can help Wayne when I go back to work."

"Does he know the war zone he is coming into?" asked Wayne, who was still nursing the swollen bump on his head.

"Keep that up and I won't let you drink beer with Karools after work," Pieter teased.

"The Madam is going to be very cross if she knows you are drinking beer every night," interrupted Martha, who was clearing the dishes from the table. "Madam phones every day to find out what is happening!"

"Ja, your mother is probably worried that Wayne will be totally corrupted here in Durban. Next time, Martha, tell the madam that I have taken Wayne to the strip bar on Point Road," replied Pieter.

"Don't listen to him, Martha," I said. "Just keep on telling the madam that everything is fine. By the way, I'm going to start some pottery lessons. Two of my friends at Nicole's school go to this woman's studio in Durban North. You should see the nice pots she's made for her house."

"Why do you want to go to some pottery lessons?" asked Pieter, getting up from the table. "How much money does that cost? You can't just go and take pottery lessons."

"It is not much money," I said. "I need the creative outlet— besides, I can make some plates for the house."

"What do you know about being creative." Pieter laughed. "You can't even read a plan! I even have to tell you how to dress. If I left you alone you would still look like some old *tannie* from Bloemfontein."

"Ja," said Wayne. "At least you look a little modern these days. But I don't know what you have done to your hair. You look like a poodle!"

"I told her that she should cut her hair short like she had it in Bloemfontein, but no, she wants to have this perm look that must have cost a fortune. That is why there is never anything to eat in this house."

"Oh, shut up both of you!" I said. "There's plenty of food here. I can't help it if you are still hungry after eating two whole chickens!"

"Hey! A man's a man and he must eat!" they replied in unison. I left the table.

*   *   *

"Pottery lessons?" asked Michelle. I was so happy to get away from The House and visit my best friend in her cozy one-bedroom apartment on the Berea, the ritzy suburb on the hill overlooking the sea and the city.

"All I ever do is cart the children to school, or fetch supplies for the site a hundred times a day. For one hour a week I can immerse myself in something I enjoy. It's so peaceful."

"What's your brother doing here?"

"Helping Piet's brother on the site. Although I think he's going home soon. The other day Piet gave him instructions on how to build a column. He built it skewed and Piet had to chop all the concrete down again. He was so *gatvol* [angry]."

"Please! What does your brother know about building?" laughed Michelle. "Your mother wouldn't let him even carry his own school-case. The maids did everything for him. By the way, I drove past the site yesterday. What were you guys thinking?"

"Believe me, Mali," I sighed, "all I can think of doing right now is taking one day at a time. If I think beyond that I'll most probably shoot myself."

The project was becoming a monster. A fire-breathing monster.

As the building progressed, so too did the drama. Most Mondays, Karools was too drunk from the weekend to operate at full capacity. That of course led to short tempers across the male testosterone field. I called these days Black Mondays.

To cope each day I switched myself onto autopilot. I was like a soldier trudging wearily across the battlefield to fulfill his commander's orders. Where that strength came from I am not sure. There were days when I really had to dig deep to draw on my meager reserves.

I truly think the ultimate reason why I did not just hightail it back to Bloemfontein with children in tow was an innate optimism that clung stubbornly to my psyche and blossomed each and every day. It refused to die. That, coupled with the unshakable love I had for my crazy husband, made me just keep going and going and going.

This drama was only the beginning. Thank God I didn't possess a crystal ball. I would have headed straight for the hills.

CHAPTER TWENTY-FOUR

_____

1983: A powerful car bomb rips through an office block housing SADF personnel in downtown Pretoria. Seventeen people are killed and 215 are wounded. The ANC claims responsibility and justifies it as an attack on a military target. Most of those killed or wounded are civilians. The whites become increasingly frightened at the surge in violence in the country.

B esides being home to the mighty Zulu nation, Durban was also home to a very large Indian population. Their ancestors were brought over from India by the British settlers in the mid 1800s to work the sugarcane fields that spread up and down the coast of Natal.

Through the years many of the descendants of these early Indian settlers became wealthy store owners and occupied a significant portion of downtown near Grey Street. The Indian market that sat in the middle of that area was a landmark, with the spicy aromas of its Mother-in-Law curry and breyani mix wafting throughout the halls. Sons and daughters of these successful businessmen attended the same sought-after private schools that I wanted for Nicole and Peter. Quite a few Indian families lived on the other side of Berea Hill, in an area known as Cato Manor. It was the best place to go to order curry *samoosas* and *bunny chows* from the street vendors.

Further down the hill from Cato Manor and on the way to La Lucia were a myriad of hardware stores, tile shops, and anything else that said "build." Many of these hardware stores were owned by Indians, or rather by Indians with white partners to skirt the law. Since 1946, Indians could not buy land in designated 'white areas' throughout all of South Africa.

Also in this area were the brickyards, acres of bricks and building blocks waiting for heavyset workers to lift and carry them to waiting trucks. Dust was everywhere. The place teemed with Zulu and Indian workers hustling back and forth with supplies for the major building sites. The roads were impenetrable with pedestrians and large trucks making their way back up the hill and over to the other side.

Did I mention dust was everywhere?

Women and children would not be in this vicinity if it could be helped. It was not a safe place. Fights broke out frequently and there were always petty thefts and stabbings, much shouting and swearing, and an atmosphere of overall chaos.

This area was a man's world, where men knew the difference between a screwdriver and a wrench—or between a flat nail and a round nail, for that matter. Testosterone ruled in that jungle.

So what the hell was I doing there on a busy Friday afternoon with two very irritable children in the back seat of my new yellow Mazda 323?

I was acting on orders to fetch Martha's bathtub. It was now time in the building process to put the bathtub in. Not later. Not tomorrow. Now! This, after I had just delivered a box of plumbing pipes for the second time because the size was not exactly right. How I would fit a bathtub in the Mazda was not open for discussion. And don't ask why the tub wasn't delivered with the other bath accessories. My orders were to fetch it. Immediately.

Those reserves of strength were reaching dangerously low levels.

"I need a bathtub, please," I said to the Indian behind the wide wooden counter. A large overhead fan was trying half-heartedly to cool the choking heat. Sitting on top of the counter in front of me was Peter, clutching a bottle, while Nicole stood beside me trying to peer over the grubby counter. Around me were men of all races, all staring at me curiously. Outside the large yard dust was flinging from every truck that came racing through the gates.

"Excuse me, madam, what did you say?" asked the Indian.

"I need a bathtub, a bath for my maid's bathroom," I replied.

"What size and what colour?" he asked.

My bloody husband had not told me what size.

"I know it has to be white." I tried to keep Peter from crawling all over the counter. "Isn't there a standard size?"

"No, madam," replied the Indian. "They come in different sizes depending on what is specified on the plan."

Specified on the plan? That was only in my husband's head.

"Well, can you give me the one that most people order? Nicky, we are going home soon, stop moaning."

"I think she means a five-foot bathtub," interrupted a Zulu builder who was standing next to me.

"Thank you," I replied, turning my head to smile at him.

"Why is your husband not here fetching the bath?" he asked. "It's not good for a woman to be here."

"I know, I know, but my husband is very busy building on the site so I fetch all the supplies. Oh, thank you," I said to the Indian. He and three assistants were busy carrying the white porcelain bathtub around the counter.

"Where is your truck?" asked the Zulu builder.

"Oh, I don't have a truck, I have a car. It's there outside." I pointed through the window at the Mazda 323. Heads turned round and they all peered in quiet disbelief through the dusty windows.

"You want to take the bath in that car?" asked the Indian and the Zulu builder together. "*Hauw*, Madam," said the others.

"I have a roof rack. We can tie it up on top of the roof, no?"

"I suppose," said the Zulu builder. "But we'll have to tie it very securely so that it doesn't slip when you go up the hill. You'll have to drive very carefully. Come Sam, let's help the lady! We'll tie it on the roof for her."

If my friends could see me now. The person they knew sat with them under the shade of palm trees sipping tea from bone china teacups. They would not know this person who was having a bathtub tied atop her car.

"Thank you so much for all your help," I gushed as I put the children back into the car before opening the driver's door. "I hope it will be okay and not fall off."

The car felt like it was on the ground. How much did this bloody bath weigh?

I pulled up from the dusty driveway into the narrow road teeming with trucks going back and forth at breakneck speed. "Sit still!" I yelled at the children as I negotiated the car onto the main road and drove back up the hill.

Phut!

What the—?

I was not a quarter of the way up the hill when the car died. Died a horrible death surrounded by chaos.

Oh no.

All around me trucks were tooting for me to get out of the way. I stepped out of the car and waved my arms helplessly. The white porcelain bathtub was hanging on for dear life atop the car. Inside, the children were hysterical.

Lovely.

"Move your car, lady!" shouted one truckdriver two cars behind me.

"What is your problem, woman?" shouted another.

Just then a very unkempt and scraggly-looking Indian approached me. Quickly establishing that I had absolutely no clue why the stupid car had suddenly stopped, he asked to look under the hood. He peered inside, then walked around to where I was standing.

"Take off your pantyhose," he said.

What?

All around were curious Zulus and Indians converging from the sidewalk toward my car. Oh please God, don't let him rape me here. And where did all these people suddenly come from?

"Why do I have to take my pantyhose off?" I asked angrily.

"Your fan belt snapped and your pantyhose will act as a temporary fan belt till you get to your destination," he replied rather curiously, perhaps wondering at the anger in my voice.

"Oh, sorry," I apologized, silently cursing myself for such gross misjudgement. "I didn't know why you wanted me to do such a thing in the middle of the road." I slid the pantyhose as ladylike as possible down my legs without lifting my skirt too high. "Nicky, try to keep your brother quiet. We're going home as soon as I drop this bath at the site."

"Mommy, why are you undressing in the road?" asked my daughter.

"Mommy's not undressing," I replied. "I am just helping this nice man fix the car so we can go home."

It was almost dark when I arrived at the site with the tub still intact on the roof of the car. My nerves were frayed and the volume in the back refused to die down. I climbed out of the car just as Pieter was walking up the driveway.

"What took you so long? It's the wrong size! Can't you get anything right?" he shouted.

God help me, but if I had had the strength of Samson that bath would have flown off the car and down his throat.

What my husband did not know was that he was helping to mold a woman who was to become nothing short of brave. And I wasn't a witch. At least I don't think so.

Sometimes Pieter called me a witch because he was frustrated at my clumsiness and my ignorance of the difference between a six-inch toilet pipe and a six-inch bath pipe. Didn't I know I was holding up the building process, costing us money? Didn't I know that my sitting and having tea with friends all day meant that the workers on the site were slacking off or building the walls askew? Didn't I know that giving the workers an extra rand or two would make them not come back the next day? Didn't I, didn't I?

But with each confrontation, each experience, a new, brave gene was added to my DNA, a new force that pushed me forward telling me, yes, you can think for yourself. You can make decisions on your own. It was just a baby step in the beginning, but it was a big step forward.

*　*　*

Peter celebrated his first birthday with a homemade chocolate cake and one lonely candle in the lounge of the apartment.

"Everyone is on holiday, ma," I sighed holding the phone, "and besides, I haven't had the chance to think about a birthday party."

"It's a disgrace!" said Mother furiously. "A disgrace that you cannot invite a few friends over and give him a party like the one we had for Nicky in Bloemfontein. I am disappointed in you, Ruchel. Very disappointed!"

"Ma, he's too young to know if there are a million friends on his birthday or if there's just his family. I can't remember my first birthday."

"On your first birthday," Mother snapped, "you had forty children with their parents and nannies. You loved every minute of it. No, Ruchel, you have to get your priorities right here. Your children are your priority and they have to have the best care, the best education, and grow up in a stable environment. This business of rushing to the building site every day is nonsense. That's a man's job. What have you heard from the school?"

"We received a letter yesterday from Durban Girls' College saying that all prospective parents are to attend a talk by the headmistress next week and after the talk, the children will spend some time in interviews with the teachers." I was now certain Mother was psychic because she always managed to phone when some crucial news was forthcoming.

"Next week! I will send her an appropriate dress for the interview. Is Piet going?"

"Yes, ma," I sighed, knowing exactly what was coming next.

"Well, make sure he wears a suit that is not too tight for him and see that his hair is combed neatly! What are you wearing? I hope a skirt and matching jacket. Remember, people are judged on their appearances, and by the sounds of things it looks like both of you will have to shape up." It was no use arguing because in some way Mother was right.

More than anything I wanted Nicole to attend this school. I wanted her to go through life with everything it had to offer, with complete confidence in herself. I wanted her to be more than me.

Pieter sensed my determination. After speaking with friends and more friends who repeatedly said it was an excellent school but very tough to get in, he took up the challenge. His daughter would not be turned down by any snobbish *rooinek*! Who the hell did they think they were? Which reminded me of why I loved him despite all the drama. He was ambitious, determined, and definitely no slouch. He was not afraid of work and if it meant he had to work harder to pay the exorbitant fees, so be it. More important, he was a family man who would love and care for us no matter what challenge reared its ugly head—or what idiot action (he thought) I performed next.

I was pushing Pieter from behind, which made us a formidable team. I knew that if Pieter were to succeed in Durban, many of his clients would be the parents of children who attended that school. We had already met two prospective parents who had put their daughter's names down at birth and had lived in Durban forever. Two couples who could eventually become his clients.

"Stop worrying, Ruchel," Pieter said on the way to the meeting. "Our daughter has her father's Afrikaans genes in her blood. She will blow them away, won't you, my darling!"

"Yes, daddy," Nicole replied while smoothing out her Mother-purchased dress. "Mommy says I must smile and answer all the questions."

"That's my girl" Pieter said, smiling.

We pulled up to the school just as the parents were being ushered into the assembly hall.

"Good afternoon, ladies and gentleman!" boomed the Scottish headmistress from the stage in front of the prospective parents. "Thank you so much for taking the time to visit our school this morning. We are delighted to have you all here and...."

Yeah, right. Every one of these two hundred parents would have missed their mother's funeral to be here today. Everyone was dressed for Ascot. The smell of competition hung in the air like a heavy cloud. You could hear a pin drop as the headmistress, in her tweed and single-string pearl ensemble, rambled on about the merits of the school. As if she had to. Everyone knew them by rote and could recite verbatim the school's history from the day it was founded.

"And finally, I would just like to add that we are very pleased to see so many of you apply to our school. As you know, we only accept twenty-five girls for the first year and they will be judged purely on merit. Our decision is final and we do not entertain any discussions after that decision is made [read: no bribery]. Thank you for coming. The teachers will now see your daughters in the classrooms below. Tea will be served in Sherwood Forest adjacent to the classrooms."

"Twenty-five out of two hundred?" Pieter mused as he walked our daughter down the passageway. "You show them how clever you are, my sweetheart!" he said as he hugged Nicole before she was led into the classroom.

"You have a very attractive husband and a beautiful daughter," said one mother as we both watched our husbands hug their daughters.

"Thank you!" I smiled, thinking that she must wonder where I fit into this attractiveness equation. "I am so nervous," I said. "I hope my daughter can answer all their questions."

"Oh, I'm not nervous at all," replied the mother rather snobbishly. "Generations of our family have attended this school. We go through the motions each time."

"But isn't it based on merit alone?" I asked, now wondering whether Nicole had even a snowball's chance.

"I have never seen them turn down families that have been here for generations. I see many of my school friends with their daughters here today."

"It sounds like incest to me," muttered Pieter as we walked around the *Sherwood Forest* area with a cup of tea in hand. In front of us loomed the imposing facade of the two-story main Victorian building that overlooked the whole of Durban. Sweeping below the building almost to the sea were the hockey fields, the swimming pool, the tennis and netball (like softball) courts, the athletic track, and the boarding houses below that. It was prime property high on the ridge of the Berea, with British old-world tradition.

Just then our daughter emerged with a slight frown on her face.

"How did it go? How did it go? Did you answer all the questions? What did they ask you?" asked her demented mother.

"I could answer all the questions except one."

"Except one?" I blurted, not caring about the hundred and fifty she could answer. "Which one?"

"I didn't know who Noddy's friend was with the beard," said Nicole, now even more worried seeing her mother's horrified look.

"That's Big Ears!" I said, shaking my head. "You know Big Ears. I read Noddy books to you when you were small."

I was Mother.

"I forgot, I am sorry," said Nicole, close to tears.

"Aaagh, Ruchel, stop it!" said my ever sane and always reasonable husband. "Who cares about this Big Ears? I've never heard of him myself." He turned and picked up his daughter, who was about to cry. "Don't worry, my sweetheart, you did just fine. Daddy is proud of you. Forget about these stupid *rooineks*! Bunch of snobbish poms! You did just fine!"

A few weeks later Nicole came home from nursery school very excited.

"Mommy! Davinia is going to wear the green uniform! When can I get my green uniform?"

I reached the panic stage. A green uniform meant only one thing. Davinia's mother had received an acceptance letter from the school.

"Yes, we are all so excited," gushed Davinia's mom when I saw her the next day in the parking lot of the nursery school. "Quite a few of us have received letters of acceptance. Ours arrived two days ago. Have you heard anything yet?"

Oh God! Two days ago? That meant we were part of the rejection batch that would arrive later. I hated her. I know, I know. I should have been glad for her and her daughter but I couldn't help it. I wanted my daughter to wear that green uniform and I hated that her daughter was getting one and mine wasn't.

Another week went by. I was totally depressed. It didn't matter that the house was making progress. It didn't matter that everyone was healthy and fine. Nothing mattered, and making things worse was Mother phoning every day to remind me that another day had passed with no word. What address did I give? I don't remember. I think it was the La Lucia address because I thought we would be in the house by then. No, I can't go to the school to ask if they sent my letter. You are not supposed to do that. I will give it another week and then phone. Yes, I promise. No, I did not wear something ridiculous to the interview. No, Piet did not drink his tea uncouthly. Yes, Nicole wore the dress. Yes, her hair was washed and tied back.

The next day after fetching Nicole at school and again greeting Danielle's syrupy mom, I picked up some electrical wire at the hardware store and traveled back north to the site.

"Nicky, don't mess your shoes, just wait for Mommy here on the top floor while I give Karools this packet." I could hear the banging and drilling down below as I negotiated between loose nails and builder's rubble but my mind was elsewhere. The thought of Nicole not being accepted was too horrible to contemplate. The anxiety sapped all my energy.

"Mommy!" Nicole shouted from the top just as I handed the package to Karools. "There is a man who wants to see you!"

A man who wants to see me? What now? Did Piet build something he wasn't supposed to? Was an inspector now here to see me?

"Tell him to wait, I am coming!" I shouted from the bottom then made my way back up the precarious temporary staircase.

At the top I saw a Zulu with a satchel hanging over his bicycle. "Can I help you?" I asked.

"*Kunjane*, madam," he greeted me, taking his hat off.

"*Kunjane*," I replied.

"Madam, I am supposed to deliver this letter to this address but I see no one lives at this house."

"Here, let me see the letter," I said, thinking it could only be a registered letter from the neighbor next door who had now decided to sue us. The Zulu opened his satchel and passed the small white envelope to me.

Oh God! It can't be!

It was The Letter. The Letter from Durban Girls' College.

I knew that because on the top left hand corner was the unmistakable green Galleon, the school's imposing emblem. "Thank you, it's for me." I smiled at the man. He could not fathom how on earth I lived in this half-finished house.

The moment of truth. Now or never. But it looked so thin. I was too frightened to open it.

"This looks like the picture I saw at the school we went to," said Nicole as she pointed to the green Galleon.

"Yes, it's from that school, Nicky," I replied, fingering the letter gingerly. All around me dust flew this way and that as banging and drilling continued at a furious pace. A bomb could have exploded next to me and I would still have been staring mutely at the letter.

"What does the school say, ma?" prodded my daughter.

My hands were shaking. Whatever the school said my daughter would read on my face. I knew I wouldn't be able to hide my disappointment if it was what I thought, a rejection letter. Oh God, please let it not be.

What kind of role model would I be to my daughter if I just collapsed in a heap of tears in the middle of the builder's rubble? I willed myself to be stoic, to accept my lot, like the Bible says.

Mother was going to blame me for not doing more, not saying more, not dressing better, not… Pieter was going to—

"Ma, what does it say?"

Please God. I drew a deep breath and gently peeled the flap open. The letter was folded in half. I took one corner and slowly unfolded it, one line at a time. My hands were trembling with fear. "Dear Mr. and Mrs. Coetzee…" Fold back a little more. "We are… pleased…"

Pleased? Pleased! "We are pleased to accept…"

"Oh my God, Oh my God! Nicky we are going to buy you your own green uniform. You are going to Durban Girls' College! You got accepted my clever, clever child!" I cried as I scooped my daughter up in a big bear hug then ran back to the car holding her hand. "We have to phone Daddy and Gansi and everyone."

My spirits soared like an eagle into the air. *Whoosh!* Oh thank you God, thank you, thank you!

I ran up the stairs to phone Pieter. "Martha, Martha, Nicky got in! She got in!" Martha was dancing and singing by the time I reached Pieter on the phone.

"It's because her father is an architect!" he quipped.

Mother immediately sprang into action and was on the phone asking for further information from the school to make sure her grandchild lacked none of the required items. Mother did not have to worry this time. We were totally on the same page.

Whoosh!

While I was sailing through the air like some madcap eagle, the house finally reached roof height. The work load at the construction site became more tolerable as I waltzed through the remainder of that year. My daughter was going to Durban Girl's College! Everything else paled in comparison.

Martha, in the meantime, had found a Zulu boyfriend, Samson, who decided to move into her room with her. We had no problem with that. The landlord did, however, because every weekend Samson would get so drunk that Martha would end up in a screaming match with him. The whole neighborhood would awaken in alarm. Needless to say, our lease was not renewed, which forced us to review some limited options open it us.

"Michelle is moving to a house on the Bluff. She says we can rent her flat until the house is ready," I suggested. "It's only a one-bedroom apartment, but at least it's something."

After living in her tiny apartment for two months, Pieter finally got approval for all the electrical in the house and announced that we would be moving in. Moving into our very own four bedrooms, three living rooms house.

Fabulous! Pop the cork!

"Piet! There's no front door!" No carpets and no tiles. Oh, and no balconies, and isn't there a window missing there and there and there?

"But we have approved electrical! Town planning rule says if you have approved power you can move into your house."

"We can't move into the house! Nothing is finished."

"Ruchel," Pieter announced with final authority. "Why is it that I have to continually remind you that I am still the head of this household and that my decision is final? I am not staying in this cramped apartment one minute longer. I'll be able to work late at night on the house without traveling. You can help as well while the children sleep."

"But where do you think we are all going to sleep? All the bedrooms are still concrete shells. None of the bathrooms have any tiles on the floor. Its not safe to sleep with no front door."

We moved in the next week.

Okay, let me clarify that a little. We moved into the one partly finished bedroom. All four of us. This bedroom at the end of the passage, overlooking the sea, would eventually become Nicole's bedroom. A loose carpet was laid on the concrete floor so that our mattress could rest on top of it. The same bedroom would also accommodate a fridge and a second mattress for the children. The bedroom had to be powered by an extension cord to the neighbor's power outlet because our house had no outlets in the walls. Electricity, yes, but no outlets. To make things worse, this bedroom had no protection from all the dust that flew around from the construction site.

Martha moved into her own concrete room, but at least it was a step up from her previous accommodations. Originally the plan said that was her room, but Pieter had changed his mind and decided to design a small apartment for her on top of the garage, complete with lounge and kitchen.

Michelle helped me move in, meaning, carrying boxes into a downstairs storeroom. "Does your mother know what this is like?" Twice she tripped over rubble.

"Are you crazy? My mother would have the armed forces here to haul me back to Bloemfontein. She thinks we are much further than we are. Thankfully she is busy attending Jenny's graduation from law school at Rhodes University in Grahamstown."

"I couldn't imagine a more suitable profession for your sister," replied Michelle dryly, showing me the scar on her arm from the time Jenny scratched her when we were kids. "Can you believe I still have that scar and I didn't even start the fight? How are you all going to sleep and eat and live in this one bedroom?"

"Don't even get me started," I sighed. "Bad enough that we had to ask the neighbor if we could use his power for the extension cord. Can you imagine if any of the mothers from Nicole's school came here? Or the headmistress? They would die of shock. Actually, they wouldn't even get out of the car. They would simply turn around and leave, thinking it was all just a dreadful mistake. We might as well reclassify ourselves as squatters!"

"Squatters!" Michelle giggled.

"It's not funny, Mali. I don't know how I'm going to keep the kids from falling over the balconies. There are no railings!"

How was I really feeling? I don't even know if I was feeling at all. It was too exhausting. The dust, the banging, the *tok* labor were all so overwhelming. The worst was when Pieter's boss and his wife made a surprise visit with a plate of food in hand two days after we moved in.

"*Ag sies tog* [Oh shame]!" was the wife's only comment as she stepped over the rubble in her new white church outfit while balancing the plate of *bobotie* precariously in one hand. But the horror on her face as she was led to the squatter's bedroom in the monstrous construction called house said much more.

Poor Martha tried valiantly to stay ahead in the cleanliness game by washing and changing the sheets each night after the dust settled. I abruptly ended my pottery lessons and started painting and tiling. What did I know about painting and tiling? Now, why would you ask such a silly question? I just painted and tiled.

The children, however miraculous it was, never fell over the internal balconies. Peter learned to walk backward down the stairs and no *thokolosi* walked through the gaping hole that for two months was the front door.

Tempers were short. But it was either short tempers or silence or sighing.

One late morning I took Peter with me to the supermarket in the La Lucia Mall. While at the checkout, Peter whined on my hip while reaching for the candy, placed deliberately at the tills to annoy tired and harassed mothers.

"You can't have any sweets! It's lunchtime!" I scolded Peter under my breath while willing the person in front to hurry up and pay for her groceries. Mine were already stacked up, ready to be tallied. Peter increased his whine volume.

"Shame," said an old lady behind me. "If you cannot afford to pay for some sweets, let me help you. Your son clearly wants it."

Deep breath. Counting one, two, three…

"Whaaah! I want!" yowled Peter, bending backward in my arms. The old lady behind me reached out to give him a chocolate.

"Please mind your own business!" I snapped at her then turned round to Peter. "We were going home. Now! No groceries. No sweets. Home. Now!"

My seething was at the boiling point.

"Help!" cried Peter as I carried him to the parking garage. "Somebody help me!"

I couldn't get out of the mall fast enough. I was surprised I wasn't arrested for kidnapping. Peter cried hysterically all the way back to the house.

"Martha!" I screamed from the top of the driveway while tooting the horn. "Come fetch your boy now! I am so mad!"

"Come, my little man," she cooed as she scooped Peter into her arms. "Martha will go and make you some tea. *Thula, thula.*"

That night my husband announced that he had resigned from work and was starting his own business: Pieter Coetzee Architects. Address : 44 William Campbell Drive, La Lucia.

CHAPTER TWENTY-FIVE

1984: *After years of bitter struggle between Mozambique and South Africa, Botha claims success against the ANC when he and Mozambique's Samora Machel sign the Nkomati Accord. In the agreement, the Mozambique government undertakes to stop backing the ANC in their territory if the South African government stops helping RENAMO, a political party in Mozambique, from attacking the ruling party FRELIMO. The actions of RENAMO, including the destruction they inflict on schools, clinics, and other infrastructure, is costing the government millions of dollars. The Accord enables the two neighboring countries to form a relationship between Marxism and capitalism and paves the way for peace negotiations with other neighboring countries in Africa.*

There's a framed cartoon drawing on the wall in our study today. It was drawn by a draughtswoman two months after Pieter officially formed Pieter Coetzee Architects in the study of the half-finished house at 44 William Campbell Drive.

This is what it looks like.

Taking up most of the frame is a very impatient Pieter sitting on the edge of an office chair twitching his foot up and down, leaning over a homemade table, and talking agitatedly into the phone. On his back are two angel wings. Agitated clouds of steam blow through his hair. On his head is a gold ring with "*Deacon halo*" written below. Above the halo is a huge tobacco pipe, with pictures of a yacht, a Rubic's cube, a bottle of red wine, and a wine glass drawn in a "pipe dream" bubble. Next to that bubble is a red picture frame with "Pieter Coetzee Architects?" written inside.

Crawling under the table is Peter, a little Dennis the Menace with "I am a demon" written on his red-and-black striped shirt. Behind the boy is a cat that looks as though it has just been electrocuted.

To the side of the red-framed picture is another framed picture of the driveway with a draughtsman looking angrily at his watch while clutching a plan and tapping his foot. "Late" is written next to the watch. Running behind him in the distance is an engineer who is huffing and puffing and clutching many sets of plans in his arms.

This is what is written in the cartoon bubble coming from Pieter's mouth:

"Rochelle, where's my #@ file on Mykonos?....Robin just hang on a minute.... Yes, of course I can give you 9,000 units on your Umdloti site, no problem, I guarantee it!!!.... ROCHELLE where ARE you? Go and print out TEN sets of Surfside, they must be ready in 12 minutes.... Yes, Mr. Stocks & Stocks, we have a problem with the earthworks—those bl...dy Engineers!.... Robin I'm coming now.... Where is the *# wife of mine.... Mr. Stocks & Stocks I'll have those drawings ready tomorrow!"

A week before his announcement, Pieter had heard through a colleague that a man from Greece was looking to hire an architect to build holiday units on a piece of land he had just acquired in Umdloti, a coastal town about ten minutes north of La Lucia. The key to winning the contract was to fit as many units on the site as possible. Pieter undertook the challenge in his spare time at night. (Did I say spare time?) He sketched and calculated and planned and drew and redrew until he was satisfied that he could fit the most units on the site. He then met privately with this Greek and was immediately awarded the contract. Nobody said he was not talented. Pieter then went back to the office, said he was resigning, and came home to start his own practice.

Just like that.

What did I think? I had no time to think. I was too busy swimming upstream.

A typical day looked like this:

After rising from my comfy bed with its incredible view of the blue ocean I would walk, bare feet on plush carpet, to my bubbling jacuzzi while soft music—no, wait. That was a dream.

Let's rewind.

After rising from my bed I would walk to the bathroom to inspect the tiling I had done the previous night, dress the children, feed everyone breakfast, take instructions from Pieter, drive Nicole to school, fetch supplies for the house, return home to continue tiling, return incorrect supplies, search for alternative supplies in strange areas, return home, help print plans for Pieter, help colour plans for Pieter, wipe dust from tables, help write letters for Pieter, wipe dust from shoes, fetch Nicole at school, arrange social activities for the children, race home to feed everyone lunch, give instructions to Martha, wipe dust off childrens' hands, take Nicole to ballet lessons, arrange social activities with another ballet mother, take plans to local authority, buy groceries, draw money from bank to pay *tok* labor, fetch Nicole from ballet lessons, tell Martha to help wipe dust off the kitchen table, cook, bake two cakes for Pieter's upcoming induction as deacon at the church, feed everyone dinner, practice phonetics with Nicole while watching Peter crawl down the stairs backwards, look for stray nails where the children walk, put the children to bed, answer the phone, make phone calls, help print plans for Pieter, help write letters for Pieter, continue tiling…. If you are exhausted just reading this sentence, you can imagine the day.

Did I stop to think? Does a mouse stop to think as it runs and runs on the moving wheel?

Word got out that Pieter's design in Umdloti was very innovative. Two large projects followed a month later. One would be almost the same number of units on a site owned by a Lebanese man, located right next to the site in Umdloti. The other would be from an Israeli man who owned the hotel on the beach across the street in Umdloti. He wanted Pieter to redesign it and add additional rooms. If that was not enough United Nations' projects, an Afrikaans man wanted Pieter to design his holiday house on the beach in La Lucia.

Pieter hired an English couple, Robin and his wife Linda, to help draw all the plans, plus an Afrikaans engineer who was a deacon with Pieter at church. The English earthworks and building company Stocks & Stocks courted Pieter for additional work.

All that took place in the study of our unfinished house, which was slowly becoming more livable and less like a war zone. The front door and concrete balconies were added three months later. For the time being I was under the illusion that we were nearing the end.

Then there were the little things, but being the good wife that I now was, it was not worth the battle. Why one task could not be finished before moving onto the next was beyond me, but if I had climbed into my husband's head I would have realized it was all about the overall and less about the details.

Pieter had grand visions for the house. Very grand indeed. Visions of a private wine cellar stocked with the best South African wines, a Rubic's cube-like solarium on top of the roof, a suspended pool with a media room below, Martha's apartment on top of the garage complete with balcony overlooking the sea. These and more were all in the "to be built" plan in his head. A plan that changed each time the sun went down and a new contract was signed. It was a work in progress. An artist's canvas. The *tok* labor never left.

And these visions did not end at the house.

The grand scheme also included his own yacht after sailing on a friend's boat at the Durban Yacht Club. Hunting with friends in the bush. Holiday homes on the coast. All things to accomplish later, but all told and retold as another nail was hammered into the door, another pot of paint was brushed onto the wall, and another set of plans was completed for submission. This was the set of plans for all to hear: at dinner tables, at *braais* with friends, in bed at night, during tea after the service at church, and pretty much any place Pieter had an audience. Even Martha and her boyfriend, Samson, now officially our gardener and general handyman, were in on the grand vision.

In Afrikaans there is a word describing this particular type of character. The word is "*windgat.*" Many people mistake the translation as "braggart." That is incorrect. A *windgat* is a person who does not believe he is wrong. A person who believes in his talents and his visions, and who tells everyone about them. Not in a bragging fashion but in a matter-of-fact fashion. A person who believes in what he is capable of doing and goes forth like a steamroller to achieve his dreams as quickly as possible. A person who is comfortable with his decisions. In short, a person with strong ego. Are there any bones of hesitancy in a *windgat*? No. A *windgat* believes he can climb the highest mountain, pound his chest harder than anyone else, then confirm to the world that he can pound his chest harder than anyone else.

King of the jungle!

Pieter's enemies said he was a *hardegat* (stubborn) *windgat*. His acquaintances agreed he was a *windgat,* but a nice one. His friends also agreed and sought his company because it was difficult not to feed off that energy.

I, of course, did not see my husband as a *windgat*. I saw him as the strong sensitive man who would fold me in his arms and hold me for the longest time. The man who would catch my eye across a crowded room and instantly communicate his thoughts with a knowing smile. The man who would dance with me long into the night. The man who would climb the highest mountain and pound his chest for his family. The man who loved me with such intensity and passion that all our arguments were minor blips on the radar screen.

In Pieter I saw the reflection of my own desires. Maybe some were not the same, but the overall goal was the same: to have again what I had left behind in Bloemfontein. A Rubic's cube solarium on top of the house? Could do without. Educating the children at the best schools? A definite yes. A yacht? Not a major priority. So I helped Pieter in whatever way I could.

Pieter and I were like those metal balls that line up in a row, swinging from side to side. If you raise one to knock the row, one will swing on the opposite side.

Tick, tick.

If you knock the whole row of metal balls out of line, it won't be long before they are lined up again and swinging in sync.

Tick, tick.

Pieter and I, like metal balls, transferred energy through each other. If we reached a point where we were all ruffled up, we would soon realign ourselves and swing in sync again.

Tick, tick. Tick, tick.

* * *

It didn't take long for Pieter to become involved in the National Party—they were known as a moderate party. He could no longer ignore the rumors and reports that were spreading across the country and felt he had to learn first hand where things stood. I tagged along to meetings out of curiosity and also because I was the good wife.

Mother was appalled. The thought of her daughter going to some Afrikaans National Party meeting to be indoctrinated with racist ideas and philosophies was about as abhorrent as if I told her I was joining the Ku Klux Klan.

"Ma," I sighed. "These Afrikaners are not the same as the ones you knew in Bloemfontein. Many go to our church. They are very liberal thinkers who want to see peace and stability in our country, with freedom for all, just like you."

"Don't think these groups cannot influence you to think otherwise."

"Ma," I sighed even more. "You haven't even met these people. They are all very nice family-oriented people who want to see if they can make the government hurry up the reform process."

"I don't know why you had to get married to that man. I had such high hopes for you, Ruchel," Mother moaned.

It was very rare to find a woman leader in the group. Most leaders were professional men from Natal who brought their wives and children to mix with other wives and children while their husbands gathered in small focus groups.

Most discussions went back and forth on equal rights for everyone, on whether the black population would gain majority rule from one man, one vote. Would that plunge the country into more poverty and violence like the rest of Africa? What would happen to those who controlled the country's wealth like the gold and diamond mines? Would that and other properties be seized, how would the right-wing Afrikaners react, and what about all the different tribes? On and on it went, all about power and stability.

In the general meeting, the microphone would be passed around for members to speak informally to the group. During one meeting, I nervously took the microphone and began by focusing on each person's rights as a human being. I spoke about the individual as he or she had to deal with the daily challenges in life. It made my point stronger that I did not talk about some ominous unknown force, but about people like ourselves who needed to educate, feed, and care for themselves and their families. It was a story about human beings struggling to gain the same opportunities as other human beings, no matter the colour.

The audience clapped and asked questions. The leaders came up to me afterward and told me that it was a very inspiring speech. The wives said I was very brave to say all those things. Pieter beamed but never said it was a good speech or gave me any further encouragement, lest I forget, I had a family to take care of. So I resumed the role of good wife.

*   *   *

Pieter's cousin, Pietie, had moved to Cape Town, gotten married, gotten divorced, then moved to Durban. In itself, that was nothing momentous. But his arrival was a confirmation that the heavenly stars actually do have a game plan in mind.

Pieter was overjoyed to have his *neef* (cousin) in the same town. A *neef* to drink with while watching the rugby matches at Kings Park, a *neef* to up the competition stakes, a *neef* to discuss politics.

As a result Pietie was often at our house visiting. At parties he was a staple. So was Michelle. And did we throw parties.

One time, in the half-finished house, we invited all our friends from the Jewish and Afrikaans communities, easily a hundred people. We had kosher sausages flown in from Johannesburg. Pietie organized his old friends in the band to play at the party while Pieter instructed Samson how to turn the sheep on the spit outside. *Braai* and sophistication happily coexisted. I spent the night running up and down the steps to see that people were talking to each other and not just huddling together in their own little groups. I know, I am my mother's daughter.

The next morning Pietie came over to our house again. An hour later Michelle also arrived. Two hours later I saw them kissing in the downstairs lounge.

What?

That was way too much for my brain, way too much for Pieter's brain, and way too much for even Martha's brain to take in. Pietie and Michelle? Pieter's cousin and my best friend? No way. Pieter drew me aside before something totally ridiculous blurted out of my mouth.

"Leave them alone," he whispered. "It must have happened last night. It most probably won't last long."

Pietie moved into Michelle's apartment behind Nicole's school
five months later and it was not long after that that she, too, fell
pregnant.

"What do you mean you are pregnant?" I asked, as we sat in my
bedroom. "You can't be!" Even Martha had to hear the rest of the
story.

"*Hauw*, madam!" she shook her head, standing in the doorway
with duster in hand.

"Remember all the problems I was having with the pill?" asked
Michelle.

"Ja, you seemed to be more at the doctor than at work."

"Well, my stupid doctor said that considering all those problems,
I would probably have a hard time conceiving so it would be better
for me to go off the pill."

"But you and Pietie were not even thinking of getting married,
were you?"

"Well, not right away. But he also agreed that I should go off
the pill if it made me so sick and guess what? Four months later I was
pregnant."

"So, ladies and gentlemen," I announced, shaking my head.
"Two very best friends, who both studied industrial psychology at
university and who are both supposedly very clever, fall pregnant and
marry cousins who are both named Pieter Coetzee. Please welcome
Mrs. Ruchel Coetzee and Mrs. Michelle Coetzee and their husbands
Pieter Coetzee and Pieter Coetzee!"

"What does *baas* Pietie say?" asked Martha.

"He is over the moon, Martha, he says he always wanted to
marry me, but was too shy to even ask me out when we were in
Bloemfontein." Michelle was beaming.

"I just can't believe it happened to both of us."

"I can't believe we'll both be married to Dutchman!"

I cried copious tears when Michelle and Pietie moved to Cape
Town three months after their first son was born.

* * *

Meanwhile, in the land of the children, things were moving along
smashingly. Peter had started nursery school at Kadimah and quickly

became part of the Five Boys. The Five Boys did everything together. Sat together in school, rode the toy cars around the track together, climbed the tree together, played at each other's houses together, ensuring that they would be joined at the hip for the three years they were together at school. There was shy Gilad, assertive Mark, quiet Sean, and boisterous Grant. Together with my rather reserved son, they would become lasting friends.

Nicole was Miss Social Butterfly, flitting from one friend to another. She was a bubbly and warm-hearted little girl with a ready smile on her pretty face. Taking her to school each morning and seeing her giggling and whispering with the other little green uniformed girls was just joyous for me. I immersed myself in all school activities—all that Durban Girls' College (which we called the DGC) had to offer, from the mother's tuck shop duty to the annual bake sale to the perpetual fundraising events. Eventually I would do just that, because my daughter was rapidly becoming not only a whiz in class but also a talent to be reckoned with on the sports fields.

Those sporting genes could only have come from her father. The closest I got to a sports field was on the upper stands eating ice cream. But Nicole was not a year at school and already it was time for the much-anticipated annual Sports Day. The parents dressed as if they were attending Ascot.

"Beat them all!" Pieter shouted from the sidelines before the gun went off. "Run, Nicky, run!" he continued as her little legs ran furiously past his video camera. It did not matter to Pieter that he was the only parent shouting. He was not quite as bad as Eliza Doolittle at the races, but the eyebrows were definitely raised. Nicole won the race hands down and the eyebrows were raised again.

Mother, of course, insisted that each milestone, each recorded event, and each photograph be duplicated and sent immediately to the growing scrapbooks in Bloemfontein. Another set was sent to Gussie and to Pieter's parents who pored over each letter as if it were a treasure from heaven.

Such joy was also always present when Gussie came to visit us in Durban. Martha would bake her special banana cake, the children would snuggle into her arms, and my heart would take a rest from its frenetic pace.

"Come on, kids, let's show Gussie what buildings Daddy designed before we go to the beach. Martha, don't forget to bring your hat," I called from the top of the stairs.

"Ruchie," Gussie said as she walked slowly down the passageway to the car. "Evelyn says I have to bring her some sea water in a bottle."

"She reminded me on the phone last night. I told her she should not drink it but you know she won't listen."

"Which beach are we going to, ma?" asked Nicole as she snuggled next to Gussie in the back seat.

"The one with the hole in the rock near Umdloti, my sweetheart."

"Ooooh, that Evelyn!" Gussie laughed. "She is too much! There is no one like her. She sure knows how to deal with your mother."

"I think Evelyn is the only person who knows how to deal with mommy," I smiled. "How is everyone back home?"

"We all miss you terribly, Ruchie," replied Gussie a little sadly. "You should bring the children and come and visit us. You can rest there a little. All this hard work you are doing here is too much for you. Come home for a while."

"I know, Gussie, I will." A tear began to well up in the corner of my eye. "I will come home as soon as this house is finished, I promise."

Pieter, in the meantime, was designing at a furious pace. His star was rising fast and it wasn't long before the study in the house became too small. Plans and scraps of paper were all over the house. Having clients come to the still-incomplete house was not a good idea when Peter and friends were playing cops and robbers up and down the stairs. The situation was made worse if Nicole was in the middle of doing her homework. Then a scream would erupt from the bedroom.

One of Pieter's clients (actually the husband of the ballet mother) asked Pieter to design an office park in Morningside, a suburb on the same hill as the Berea. Once complete, there would be enough space for Pieter to take half of the double-story building. This was a huge move for both of us.

Our house still lacked covers on the plugs and doors on cupboards. But as they say in Afrikaans—and this really gets lost in translation—*ons gaan maar aan* (we just go on).

Pieter named himself president and I was given the title of secretary. Now, I had no clue what duties a secretary was supposed to perform. If it was answering phones, printing plans, and filing, then fine, I was already doing that at the house. If it was typing, shorthand, and accounting skills, then not fine, they were skills way over my head. So I enrolled in a three-month crash course at the local college.

We have a photograph of me sitting at the typewriter, with Pieter, his Afrikaans architect Evan, and his Indian draughtsman Raj standing confidently behind me for the official photograph of Pieter Coetzee Architects. What was I thinking, with my sequined T-shirt and permed hair? Ridiculous.

Still, I was now the official secretary of the company. Mornings only, mind you, because Mother insisted that the children needed me in the afternoons for carting them about and homework duties. So mornings only it was, with duties that included answering the telephone while taking shorthand and serving tea to the clients. I enjoyed this because together, Pieter and I were building a company. It was just Pieter's lack of acknowledgement that sometimes caused the metal balls to swing out of sync.

* * *

Six months after we moved in, we decided to throw an official party at the new office.

"Make sure you invite all the government officials, Ruchel, and that we have enough food," Pieter ordered. He paused during a phone conversation to give me the instructions. "Don't forget Fanie the bank manager. And my lawyer! Tell Martha to see that Samson is not drunk that night. I will be with you in a minute, Albert, I am just giving my wife some instructions for the party. *Jy beter kom* [you better come]. Ruchel, I am not finished with you. Make sure you tell Raj that I want the height of the wall changed to five feet. Albert, *wag 'n bietjie* [wait a minute]! Ruchel, get me Frank on the line, I need to speak with him now."

The date was set and government officials were coming, thank God. Martha and I prepared and cooked the food three days ahead. That evening a very sober Samson set out all the tables and chairs while Pieter dispensed instructions like an army general. "A hundred people are coming, this is an important party, the office has to be tidied up, put the beer in the ice bath, hurry up, there is no time!"

"*Mies* [Madam]!" called Martha from the top of the stairs with broom in hand. "Phone for you, the madam is on the line."

"Tell Mother I can't speak to her now, Martha. I have to fetch the children just now and have not even finished decorating the table. Tell her I will phone her tomorrow after the party."

"Madam says it is urgent and she wants to speak to you now!" Martha insisted.

"Oh man," I sighed as I ran up the stairs to pick up the phone. "Hello, ma?"

"Gussie died early this morning," I heard her say softly.

"NO!" The world around me stopped. "How?"

"She went in for that operation on her hip and everything was fine but last night a clot went straight to her brain." I could hear the tears in her voice.

I had no words. Tears streamed down my face as I collapsed to the floor. Gussie? My Gussie? This couldn't be true. She was only seventy-two. I still had so much to tell her. I still had to give her one last hug. I still had to say how much I really loved her. I still had to visit her. I still had to...Martha, hearing the conversation, rushed to hold me while instructing Samson to call the *baas*.

"The old, old madam died," I heard Martha tell Pieter as he rushed up the stairs.

"There, there, Ruch," Pieter said as he held me tightly and rocked me from side to side. The sobbing would not subside. I wanted to just cry and cry. Cry for all those unsaid words. Cry for all those lost hugs. Cry until my body was depleted from all the tears.

Pieter said I had to be brave. That we would travel to Bloemfontein tomorrow for the funeral. He said that the party must go on, that all these people were coming and we must not show sad faces. No sad faces. I tried hard but my heart could not help but burn with sadness right through my body. It was the longest night.

We traveled to Bloemfontein numb with sadness.

I thought back to the time I sat in Gussie's kitchen watching her roll the rice and meat mixture into grape leaves one by one. Small little parcels packed neatly one on top of the other while the aroma of fried onions wafted over us. I thought of the times I sat under her arms as she told the story of Oupa and the two bags of gold and how she kept his little suitcase with his shirt packed neatly inside when he first arrived in South Africa. I thought of the times we used to sing *"It's a long road to Tipperary, it's a long road to go..."* as we all traveled to Durban. I thought of how she would always hold me when tears threatened to erupt.

Those tears were here now and Gussie was not here anymore to make them stop. She would never be here again to hold me, comfort me, soothe the pain that was threatening to tear my heart into a million sad pieces. The memories flooded my tired brain like a burst dam. I desperately tried to hold onto her kind gentle eyes and loving heart but she slowly faded into the distant white light.

The funeral was unbearably sad. My emotions overwhelmed me as I watched Mother for the first time uncontrollably break down. Then tears came streaming down Father's cheeks and I cried even more. Evelyn was inconsolable as she and the whole staff in their long church robes slowly walked up the aisle singing mournful Sotho songs of years gone by.

"She was loved throughout the community," boomed the old Reverend who had baptized me in this same cathedral. "Her Sunday lunches were legendary and I for one will miss those sorely...people used to call her Baby...she is now in heaven with her beloved husband, and the angels."

I was awash in tears as Father leaned over to hug me. Relative after relative, some I had not seen in years, came forward to say what beautiful children I had and how I had grown. Mother's friends busied themselves around the table making sure everyone had enough to eat. But it was not the same. The food was not the same and I cried even more. I wanted my Gussie's food. I wanted my Gussie's hugs. It would be no more.

No more.

CHAPTER TWENTY-SIX

1985: *It is politically fashionable in the United States to demonstrate in front of the South African Embassy in Washington. The cause is to abolish white supremacy in South Africa. The result is major foreign disinvestment, heightened antiapartheid rhetoric, and constant television coverage of the rioting and demonstrations in South Africa. This leads the South African government to ban all television coverage of any uprisings back home. Apartheid is being vigorously opposed not only internationally but also domestically as major strides are made by Afrikaner organizations, churches, and academia who realize that it is better to talk than to take action through the barrel of a gun. Because of the sensitivity of the subject, most of these preliminary talks with the ANC leadership are held in secrecy. The parties involved do not want to inflame the anger of the blacks or the fear of the whites. These talks, including those by English-speaking whites through big industry such as Anglo-American, continue despite increasing violence.*

Botha's reaction to negotiations is cautious to not inflame the wrath of his more conservative members, who are becoming increasingly alarmed at the rapid reforms taking place through his government. Before Botha's speech to the National Congress in Durban in August 1985, televised live across the world, Foreign Minister Pik Botha (no relation) hinted to international leaders that major reforms will be announced. President Botha thinks long and hard about how much can be said at the meeting. The result is that Botha buckles to the pressure of some of his members and fails to cross his Rubicon. His finger-wagging promises of continued reforms are lost on the crowd when he warns the outside world that they must not "push us too far." These hidden suggestions of reform do not satisfy anyone and instead heighten the condemnation of South Africa both nationally and internationally.

P ieter and I attended the conference, held in the downtown city hall. By now, like many others, we were eager to see some real reforms and an end to the violence—even as we were unaware of the full extent of the violence owing to the limited media coverage. We knew the only way forward was to dismantle apartheid. It was with an air of expectancy and hope that we walked into the crowded hall. International press correspondents were waiting to televise the event to three hundred million viewers around the world.

The hall was packed with Afrikaners and English alike. There were actually two types of Afrikaners there that day—the city Afrikaners who, like Pieter, were urban professionals and open minded, and the real Boer who, like his family, were far more rural and conservative. The city Afrikaners were refined; they would barbecue fish, drink Cabernet Sauvignon, wear Pierre Cardin golf shirts, and send their sons to play cricket with the best of them. In the eyes of the real Boer, these city Afrikaners were "sissies."

A real Boer was a farmer, a blue-collar worker, or a government official. He typically wore an old wide-rimmed hat that was stained with sweat. He drank brandy and coke three fingers strong with no ice midday. His wife could sew any and everything and his only suit had to suffice for church, weddings, and funerals. A real Boer refused to speak English but he could speak the language of his black staff. A real Boer had lots of children to help on the farm and owned at least one twenty-two rifle and four other guns that he kept in the bedroom.

This mix of modern Boer and old school Boer was Botha's audience as he stepped up to the podium that cold August day. Sitting on either side of us were Fanie the bank manager and Kobus the engineer, with their wives. At the end of the row I could see one or two parents I knew from Nicole's school. All were there to learn whether this was it, whether to leave or stay. The speech was dubbed the Rubicon speech because the audience, and the world, expected Botha to cross the point of no return, spelling out the final radical reforms for a new South Africa. It was eagerly anticipated.

After much preamble and introductions, Botha began wagging his finger and boomed into the microphone.

"We will not give in to hostile pressure and agitation from abroad! Do not push us too far.… We are not prepared to lead white South Africans and other minority groups to abdication and suicide."

I was stunned.

"What the hell is he talking about?" I whispered to Pieter. "Can't the idiot see that we have to dismantle all apartheid as soon as possible? This is a nightmare!" Many in the audience just stormed out of the hall shaking their heads in disgust.

Some of our friends chose to leave the country, especially in the wake of the plunging rand. The international monetary community had devalued the South African currency from an already depressed fifty-two cents US to thirty-three cents US. Over the following weeks the situation went from bad to worse. The United States imposed limited economic sanctions while the nightly scenes of violence in the townships were beamed across the world. Our own SABC television chose to show little of the violence. It was not long before the government banned all foreign television news reporters from filming in the townships.

The explosion of unrest increased, from one hundred forty-nine dead and six hundred fifty-one injured in 1984 to eight hundred twenty-four dead and two thousand six hundred fifteen injured in 1985. And these were the reported statistics. The townships had become ungovernable.

"What do you mean you are leaving?" I said in a panic over the phone to Michelle. She had just given birth to her second son in Cape Town. Now she was telling me that Pietie had been granted a transfer with his company to Australia. They were leaving in a week's time.

"We can't live here anymore, Ruch," she said sadly. "The violence is becoming worse here in Cape Town. The other day I was nearly killed while driving past a township on the way to the airport. You should have seen all the squatters spilling onto the sidewalk of the main highway. Blacks were running everywhere, throwing rocks at the passing cars. One of the rocks smashed my passenger window. Thank God no one was hurt. But we can't live here anymore."

"A lot of people are talking to the ANC right now," I chipped in, trying to make her change her mind. "We can all ultimately come to some agreement. It can't go on like this forever."

"Are you dreaming? We're not waiting around to see if that happens. We're leaving now. I'm going to miss you terribly, my friend," Michelle said.

"You have no idea how I'll miss you!" I replied, close to tears. "Promise to write the minute you get there!"

It was déjà vu all over again. What bad omen would rear its ugly head now?

Martha refused to go into the township. Many nights she would have two or three of her friends stay over. To some degree the violence was contained in the townships and the government continued to promise control and reform. We believed them. I think we believed them because we never got the whole picture or saw for ourselves the extent of the violence.

We found a small measure of hope when a few top South African white businessmen decided to meet with exiled ANC leaders in Lusaka, Zambia, for talks. When one of them, Anglo-America's Gavin Reily, came back and said the talks were "useful" and "might lead to some fruitful conclusions," our hope soared.

We listened carefully for any news of talks with Mandela. Because news was censored, we still had no visual image of what Mandela looked like, or a clear report of what he said. Was he really a criminal or was he a saint? All we knew from the scant reports through Pieter's contacts in the National Party was that he had to be released. Why? Because economically businesses were hurting from the international sanctions imposed on South Africa. I can remember thinking at the time that it was ridiculous that the National Party was taking so long to release him.

We were not informed of the political maneuvering of both Mandela and the National Party—the only story we got was that Mandela was refusing to be released. With very little 'behind the scenes' knowledge, it was difficult to understand the full story.

Time and again, Mandela was offered release from prison if he called for an end to violence. He unwaveringly turned those offers down, refusing to leave Robben Island until South Africa enacted a law granting "one man, one vote." He said it was Botha who could end the violence by dismantling apartheid.

It was not until almost a decade later when I read Mandela's "Road to Freedom" that I truly understood the raw pain and suffering of the struggle for democracy. I remember feeling anger at discovering the lack of knowledge at the time. Not guilt, but anger that I was not in a position to do more, or to know more. Angry that I was not aware of the atrocities carried out in parts of our country. Angry I was not in a position to have a platform to speak out and implement change.

*   *   *

In the meantime Pieter's star was rapidly rising. He had secured a major contract from the House of Delegates to design and build low-cost housing for the Indian community. His revolutionary design, which incorporated the religious beliefs and needs of Indians, was heralded in the newspapers as a step forward in making affordable housing available to all citizens of South Africa. A picture of him and Minister Rajbansi was splashed across numerous publications.

The lion strutted to and fro across the vast plains of the veld!

Of course, this success needed to be taken to the next level. I immediately added 'good sweet public relations wife' to my list of rapidly growing titles. This would be my promotion.

"We have to hire a secretary!" I announced in the office one morning.

"What for?" replied Pieter. "Stop going to all these lunches and tea parties and you will have enough time to do the work here!"

"You need someone full day in the office to answer phones and do the filing," I shot back. "I am busy with the children in the afternoons and besides, how do you think you would have met one of your biggest clients here if it wasn't for me being friendly with Nicky's ballet friend's mother?"

"You just introduced me to him," replied Pieter. "I did all the work."

"So who do you think had to entertain the House of Delegates architect's wife in Mauritius the whole day while you and her husband fished and got drunk? Who has to cook and entertain your clients at dinners every weekend? Who—"

"Aagh, Ruchel! Stop making excuses. That is not work. You don't know what work is. Martha cleans the house, the children are at school, and you go to tea parties all day. What work are you talking about?"

Aaaargh!

It made no difference what I said. In Pieter's eyes I was just a lady of leisure. Dinner miraculously landed on the table each night, cement miraculously landed in the hands of the tiler who was tiling the whole house again, a few clients miraculously landed at Pieter's doorstep, the children miraculously were transported from karate lesson to tennis lesson to music lesson, ensuring well-rounded, well-mannered future adults. These and all the hundreds of other miracles were just that—miracles.

So I promoted myself and went ahead and found someone to replace me in the secretarial department. Pieter protested but when one of *Die Manne* complained that he could never reach Pieter on the phone in the afternoons, Pieter finally relented.

I interviewed and trained a young Indian lady, Salome, who seemed eager and pleasant enough to learn how to deal with the half cryptic instructions from her boss and not take offence if he forgot to greet her in the morning. At least she did not have to take instructions in the middle of the night or while cooking supper and helping with homework.

Timid and shy, Salome grew bolder as time went by. But in the beginning I know she must have gone home each night and regaled her parents with the crazy antics of her boss. Like the time Pieter asked to taste some of her lunch, then told her that he wanted the same for lunch at least once a week because his wife could not cook curry like that. Or the time he came back to work from a long drinking lunch with the House of Delegates architect and promptly fell asleep on the floor of his office. Salome finally got the hang of warding off all inquiries until he eventually woke up from such naps.

For my new role, I became a chameleon. Picture a ladies' luncheon, held under the shade of purple bougainvillea in the garden of a huge mansion. I'm wearing a heavily discounted designer dress, sipping tea while commenting on the fashions shown by models sailing between the tables. I liked good clothes but Pieter hated to spend the money, so I always had to find the middle ground of creative financing within the household budget. So there I would be, talking and networking as if that was all I had to do. Lovely! Smiling and watching a pink fuchsia cocktail dress sweep by, thinking, how can I pick up two bags of cement on my way home without ruining my shoes? So lovely!

*   *   *

By now Peter had graduated from nursery school and was selected by the private all-boy's school Clifton Preparatory. Because I was well versed in how things worked in the land of private schools, Peter's name was down at birth. With his sister already in Durban Girls' College, I knew I would not have too much of a problem getting him in. He breezed through his interview, and tears flowed down my cheeks as I watched him walk in his little khaki uniform and black socks toward his new teacher. The headmaster said he was delighted to welcome such a well-mannered little boy into his school and hoped that my husband and I would become involved in the school activities. Of course, of course, I said, as I smiled sweetly and waved goodbye. Of course.

This was my life. It had finally settled into a predictable pattern, with me exceeding all expectations in the wife and mother departments. Even Mother's phone calls were less frequent. It was as if she were slowly coming to grips with the fact that her daughter could actually perform some of these duties. Martha seemed to control the household pretty much her way, making up the cleaning program as she saw fit. In between cleanings she would bake cakes for church meetings in her new apartment above the garage. Every time I met a new friend of hers, I was told that I spoiled Martha—and this from one of her friends! I was just happy that she was happy, and when she was happy, the world was happy. The same with Pieter and Mother. My life's purpose was to ensure that everyone was happy.

Samson was now no longer Martha's boyfriend but he still remained our gardener. Drunken gardener, that is, but when he was sober he was still a good and trusty handyman. Even the neighbor's retaining wall was finally built with the help of Samson and *tok* labor. We never heard a word from them and it was not long after that we saw the For Sale sign outside their house. Life could move forward when the sky did not fall in.

Now, in case you think my bum had disappeared into the sunset, think again. Just because no drama was rearing its ugly head didn't mean that I was not constantly in search of the perfect diet. Food and I had a love-hate relationship. I was as picky as my son when it came to eating (I wonder where he learned that?) so invariably three variations of dinner would be cooked each night. One that Pieter, Nicole, and Martha would eat, one modified so that everything was separated and sauce free for Peter, and one that would exclude either the fat or the starch or both for me. Peter and I refused to touch *pap* and anything else related to that gooey family. But we did have a wonderful arrangement with cheese rolls. I loved the melted cheese on top and he liked the fresh bread below, so we duly separated the few rolls I bought while we waited in the car for Nicky to finish class.

It was one of those afternoons. Peter had finished school a half hour earlier and we sat in the car eating cheese rolls and going over his day at school.

"I want to wait by the gate and carry Nicky's suitcase," Peter announced when he saw the junior girls start to walk out.

He had done this often, so it was no biggie. Since I was parked on the opposite side of the road I got out and walked him to the Lollipop Man, as we called the crossing guard, to see him across the road. Peter loved to hide behind the ancient metal post of the school gate and pop out just as Nicole walked through the gate. It made both of them laugh.

I sat in the car going over the notices from his school about upcoming functions and what each parent was expected to bring. Cars were two deep on either side of the busy road as parents double parked to pick up their children. Every now and then I would glance up and see Peter as he stood patiently peeping from behind the post to look for his sister. Children were crossing the road and climbing into cars in front of me. The noise was deafening, with cars tooting and children shouting as other cars whizzed by on the busy road.

Suddenly there was a screeching of tires and a scream. Then a deathly quiet as traffic came to a halt.

I sprang out of the car and tried to see what had happened. I could not see Peter or Nicole. Where were they? Sweat began to pour from my forehead as foreboding washed over me. I rushed across the road with my heart in my throat.

What happened? What happened?

My heart threatened to burst out of its casing.

In the distance—look.

What? What is there?

Two little feet with black shoes and black socks under that car. Look.

"Oh God, no—"

"My son, MY SON! Oh God, PLEASE HELP!!!"

I faintly hear the buzz of voices jumbled together. "Someone call the ambulance…There is no pulse! What happened? I don't know… This motorcyclist did not see the Lollipop Man's sign up, her son was the first to walk across…Where's Nicole?…Madge took her home, she would have become hysterical seeing her brother…Make room for the vice headmistress…Give her space to see if she can get a pulse… Move away from the scene please…Shame, he looks so angelic lying there…I heard the motorcycle hit him and saw him fly into the air… He must have landed on his head and rolled under the parked car over there…Oh, here is the headmistress now…She is comforting the mother, who seems to be totally in shock…Poor thing…"

Why are all these people standing here talking like that? How can I be standing looking at myself bent over trying to get my son to breathe? Why am I not doing more? Why am I not in my body? They say they feel no pulse but no one seems to help. Call an ambulance someone. But wait! Who is this soldier? Why is he bending down and placing his mouth over my son's mouth? Why do I sit there all hunched up doing nothing? The soldier is coming up for air and feeling my son's pulse. Why are the other people crying? What? Someone says they feel a slight pulse? What's that noise? That red flashing light? What? He has a slight pulse? He has a pulse?

"He has a pulse? You feel the pulse?" I sobbed as I watched the paramedics lift my son into the ambulance and hook him to an intravenous drip.

"I'll come with you, Ruchel," said Chrissie as she instructed another mother to take her daughter home with her.

"Where's my daughter?" I sobbed as I climbed into the car.

"Don't worry, Mrs. Coetzee," said the headmistress gently. "One of the mothers has already taken Nicole home with her. My secretary is phoning your husband."

"Oh God, please help my son!" I cried as the ambulance door shut. Chrissie put her arm around me.

"Please God, help my son!"

The phone rang in Pieter's office.

"Could I speak to Mr. Pieter Coetzee urgently, please?"

"I am afraid he is not in at this moment," replied Salome. "May I take a message?"

"This is the office of the headmistress at Durban Girls' College and there has been a rather serious accident. We need to reach Mr. Coetzee urgently."

"Mr. Coetzee is not in town," replied Salome, now worried. "He is in Howick on site for the House of Delegates. There is no phone to reach him there. Can I inquire what the accident is about and then see if I can send one of the staff to drive out to Howick and relay it to him? I am afraid it might take a while as Howick is an hour away."

"You can tell him that his son was in a serious accident and has been rushed to Addington Hospital. Could you please inform us when you reach him? Thank you."

Salome panicked.

"Raj! Raj! Come here quickly! I have to reach Mr. Coetzee. The school says that small Peter was in an accident and it is serious! What are we going to do?" She was on the verge of tears.

"I will phone the site office, I have the number," replied Raj, picking up the receiver. "Hello, hello?" he shouted into the phone. "Is Mr. Coetzee there? This is his office, it is urgent! His son has been in accident! He is in danger!"

"*Bliksem*!" replied the foreman. "Dube, *hamba, hamba*! Tell Mr. Coetzee his son is in bad accident. Very bad accident! He is in house number 198 with the other *baas*. *Hamba*!"

"*Hauw*!" mumbled Dube. He sprinted away to find house number 198. "*Baas, baas*!" he shouted as he approached Pieter and the rest of the team. "*Baas*, Mr. Coetzee!" He was panting as he entered house 198. "Office says *baas* son is dead!"

"What?" said Pieter in shock. "What did you say?"

"*Baas* must hurry to office. *Baas* son is dead!"

"We can drive you back to Durban," offered the foreman on the site. Pieter tried to get details from a very distressed Salome, who couldn't make out where her boss had heard that his son was now dead. She was too frightened to correct him. All she could remember was that he had been taken to Addington Hospital, the large general hospital on the beachfront in Durban.

That ride to Durban was the longest journey of Pieter's life.

My ride in the ambulance was even longer.

"Oh God, please help!" I cried as I watched them wheel my son into the emergency room. His face looked so pale and angelic as he lay there unconscious. I was dying inside. Chrissie kept her arm around my shoulder, offering words of comfort. I couldn't think. I couldn't listen. This was my child and it was my fault. I should never have allowed him to cross a road. It didn't matter that other children crossed roads. I should not have allowed my son to cross any road. Mother was right. I was useless. I was not fit to be a mother.

After what seemed like eternity the doctor cautiously approached me. "Mrs. Coetzee?" he inquired.

"Yes, doctor, how is my son? Is he going to live?"

"We have to give him some time," replied the doctor calmly in case I collapsed into a heap of uncontrollable hysteria, which was a distinct possibility. "Right now his vital signs are stabilized but he still remains unconscious."

"Unconscious? Why?" I sobbed.

"We are not sure at this moment. On a scale of one to ten, with one being the worst case, your son is a three."

"A three? What does that mean? What does that mean?" I was beginning to lose control.

"It means," replied the doctor gently, signaling Chrissie to make me sit down again. "It means that the next twenty-four hours will be the most crucial to see if his level of conscious raises or not. We are now going to transport him to a bed on the seventh floor."

"Oh, Chrissie!" I said in tears. "My son, my son! Oh God, Pieter. He is going to kill me. Don't let anyone phone my mother, please!"

Just then Nicholas' mother, Carol, rushed into the hospital.

"I've just heard! I am so sorry, my friend," she said as she hugged me. "I was fetching Nicholas from swimming practice, the headmaster told me. Where's your husband? Do you need me to phone him?"

"The headmistress has called, I'm sure he'll be here soon," said Chrissie, hugging me tighter. We all sat frozen in Peter's room, watching the fluid drip slowly into his arm.

Dip, drip...

Nurses came in to tell me that their switchboard was jammed with people phoning to find out about Peter and could I please ask the schools to tell the parents that there was nothing to report right now.

"I'll phone the school," offered Chrissie, who walked back to the nurse's station on the same floor.

Drip, drip…

Just then Pieter rushed into the room.

"What happened? What did you do to my son?"

"He was hit by a—" I started to reply but Pieter interrupted me as Carol quietly left the room.

"I know what happened," he said angrily, pacing up and down beside Peter's bed. "I have already spoken to the doctor and the headmistress after I thought he was dead. How could you let him cross the road by himself? How could you? I told you a week ago not to park on the opposite side of the street. No, don't answer. I don't want to talk to you right now."

Okay, I knew he was in shock and I knew he would express his hurt through anger because I had seen this reaction before. But it was as if a bullet had been shot into my heart. I was dying inside and my husband was dying inside and there we were, sitting on the opposite sides of the bed, not saying a word to each other.

Drip, drip…

Chrissie and Carol came back to say that they were leaving and would be back in the morning.

"Don't worry about Nicky," said Chrissie. "Madge took her home with her. I've just spoken to Madge and she says that Martha is with your daughter now. Just phone Martha sometime tonight as she is also worried."

"I will. Thank you, my friends," I replied tearfully. Pieter still did not say a word.

Drip, drip…

Day became night. The nurses came in, complaining that their switchboard was still jammed.

I walked slowly to the pay phone down the hall.

"Don't tell mommy but Peter has been in an accident," I finally blurted to my sister, who was now practicing law in Johannesburg. It was near midnight and I couldn't hold out on telling the family any longer. I had to hear at least from Jenny, who was always the one with the sage advice.

"You have to, Ruch!" she said after hearing what happened.

"No, she'll panic and the doctor said we have to wait twenty-four hours. I'm hoping he will improve."

"What if something happens to him tonight and mommy finds out that you didn't phone her. I'm going to phone her!"

"No, don't!"

It wasn't that I did not want to speak to Mother. It was that I could not speak to her. I was so ridden with guilt and sorrow that nothing short of my son waking up would alter this terrible emotional state I had sunk into. I reached out to Jenny several times through that night, to seek her strength and guidance.

Jenny phoned Mother. It was two in the morning.

"What! Jenny, speak up! What did you say?" shouted Mother. "Peter? Oh God! Where is he? How bad is it? You don't know? I'm not waiting for Ruchel to phone me. NO! I am going to Durban now! I know there are no planes at this time of the morning, Jenny. I don't care about safety. I will phone when I get to Durban."

"*Hauw*, madam Shirley!" said the gas attendant as Mother tooted for him to fill the car. "Where's madam going this time of the night?"

"Fill her up, John. My grandson is in hospital in Durban. Check the oil and the tires. It is going to be a long drive. And bring me three tins of Coke, please."

In the back seat of the car were clothes hastily thrown into a travel bag. Outside, the night was dark and eerily quiet. It would be a long six-hour journey on roads that were not safe for a woman during the early hours of the morning. That was the least of Mother's worries.

"Where is my grandson!" demanded Mother as she barged through the front door of the hospital at half past seven the next morning. "Where's the doctor? Nurse! Get the doctor on the phone immediately! I want to speak to him now!"

From down the hall I heard Mother asking the nurses if they had changed his bed sheets or checked on his status in the last five minutes.

"Wake the doctor up, nurse! Show me the room."

A thunderstorm burst into the room.

"Ruchel!" Mother commanded as she made a beeline to where Peter was lying. "Why did you not phone me? What happened here?

Piet, you have to go home, I am sure Nicky is in a terrible state and she will need one of you there. I am here now and I am going to see that the best doctor is called in immediately!"

Pieter knew it was no use arguing and, besides, he was emotionally drained. He needed to sort things out at home and at the office. He had mumbled no more than a few words to me as the initial shock began to slowly subside. "I'll be back in a few hours," he said as he left the room dejectedly.

Mother began to fuss around Peter's bed. She ordered the nurses to change his bedsheets and check on the IV. She instructed the doctor, once he arrived, to check his eyes, his pulse, his heart, his everything. She checked under the bed to see if the floor was clean. She called the nurse in again to check his IV. She paced the room and then told me that in the future I was never to let Peter cross a road by himself again even if all the other children in the world crossed that same road. She said I had to tidy myself in the bathroom and brush my hair because I looked too dreadful. She said that Peter would be home soon and that he would be fine. She said that he'd soon be reading his favorite comic books, *Asterix* and *Obelix*. She told Pieter to bring copies of them to the hospital when he returned. She said if matters did not improve in the next few hours in this hideous hospital, she would take him home to his own bed and hire a private nurse. She said—

I didn't feel so alone anymore.

Pieter returned with a handful of comic books.

"The phone has not stopped ringing since I arrived at home this morning," he said as he bent over the bed to check his son's status. "I don't even know all these people. And all the flowers! Who are Molly and Devorah and Marilyn, Ruchel?"

"They're mothers at Nicole's school. We sit together during athletic events. Marilyn is Gilad's mom from nursery school, you know her," I said, thinking how nice it was that people who I hardly knew or had not spoken to in a long time had phoned.

"Well, I told Martha to take messages. She is in such a state. And I didn't tell Nicky too much. Already she wants to come here to the hospital but I said I'll bring her brother home soon."

"Poor Martha, and my poor darling Nicky," said Mother, who was now busy reading *Asterix* to Peter. "At least Piet agrees with me that Peter will recuperate better at home."

"Ma," I said, "he hasn't even regained consciousness. How can you both decide to take him out of here?"

"I know my grandson is listening to me. He will wake up, you will see!" She read and spoke to him in the full belief that he could hear her, and we followed her lead.

I was still in deep, deep pain but somehow the strength of these two roaring lions propped me up.

Pieter left again to take care of matters in the office. Not five minutes had passed when Marilyn brought Peter's four best friends from nursery school into the room.

"Oh my God," I cried. "Look, Peter, look who has come to visit you. Mark and Gilad and Grant and Shaun are here to see you." The boys clambered around the bed trying to shake Peter awake. Mother tried to keep them from climbing all over him.

"Hey, Peter, wake up!" Mark shouted near his face. "Wake up!"

"Hey, Peter, it is me, Gilad!"

"I know it is you Mark...Gilad...." mumbled my son.

Did I hear my son? Did he speak? Oh please God! Please give me back my son. Oh God, I beg you! Please let this be true.

The boys retreated behind Marilyn as Mother rushed to his side.

"Peter!" Mother bent down to call him. "Gansi is here and mommy is here, my darling. Can you hear me? Look I have your favorite book *Asterix*—show your Gansi where is *Asterix*, please, my sweetheart."

"*Asterix* is there, Gansi..." Peter slowly pointed to the correct picture in the book that Mother held in front of his face. "But I already have number twenty, Gansi. I'm tired, mommy."

"Oh thank God, he has come back to us and there is no brain damage!" exclaimed Mother. She rushed out of the room to call the nurse and doctor, and I called my husband.

Everything went at breakneck speed after that. The doctor and nurse rushed in and tested all his vital signs, then declared him fine. Mother insisted that Peter be taken home immediately.

Surrounded by everyone who loved him, he recuperated far quicker than expected. The doctor conceded this after his first visit. Nicky did not leave her brother's side and refused to go to school for three days after we brought him home. Martha's friends from church made a steady procession to our home to pray for his full recovery. The house was filled to the brim with flowers and good wishes from family, friends, acquaintances, and politicians. The phone never stopped ringing.

Thank you, God. Thank you for giving my son back to me. Thank you for that second chance. By His grace... *A re bineng sefela sa mashome a robeli a metso e robong.* Let us sing the eighty-ninth hymn. Let us joyfully sing of our deliverance, let us joyfully sing His praises.

CHAPTER TWENTY-SEVEN

———————

1986: South Africa abolishes the pass laws, mixed marriage, and immorality acts. Ladysmith Black Mambazo and Johnny Clegg (the "White Zulu") and his Juluka group play to thousands of adoring South African fans of all races and to international audiences as well. The world sees "The Gods Must Be Crazy," a clever comedy that stars a Kalahari Bushman. Drag artist Pieter Dirk Uys and his alter ego Evita Bezuidenhout poke fun at the government. The state of emergency is lifted. A month later, Winnie Mandela tells a huge crowd at Kagiso in the Transvaal that "the time for speeches and debate has come to an end. We work in the white man's kitchen. We bring up the white man's children. We could have killed them at any time we wanted to. Together, hand in hand with our sticks and our matches, with our necklaces, we shall liberate this country."

Dire Straits was playing faintly in the background as Martha began clearing the plates from the dinner table. In a rare moment of calm, I read that morning's newspaper, while Pieter hung paintings we had recently bought from an art show.

"What is she talking about?" I asked Pieter. He leaned over my shoulder to read out the headlines about Winnie Mandela's speech. "What's this about necklaces?"

"It's a nickname for the way blacks are killing each other in the townships. They fill a rubber tire with petrol, place it over the person's head and then set that person on fire."

"You must be joking! Are you telling me they're putting rubber tires over people and burning them alive? That's unimaginable! Why are they killing each other if they are supposed to only hate the whites?"

Of course, "they" referred to unknown blacks and not to those like Martha and others who were close to us. Even Martha used to say "they" while shaking her head at the township atrocities. "*Tsotsies* [gang members]!" is what she called them. "*Tsotsies!*"

"I heard that some gangs suspect others of collaborating with the government, so they kill them," said Pieter. "It's not good if Winnie encourages these same people to kill whites like that. I think the right-wing Afrikaners will retaliate and start a war."

"Then it's not safe to live here anymore. Michelle was right!"

"Aagh, Ruchel," said Pieter. "You panic for nothing. Fanie tells me that the government won't allow that to happen. Besides, when I was at the National Party retreat in Cape Town, they all said we were on track to slowly abolishing all apartheid. This will finally appease not only the majority here but the international community as well. Mandela will be released from prison and we will all be able to go on with our lives in peace. Did I tell you I met FW de Klerk? Actually a bunch of us threw him into the pool one night after a couple of beers. It was so funny. He took it in the spirit of the evening. Nice guy. I think he'll be the one to eventually replace old PW."

But the government responded to Winnie's remarks and the call for a black boycott of white-owned businesses by imposing a second, far more stringent state of emergency over the country. Journalists were banned from areas of unrest, all reports about such areas were censored by a newly formed Bureau of Information—it should have been called "The Bureau of No Information." Hundreds of activists were detained in a nationwide swoop.

It was a constant topic a dinner parties.

"These sanctions are not going to help the country," complained Pieter while pouring Backsberg Pinotage for our dinner guests. "*Boere sal net a plan maak* [Boers will make a plan]!"

"*My ouers is gatvol vir die Nationale Party* [My parents are fed up with the National Party]," replied Jakobus, taking a sip of his wine. His wife was helping me pass the lemon meringue pie around. "*Hulle gaan oorstap na die Konserwatiewe Party* [They are going to cross over to the Conservative Party]. Och, this pie is delicious, Ruchel. Antjie, get the recipe."

"What will happen if more people vote for the Conservative Party?" asked Mercia.

"*Daar sal groot kak in die land kom* [The land will be in deep shit]," replied Jan.

"*Sal nooit fokken gebeur nie* [Will never *&%$# happen]! added Pieter. "*Die Verkramptes het geen kans nie. Die souties stap oor na die Nationale Party* [The Conservatives have no chance. The English are crossing over to the National Party]!"

The real Boers, of course, did react. They reacted with their vote by making the Conservative Party the official opposition party in Parliament. More blue-collar whites swung to the right, accusing the National Party of being "soft on security." The only saving grace was that many of the left-leaning whites voted for the National Party, which meant the majority of whites wanted a change.

Our hope has not yet died. We still believe we can pull through this upheaval and emerge a peaceful nation. We love our country and do not want to abandon it like the proverbial rat on a sinking ship. The house is not even complete! We still have so much to accomplish, so many dreams, so many goals. What could better than a good South African Cabernet under the oaks of a Cape wine farm with close friends? What could be better than sunsets over Clifton Beach in Cape Town, or cool mountain air in the Natal midlands? Dark blue thunderstorm clouds over the endless fields of the Free State, the smell of the veld after the rain? What was better than the drumbeat of Africa itself? That is where our soul is firmly planted. That is who we are.

We would ride out the storm. We are that confident.

*   *   *

The Cape became our playground each vacation. We soon bought our first timeshare at the Beacon Island Hotel in Plettenberg Bay. From the two-bedroom suite on the fourth floor overlooking the sea, we have a perfect view of the resident mating whales. It even has a glassed-in shower on the balcony. That is why we bought it—that and the raised bed with its sweeping view of the ocean. We just couldn't get enough of going from the shower to the bed to the lounge to the shower again—all so naughty and delicious between chocolate-covered strawberries and champagne.

We were fast becoming the golden couple as Pieter's star continued to rise. The raw love and energy that bound us together, the craziness, the childlike love of life and ambition, all that and more was what attracted so many friends. We were different. It was the formula

of our personalities—the dashingly handsome rough Afrikaner with
the naughty-but-nice English private school girl, as Pieter called me.
We never grew up. We belonged to each other, dancing to a secret
rhythm, through rich and poor, in sickness and in health, no matter
what.

Its a bloody miracle I never strangled him.

Let's talk about hunting.

In chauvinistic South Africa where the lions ruled the land, how
many women do you think would go hunting in the wild with a rifle
strapped to their shoulder? Very few.

Most men use this time to bond and act out all their juvenile
fantasies with a beer or two in hand. Especially after the hunt each
night. To have a woman present while they are making beer holders
out of the testicles of the slaughtered deer is just not kosher, darling.
Besides, where can a woman divert her eyes or ears in the middle of the
veld when the men hold their pissing or farting contest? No thank you.
Not worth the equality battle. Much better to stay at home with the
children. It's saner and there are no snakes or hairy spiders at home.

"What do you mean you want to take our son hunting with
you? Are you crazy? He is only nine!" I said. I was horrified that Pieter
would even contemplate such a thing. This was my son we were talking
about, the son I nearly lost. No way.

"You cannot baby him forever, Ruchel. He needs to be with his
father doing men stuff." Pieter shot back. When he was this determined
nothing would stop him, no matter how I carried on.

"God help you if anything happens to him!" I threatened as I
packed cut-up raw vegetables, bread rolls, nuts, and all the other food
I knew my son would eat. "See that you do not let him out of your
sight and see that he eats this food!"

"Let's go Dad!" shouted Peter excitedly from the truck. "Bye,
Mom!"

"Bye, my darling! Be careful and stay close to Daddy!"

Three hours later they pulled into the campsite.

"Dad, can I bring a friend next time?" Peter asked, helping his
father unload gear. "Christopher wants to come and hunt with us.
He says his father would never take him."

"What do you expect from a *rooinek*!" laughed Pieter. "Before any
of your friends come with us, you better learn the rules of hunting,

my boy. Daddy will teach you. It's very dangerous out there. You have to respect the animals."

Peter climbed into the small caravan that was permanently parked there.

"Dad! There's a scorpion on the bed! There're lots of black widows on the trees outside! I don't want to sleep in the caravan!"

"It's just a baby scorpion." Pieter climbed into the caravan and swept the scorpion outside. "Look, there are no more in here. The black widows won't harm you if you leave them alone. You see what I mean when I say you have to respect nature. Just follow me and you will learn."

The open veld stretched for miles around. Peter watched his father and two friends check their guns and then ask the farm laborers where they had last seen the *impala*. All around them birds and crickets danced in trees. Broken white skulls and bones lay scattered in the dusty veld while the hot breeze rustled the tall dry grass. The intense scent of wild sage stung the nostrils. It was a wilderness devoid of other human beings, a place where an animal could leap right out at you at any given second.

Just then a group of *impala* came into sight in the distance. Peter stayed close to his father as they all walked slowly through the tall grass. A shot rang out and one of the *impala* fell to the ground.

"*Bliksem*, Jan!" said Pieter, "*Dis 'n treffer daai* [That's a perfect shot]!"

"Not fair!" moaned Peter. "I wanted to shoot first!"

"Don't worry, my boy, there're lots of *impala* here," Pieter said. "We just have to be patient. Hunting is all about patience."

A little further up, behind a clump of spiky bushes in the distance, they spotted a group of *impala* grazing.

"Okay, shhhh…you must be very quiet now. Remember how Daddy showed you how to hold the gun? Yes, that's right, my boy. Slowly now, look through your viewfinder. Aim… Keep your hand steady."

Standing with his little legs slightly apart, Peter cocked his head to the one side to squint through the lens. Once satisfied he was aiming correctly he squeezed the trigger.

Bang!

Two *impala* fell to the ground.

"Goeie donner [Damn]!" whistled Jan as Pieter swooped his son up into the air, hugging and kissing him.

"That's my boy!" Pieter laughed. *"Dis my seun* [That's my son]! Two *impala* with one shot! *Kan jy dit glo* [Can you believe it], Jan?"

The farm laborers smiling from ear to ear ran up to Peter. *"Hauw, klein basie, hauw!"* They laughed as they all patted him on the back. *"Twee bokke met een skoot* [Two antelope with one shot]? *Shoh, shoh, shoh!"*

Tradition! Father and son tradition in all its glory! Peter was now one of *Die Manne.*

After having dragged that *springbok* across the kitchen floor on my twenty-first birthday, Pieter agreed to cut up the animals on site and take only certain pieces home. The farm laborers loved this arrangement because they scored not only the head, inside organs, and skin, which they coveted, but some of the meat as well. For the most part this worked beautifully. Beautifully, that is, until the stars above decided to have some fun.

On the next hunt, *Die Manne* were not very successful the first two days. The Kudu were scarce and could not be tracked anywhere, which was maddening. Late on Sunday afternoon, just before they were about to return home, the stars placed a Kudu right at the exit gates.

Of course Pieter shot it. "Too late to cut it up, it will be dark when we get back home," shouted Pieter to the farm laborers. "Just cut open the stomach and take the insides out," he instructed. "The skin together with the wind at the back of the truck should act as a refrigerator until I get home. *Hamba! Hamba!* It's already so late."

I raced outside, hearing all the commotion in my driveway.

"You are not dragging that thing into my house!" I said as I saw the cow-size deer lying on its side. "It's 9:00 PM! The children have to go to school tomorrow. What do you think you are going to do with this thing?"

"Ruchel, there's no time to argue!" Pieter said, shouting for Samson and Martha to come and help. "I am not wasting this prime meat. It cost me a lot of money. We'll just have to cut it up here and put it in the fridge until I can take it to the butcher tomorrow. Take everything you have out of the fridge. Samson, come help me drag this Kudu off the truck. *Hamba, Hamba!"*

"Cut it? Where?" I was horrified. "How are you going to fit a cow into my fridge?"

"Out of the way, Ruchel! Samson! Too steep to go around—gotta go through! Help lift the back legs. Martha! Get my *panga* [long knife] and my two sharp knives. Ruchel! Stop standing there! Go clear out the fridge!"

I stood frozen as I watched the Kudu dragged, dripping blood, through the front door, down the carpeted stairs, through the kitchen, and out to the side of the house to the patio that was reserved for the washing lines. Of course clothes were still hanging out to dry.

Pieter and Samson hung the dead Kudu by its feet on the washing line. They sliced and diced like two Samurai warriors, and carried little piles of raw meat to the kitchen area. Large ribs lay in buckets filled with vinegar water while other portions of the Kudu were plopped onto the kitchen table to be chopped into smaller pieces. Blood dripped all over the tiled floor. Martha and I bagged and tagged the meat until after the sun rose the next morning.

Did I contemplate murder? Of course, but then more blood would have been spilled, which would have created more chaos. So instead of murder that night I performed damage control during the Samurai production. Martha and I continued to clean long after Pieter collapsed into bed.

Maybe it was the look of absolute horror on my face, maybe it was all the blood, but after that night all game meat from then on went straight to the butcher. The carpets on the stairs were replaced, the tiles were scrubbed clean, and new washing lines were erected.

Only after all that did the stars return to their silent twinkling.

* * *

I was constantly reminded that it was essentially a man's world in chauvinistic South Africa.

And that was my husband. King of the jungle, a lion that roared long into the night, a lion that ate voraciously, laughed voraciously, and made love voraciously.

Pieter paced the jungle together with his fellow lions in an insatiable quest to conquer. They gathered together in pubs at night plotting their next moves on the African landscape. They huddled at church, on the golf course, during hunting or out sailing, all the time ribbing and lightly punching each other in camaraderie. The strength of that inner circle was arresting.

There were lions above the inner circle, especially those in government, who had the power to make demands on this eager pack of young lions. And of course, the inner circle of lions had to comply to maintain their place in the jungle.

"Kobus says we must organize some girls for the night," said Pieter to his quantity surveyor. "He is flying in from Pretoria. There is a good chance that he will give us the job for those eight hundred houses in Richards Bay. The Post Office is now looking to build low-cost housing there, and we have to show him that among us all we can manage the entire project."

"He's married," replied the quantity surveyor. "Doesn't he get enough at home?"

"Who cares? All I know is that Kobus says that in order to get the job we have to line up some girls for him," continued Pieter. "I hear Smugglers Inn in Point Road has a VIP club upstairs. Let's take him there."

Prostitution in South Africa was illegal but Point Road, a beach front area near the harbor, was as famous as the red light district of Amsterdam for its girls. Smugglers Inn used to be a seedy old sailor's bar but an intrepid entrepreneur turned it into an upscale, exclusive, gold card, members only club upstairs that could put Parisian bordellos to shame. The police knew but didn't want to know. Inside, members met in a central lounge-cum-bar before retiring to one of the many themed bedrooms with a girl of their choice. Everything was expensive.

"What do you mean you spent five thousand rand with your new gold card?" I yelled as Pieter mumbled drunkenly after returning home late that night. I thought I was having a nightmare. The bedside clock said 4:00 AM. "You only received that card yesterday!"

"Bloody Kobus never had a card and the others only had cash so I had to pay the membership fee to get us all in," slurred Pieter. "They wouldn't let us in if we weren't a member or with a member. Mind you, I must say that they've done it out *lekker* inside though. Topless girls served us at the bar. You should come and see. Jan and I stared at this one girl's breasts the whole night while we waited for the guy from Pretoria to finish in the bedroom. Some of the other guys from our group were naughty. They also went into the bedrooms with some girls."

"Who?" I asked.

"Oh, there was ..."

Did I believe what he was telling me? Yes. More importantly, I trusted my husband. Some said I was too naïve and let my husband get away with murder by coming home at all hours of the night. Others said I spoiled him by letting him do what he wanted.

But I knew my husband inside and out. He could not tell a lie even if he tried, and I was comfortable in his love. I trusted him. Also, I never failed to remind him that should that fine line of trust be broken he would not see me or the children, ever again. He never gave me cause to test that threat.

Besides, he was extremely possessive and hated if another man even looked at me other than as a friend. It was all part of his being a man, a lion, and I did not see the point of trying to change that in fiercely chauvinistic South Africa. I was just angry that he had spent so much on one night, since I was the one juggling the household bills.

Two weeks later Pieter returned home after spending time at the yacht club. His face was white.

"What's wrong?" I asked. I was chopping onions for the *bobotie* that night. The children were upstairs doing their homework.

"I saw two of my friends at the yacht club, they looked terrible," said Pieter, fidgeting. "I asked them what was wrong. They said they heard that some idiot from Smugglers Inn pissed the cops off so they raided the place and seized all the records. The cops gave the names of all the members to the newspaper."

"So what are you trying to tell me?" I asked suspiciously.

"That my name most probably will appear together with all the others in Sunday's newspaper as being one of those who went to Smugglers Inn."

"What!" I nearly chopped my finger off. "Are you telling me, are you saying—"

This was not funny. It was one thing to know privately that your husband went to such a place with a group of friends. It was another to have it blared all over the city. Most wouldn't believe that my husband took a client there and stayed at the bar. Some people would stop associating with us, especially parents at the children's schools. And my friends? What would they think behind my back? And Mother? She would definitely have something to say. No, this was a disaster.

Sunday could not come fast enough. The newspaper had hardly hit the driveway when I ran outside in my pyjamas to fetch it. In the dawn light I ripped open the plastic and stared at the headlines: *Top Businessmen Caught With Their Pants Down.* The list of names was right below.

"Coetzee, Coetzee," I mumbled as I ran my finger down the names. No Coetzee. Okay, this is good. This is very, very good. I started to read the other names. None of Pieter's buddies, either, but look, one of the fathers at Nicole's school. My, I had no idea.

"Your name is not in the paper!" I shouted as I ran back into the house.

Pieter immediately got onto the phone. The buddies also had no clue. Weeks later, a magistrate in church said Pieter owed him a free hunt. Pieter said fine but that he didn't know why he owed him one. Later, while aiming at a Kudu in the middle of the African bush, the magistrate said that, next time, Pieter and his buddies should be more careful. He'd had a hard time deleting their names from the list before it went to publication.

Such a man's world!

Of course Pieter had to have the mother of all toys. A Bruce Farr thirty-eight foot yacht christened *Madame Pazzazzz.*

Expensive? Bloody expensive!

We could have gone for a much smaller yacht. But the deal from Pieter's client who owned the yacht was so good, and the desire on Pieter's face so naked, that accelerated creative financing on the home front was the only solution. This yacht had just returned from Rio de Janeiro and was in superb condition. We were already members of the oh-so-British Point Yacht Club. The purchase of this yacht was the talk of the club for at least a week.

"She's to be a family yacht, the whole family can go out for a day's sail," reasoned Pieter. "We can end the day with a glass or wine, and watch the sunset on deck."

It started out so well.

Madame Pazzazzz had beautiful interiors with polished wood and a place to keep books during lazy afternoons as you suntanned on the deck. I could taste the dream as I ran my hand across her blue-striped hull. I even enrolled myself at the local sailing academy to learn how to become a qualified deckhand. My teacher was a British old timer, a perfectionist, who I aimed to please. By the end of the course I had learned how to coil the sheets (the ropes) in neat round circles, what direction port and starboard were, how to gently pass an oncoming yacht on the starboard side, how to respect others on board, how to never put your head in front of a boom, and how to be a good and tidy sailor.

Pieter said, aagh, he knew all that stuff because he had already sailed with his buddies on their yachts. He said you didn't always have to coil the ropes so neatly, that's just the bloody *souties* for you. He said he'd already sailed to East London along the wild coast of Africa in a friend's yacht so he was more than qualified. He said he would eventually take his captain's course, later, and that I should stop panicking.

Fine.

Our first family sail into the ocean was the following Sunday. The children and I were nervous but excited. I was not too confident that Pieter and I could handle the yacht ourselves, and was glad to see three of his club friends ask if they could hop on board as well. The swells off the coast of Durban were always rough so a person had to be well qualified to take a yacht out of the harbor. Also, someone on board had to have a captain's license to ask for clearance from the harbor authority. It was good to have someone like Terry, who did have the necessary license and experience.

We pulled into the wind to hoist the sails. I was so proud of myself as I pulled the sheets down and tied them neatly around the cleat. A gust of wind suddenly blew life into the sails. Gulls squawked overhead. Peter chose to stay inside the cabin while Nicky stood by her father at the wheel, watching in awe. Once out of the harbor, we could see the expanse of the wide blue ocean. Sea spray washed aboard as the yacht tilted from one side to another, surfing the waves. It was exhilarating.

"Look at the yachts, all clumped together, there, in the distance?" I asked innocently.

"Oh, that's the Sunday bay race around the buoys," replied Pieter nonchalantly. "Terry says we should join them. It will be fun."

"I thought we were going to take it calmly?"

"We are. Terry is a Springbok sailor, he's raced quite a bit—says it'll be exciting. Just sit at the back, here, behind the wheel with Nicky. Enjoy yourself. You'll be fine."

Fine?

At that precise moment the yachtsmen suddenly morphed into terrifying monsters, shouting and screaming to pull one sheet here and let loose another there. Round and round the buoys we sailed at a speed that defied logic. Books and cups went flying below deck. Peter started to cry, so I hauled him out onto the deck to sit with Nicky and me behind the wheel. We lurched high into the air, then dipped so low into the water that my knuckles were white from gripping the side rails.

We won the race.

Pieter was elated. "See, it was not so bad! Now we can all go have a drink at the club. What an exhilarating ride!"

That poor, exhausted yacht. The inside of the cabin looked as though a hurricane had struck. A winch handle was lost overboard, and a strip of wood was chipped where it had been hit by a metal object.

Another dream shattered. This was not going to be a family sailing yacht, where we could sip wine and watch the sunset. This yacht was going to become the *numero uno* racing yacht, whatever it took. *Madame Pazzazzz* became Pieter's all-consuming mistress.

I left The Boys to party upstairs in the clubhouse and returned home with the children.

I thought long into the night. I thought about who I was as a person, what it was I wanted to achieve personally. Was I brave enough to achieve something on my own? Something that could define me as an individual?

I didn't find the answers that night but I did realize that I couldn't continue to exist in the shadow of my husband or my mother. I had to step out and make a mark on the world myself, for my own good. For my own sanity.

CHAPTER TWENTY-EIGHT

1986: An explosion rocks the Durban beachfront on a crowded summer weekend. Three women are killed in front of Magoo's Bar, and sixty-nine are injured. Robert McBride of the ANC's military underground wing (MK) known as "The Spear of the Nation" is arrested and found guilty for the car bombing. Allegedly he targeted Magoo's because the MK believed security police frequented the bar. The South African Sunday Times newspaper highlights graphic pictures of glass shards and blood spattered car parts on their front page. McBride later states "It was the first time the conflict in South Africa was brought home to white people."

In another section of this liberal English newspaper British born South African journalist Jani Allen is fast becoming a rising star. Her popular interviews with celebrities increase the paper's circulation. Many of her readers however are horrified two years later when she follows up her interview with the ultra-right wing Neo-nazi AWB leader Eugene Terre'Blanche with an article where she declares that she is "impaled on the blue flames of his blow-torch eyes."

T he news of the bomb explosion on the beachfront spread like wildfire throughout the community. Discussed on the phone, at school, at work, and at dinner tables. Did you hear about it? Did you know who was killed? Did you see the damage? What did you think?

Mother phoned the minute she heard to tell us that from now on the children could not go to the beachfront at night. Period. I had to listen to a long lecture about how dangerous it was to live in Natal with Zulus fighting in the townships and why we should be moving back to Bloemfontein where nothing ever happens. Then of course I had to listen to the counterlecture from Pieter who said he was not moving back to Bloemfontein ever again. Then Michelle called from Australia, telling me she didn't care where I was, as long as I was out of South Africa. The blast was at the highly popular "Golden Mile" seafront, down the hill from her old apartment in Berea.

Earlier that year, the government abolished the much-despised centuries old pass laws. I read about it while waiting for Martha to get a prescription from the hospital for her asthma. It made me think about the time Pieter had to use one of his government connections to make sure Martha could work legally in Natal. I think I said "finally" and "bloody ridiculous law" in the same breath that day.

The country moved backward and another day we moved forward. Backward and forward like a pendulum.

The following year a South African Airway Boeing 747 plunged into the sea off Mauritius killing all people on board. I remember consoling a friend who lost a sister in the tragedy. She felt the whole accident was suspicious. Her family was making plans to move to London because they did not want to live in a country that was becoming more dangerous with each passing day.

I remember thinking that she was distraught and overreacting, because apartheid was on its way out.

That same year a group of more than fifty mostly Afrikaans-speaking businessmen, professionals, and academics flew to Dakar in North Africa to meet with the ANC. Just like that. No one stopped them or put them in jail. That was a huge step in the minds of most South Africans. Those types of people were usually arrested for "conspiring against the government." They came back and reported that although there were some tough debates with ANC leader Thabo Mbeki (past President of South Africa) and his team, they did agree on one vital issue—that South Africa had to become a nonracial democratic country as soon as possible.

President Botha made a point of condemning the group of fifty as "political terrorists," but the people continued to move forward and speak out. Even Pieter knew about the meeting before it was reported, and said it was a step forward.

My country was pretty much despised by the rest of the world. I loved my country and did not want to run away. I believed there was still hope. I was a South African girl, a sometimes English, sometimes Afrikaans, sometimes Pulani girl, but always a South African girl.

I was also a girl who never really grew up. I was not like the other more demure mothers. It was not me. I did try, but that coiled spring in my soul just wouldn't let me change.

Turning thirty was big for me. Unlike other birthdays, I wanted to give significance to this passage of time. I wanted a tent with tables dressed in yellow, and white bone china with lots of pretty flowers in the center. I wanted a string quartet playing soft music as the guests arrived. I wanted Martha and her friends to help me bake cakes and make *marmite* sandwiches and thin cucumber sandwiches cut up in triangles with no crusts. I wanted the silver teapot on the silver tray with coloured sugar crystals in the silver sugar bowl. I wanted the guests to wear hats and the champagne to flow. I wanted to be the princess inside the palace gates again for a few brief hours.

"It's a waste of money!" complained Pieter as I told him my ideas a few weeks before. "Where do you think you are going to put this tent? I'm not paying for you to have this party at some club to impress your friends!"

"I'm not going to have it at the club," I said quickly. "I'll have it in our garden. A friend of mine can supply me a small tent at a huge discount."

"Ruchel," Pieter sighed. "Have you seen what it looks like outside? Look! There are workers knitting together enough steel for a two-story building for our pool. There's no way they'll be finished by your birthday in two weeks time! Can't you see that?"

"I know. But I've already thought how to do it. Just ask the builders to make a pathway with some wooden railway sleepers so that my friends don't slip as they walk down the hill. It will be fine."

When the day came you had to see it to believe it. At the bottom of the garden, nestled between the banana and pawpaw trees, was a small white tent with tables decked out in yellow and white. A three-person string quartet I had found at the University, played their violins as my girlfriends negotiated their way down the hill between builder's rubble and dust. Pieter's staff from the office made sure they didn't slip. Martha and her friends wore starched aprons and white gloves to pour Earl Grey into Queen Anne bone china. My friends loved it. And I was a princess for the day!

"Oh God, Ruchel, you are too much!"

"Where did you find this string quartet? They are fabulous! I must have them play at my parties!"

"Cucumber sandwiches served on bone china in the middle of a war zone? Unbelievable! Wait till I tell my friends!"

I loved my thirtieth birthday party

Michelle by this time had returned from Australia—without Pietie. She found her feet again in our two-bedroom apartment at Club Mykonos with her two boys. Despite her fear of violence, she too was a South African girl, and needed to regroup on home soil.

Pietie returned to Durban as well, and became one of *Die Manne*. It was amicable with Michelle, and both still appeared at parties. Not long after, Michelle divorced Pietie, found a job as a journalist for the *Natal Mercury*, and moved into an apartment on the Berea.

"He was not motivated to do anything and eventually we just grew apart," she complained. "Sometimes I don't know how you put up with that crazy husband of yours."

That crazy husband of mine was just what I wanted. I was addicted to him. I could not imagine dancing through life with anyone other than this sensual chauvinistic beast. So if he was impossible at times, I learned to brush it off so we could continue our rhythmic dance through the jungle.

Pieter and his cohorts were a team, and the wealthier *die manne* became, the more expensive their toys became. If the whole group were Afrikaans, then they were *Die Manne*. If some Jewish and English buddies were thrown into the mix, then they were a step up from *Die Manne*—they were The Boys. Pieter straddled both teams and the metamorphoses were sometimes hysterically funny to observe.

If the sport was hunting, it was *Die Manne* with all their rough and ready outdoor activities. None of them would think twice about eating the testicles of a slaughtered *springbok* to show who was a real man. It was the ultimate intiation ceremony in my husband's Camp Pierre Hunting Club. Then they would take the skin of the buck's balls, sprinkle it with coarse salt, mold it into a cup holder, and wait for it to dry while they told *Gatiep and Meraai* and *van der Merwe* jokes to each other. That is what the *real manne* did while the dried-out ball sacks waited for someone to put cold beer cans in them.

Now, if the sport was sailing, golf, or tennis, it was usually The Boys because in Natal yuppie professionals dominated these sports.

When you were a yuppie professional you had to try and not behave too much like a hooligan.

The difference between *die manne* and *Die Manne* is best illustrated in the dance of the South African male at that biggest of all sports in South Africa, rugby. Everyone attended rugby at Kings Park Stadium or other stadiums dotted around the country. Everyone! The rougher crowd, *die manne*, sat in the bleachers with their smuggled-in brandy oranges.

Brandy oranges? Here is the recipe: Take a syringe filled with brandy and squirt it into an orange. Take same orange to the stadium where alcohol is banned, pass indifferent policemen at the ticket gate, and proceed to your assigned seat in bleachers. Before the game begins, suck on said orange until all brandy is consumed, then throw the orange at annoying fans of the opposite team or idiot players on the field. If your supply of oranges runs out during the game, steal from neighbor sitting next to you and repeat the process.

Now that Pieter was one of *Die Manne*, he was beyond such juvenile behavior. He watched the game from a private suite where cold Castle beer would be served while you played nicely with your friends. No lewd comments, no getting drunk on *spook en diesel* (rum and coke). Occasionally you would invite your lovely sweet wife to talk to the other lovely sweet wives while you alternated between Castle and Perrier; typically when the bank manager or the government officials and their lovely sweet wives were invited. That was the ritual, as predictable as the mating season.

So *Die Manne* played nicely at these rugby matches.

With his English friends, The Boys, Pieter also tried to play nicely at the yacht club but it was difficult. The music was so loud on *Madame Pazzazzz* that it frightened even the most hardened seagull. With the music came the girls, all clambering around the yacht in their tight shorts and push-up bras begging for a ride on the next sail. The Boys loved the attention. Loved the whole testosterone-filled atmosphere.

Every Wednesday night there was a bay race in the harbor followed by heavy drinking in the pub late into the night. On a workday? Oh, that was all part of the show, darling, and cousin Pietie was right up there with him, never missing a beat. Boys with their toys who could leave work after lunch to head down to the PYC, the Point Yacht Club, to prepare their yachts for the Wednesday night race.

And these nights always came with a carnival atmosphere. Bronze muscular men clambered up and down the masts while others unfurled sheets from stays on the sidewalk. Girls cajoled owners for rides. Crates of beer were carried onboard by boys still climbing the social ladder. They jockeyed for positions as crew on the fastest yachts. "No" was never part of their vocabulary.

And the owners? Preening of course. Preening! And my husband? Right in there, darling, with the best of them, on his beloved *Madame Pazzazzz* with her big fat red lips logo plastered smack on her stern. All thirty-eight feet of her lying patiently for her master to release her from her bondage.

"Hey, Willie, put the sail cover in the hatch below," Pieter shouted above the music while unknotting the ties on the mast. "Freddy, make sure we win tonight. Louie! Stop letting so many girls on the boat, china. We have enough people already." (Men called each other "china," a South African, English, Jewish-derived term for "my friend.")

"He's so sexy with those bedroom eyes. Is he married?" whispered one girl on the boat to a friend as she stared at Pieter.

"I heard something about him being married but I have never seen a wife at a Wednesday night race," replied the friend. "Maybe it's just a rumor...you should see him dance in the pub after the race. Everyone wants to dance with him."

"Does he have a girlfriend?" whispered the girl seeing an opening.

"No, he's so aloof. He just dances and drinks with his buddies, then he goes home."

A mystery man.

Pieter often begged me to come, said everyone wondered where I was on those Wednesday nights. Why didn't I go?

Because... Every Wednesday, Peter had karate lessons at 4:00 PM, Nicole had swimming practice at 6:00 PM, and both children always had homework. I was too exhausted to party till late at night with a bunch of hooligans who raced around buoys as if they were in the Indy 500. Why else? Because... if I heard another UB40 song blaring in surround sound from the cockpit, I would bury myself. Because I would be a wreck each time I saw a beer spilt on the deck or a nick cut in the wood.

Because my husband was king of the jungle and this was his time to have fun.

*   *   *

1988: *Barend Strydom, a twenty-three-year-old member of the extreme right-wing Afrikaner Weerstandbeweging (Afrikaner Resistance Movement, or AWB) and a self-confessed member of the Wit Wolwe (White Wolves) spends fifteen minutes on a Tuesday afternoon gunning down blacks in a Pretoria shopping center. Seven are killed and sixteen injured.*

I read this story in the *Natal Mercury* and then watched it unfold on SABC that night. This was huge. Huge.

Why? Firstly, because this report could not be hidden by the government. And secondly, here for the first time was an extreme right-wing party member reacting to the dismantling of apartheid in the most public of displays. How could a person be filled with so much rage so young? Were we living with a racial time bomb?

Did I know what was happening? How could I?

I had never gone into the heart of a township, never personally witnessed the violence. I read about it in the limited statistical government releases, with no human detail, in a newspaper filled with stories on violence in Iraq, China, Zimbabwe, and other places.

What I did not know about was the dark forces sent into the squatter camps and townships to snuff out activists in the still of the night. Or the death doctors who bathed in the blood of their victims then gave the victim's bones to the witchdoctors. Or the body parts of sons and daughters that were shipped off to mothers as a warning or how others were set alight with a rubber tire around their necks because they were "traitors" or "activists." Or the kangaroo courts popping up in townships now reduced to slums with no running water, sewage, or electricity.

I did not know of the thugs and gangs who took over as conservative groups pleaded for a return to order. I did not know of those in jail who were subjected to unimaginable torture. Horror was the plague of the townships.

All unreported. It never reached my ears or eyes until many years later.

So what did I read that year?

1989: *F. W. De Klerk replaces P. W. Botha as president. The general election that follows confirms that the white opinion has polarized dramatically. The National Party loses ground both to the extreme right and to the realists who think the country is headed for total destruction. Pressure to release Mandela increases tenfold. Walter Sisulu and six other ANC members are released from prison.*

The dismantling of apartheid was now on an accelerated course. Hope glimmered through the dark apocalyptic clouds.

A number of friends who had witnessed violence or death in their homes left the country they loved. Others chose to brave it out because, like me, they believed the violence would end.

I was not prepared for violence on my own doorstep, forcing me to assess my immediate situation.

I heard the stories. A friend's cousin was pulled out of her driveway only to be confronted by two black men who shot her and her two children then drove off with her car. The son of the maid of the lady next door was labeled an activist, so they slid a tire over his shoulders and burned him to death. The maid was traumatized and the lady tried to go to the police to seek justice for her but it was hopeless. The police had their hands full.

The mood at dinner tables across the country became somber. South Africa was a powder keg of anger.

The only thing missing was the match.

CHAPTER TWENTY-NINE

1989: *Increasing violence has forced the South African government to renew the state of emergency every year since 1985. From the government's perspective, the country has plunged into chaos. Of the myriad subsecurity organizations that rose during the P. W. Botha regime, one particularly evil organization is the Civilian Cooperation Bureau (CCB), which was responsible for some of the most heinous crimes. This secretive organization not only assassinates, blows up, or poisons their victims but they also murder many of their own agents who are losing their will to carry out that work. Accounts that come out many years later during an inquiry tell of bodies dumped at sea by helicopter or burnt on open fires while the agents watch and hold a picnic barbecue on another fire. These same agents also help incite the hostilities between the Xhosas and the Zulus that result in the increased violence in Natal. Some of their killings, such as the assassination of Dr David Webster, a Witwatersrand University social anthropologist, make headlines but all too many never surface.*

As one of his first tasks as President, F. W. de Klerk chooses to dismantle all the security organizations in the government that have plunged the country into a police state.

Pieter during this time was busy conquering unimaginable seas while racing around every buoy from Durban to Mauritius.

I, in turn, had realized that I had two selves at odds with each other.

The dominant self lived the life of good wife, mother, daughter, cook, hostess. The other self, periodically came to the fore in short bursts of defiance. Its patience was running thin and its desire to express itself more often became a need.

I joined a book club and became a voracious reader once again. I read books about women who had arrived in America penniless and created an empire. I read about women who lunched at the Russian Tea Room and vacationed on Martha's Vineyard. I read about women who wore Chanel suits while carrying a briefcase, and crossed oceans to make deals in boardrooms in London and New York. I read about women whose opinion mattered.

I wanted to be that woman. A woman who carried her own briefcase and made deals in the most powerful boardrooms in the world.

"That's not you!" My dear friend Michelle laughed as we walked in the mountains of Sani Pass.

"Ruchel, you're crazy," said my friend Denise. "You're the wife of this illustrious architect, Pieter Coetzee. You, my friend, look after your husband and your children and attend frivolous luncheons and fashions shows with yours truly."

It was true. I did attend frivolous Ladies' Day events. I did dress up in Ascot finery and sip Earl Grey with Denise and her husband at their suite at the Durban July (think Kentucky Derby) each year. I made the society pages—which delighted Mother no end—and participated on the boards at the schools. I made sure my children excelled and helped my husband climb further up the ladder.

I simply needed more.

Denise was not convinced. "Can you imagine if I said to my husband that I was going to open a business making floral arrangements? It's my hobby. He would think I had lost it."

"Rubbish!" I replied. "He would be proud of you, you are so talented. Remember how the editor loved the flowers you arranged for me when they came to shoot my house for *Femina* magazine? The house looks great now that its finished, but the photos would never have come out so well without your arrangements. They even credited you with a caption beside the photo, 'Flowers by Denise Jonas'. I mean, that is an honor."

"I know," said Denise, "My husband's comment was, 'That's nice.' Nice. Not, 'you should open up a floral shop.' Our husbands assume our entire life should never be more than taking care of them, family responsibilities, and social events. And when would you have the time? You are dreaming!"

"No, I am not!" I replied. "One day I will have a company of my own. I will call it Successful Images. I'll travel to New York and

London with my briefcase and have meetings in big boardrooms. Look, I even know what my logo will look like." I drew an "S" and an "I" to look like a dollar sign but with curves that looked like a woman dancing.

"Right!" laughed Denise. "I can just see your husband's face! Come my friend, let's go back before we are missed."

The dream was firmly planted in my mind. One day I would be that woman. Don't ask me what I was going to do or say in those boardrooms. The vision of me with a briefcase was revolutionary enough. All I knew was that I would one day have this company.

*   *   *

"Martha!" called Nicole from the top floor. "Martha, can you come upstairs and help me with my Zulu homework, please?"

"Nicky, Martha has her church meeting tonight and I have to go to book club," I called out from downstairs. "See if daddy can help you when he gets home."

"*Hauw*!" laughed Martha. "The *baas* helping Nicky with the Zulu homework while the madam is out? No, not good. Nicky, bring your homework to my room. I will help you while I am setting out the tea cups for my meeting."

"Can I have some of your *pap*?" Nicky asked in a much more upbeat tone. Nothing pleased her more than to sit in Martha's lounge and eat *pap* while Martha solved all her worldly problems. After all, there were secrets that needed discussion and analysis. Secrets that would never leave the safety of Martha's walls.

"Martha! Martha! I want some banana cake!" came a voice from outside.

"Okay, my little man," cooed Martha, wrapping her arms around Peter as he ran into the kitchen. "Wash your hands and Martha will cut you some cake."

"I found more bananas on the trees. Samson says we have to wait until they turn yellow before we can use them for banana cake," Peter continued from the sink.

"I better tell Samson to check for snakes around those trees. I am sure the *boomslang* is still slithering around there somewhere. I have never seen madam scream so much," Martha laughed.

"If you hadn't swept the snake outside with your broom, Martha, I would still be standing on the bed screaming. Where is Solomon, by the way? I haven't seen him all day."

"Still trying to sober up," replied Martha. "*Baas* says the people at the boat thought he was dead. *Baas* says the people at the boat called the ambulance when they found Solomon lying on *baas'* boat but *baas* just threw a bucket of water on him and brought him home this morning. *Baas* says he told Solomon to just clean the boat and not drink the beer left over from the races but Solomon didn't listen to *baas*. *Baas* was very cross this morning."

"And he moans because I go to book club once a month for a couple of hours."

"*Baas* is jealous and thinks that madam will listen to the other madams and not to *baas*," replied Martha as she popped another batch of banana loaves in the oven.

"Ridiculous!"

"Go and enjoy yourself at book club, Madam." Martha handed me a cup of tea. "Don't worry about *baas*. I made curry stew this morning with the meat from the hunting. *Baas* always calms down when he eats my curry stew."

"Bless you, Martha," I replied. I took a much needed sip of her tea. "I don't know what I would do without you."

Tea featured big in our household. It soothed frayed nerves. Peter consumed tea by the gallon while reading *Asterix* on his bed. Nicky served it to her dolls and then for her friends. It was *Rooibos* tea, red bush tea, and shouted Africa each time you took a sip.

Martha was the force that kept the sanity in the house. She was the light as our ships pulled into harbor at night. Martha and her *Rooibos* tea were my rock.

* * *

"Madam!" called Martha from the top of the stairs the next week. "Phone! Sounds like the *baas* that goes hunting with our *baas*."

"Tell him that he is coming home at seven tonight," I shouted from the kitchen, where I was slicing apples for Peter.

"He wants to speak to you," replied Martha, waving her hand frantically from the top of the stairs for me to hurry up.

"Hello?" I said.

"Hello, *Mev.* Coetzee? *Dit is Fanie, die bankbestuurder hier* [the bank manager]."

"Oh hello, Fanie, please call me Ruchel. May I give my husband a message or tell him to phone you?"

"Oh no!" he said. "I actually wanted to speak with you..."

Oh?" I said. Why in heaven's name would Fanie the bank manager call me except to complain about my crazy hooligan.

"...to come to a meeting," Fanie was saying.

"Pardon me, Fanie, what did you say? Pieter has to come to a meeting?"

"No, I would like you to come to a meeting at the Durban Club next Tuesday at twelve noon if you can spare the time."

There were several things wrong with this picture.

First, no wife attended a meeting by herself with a bank manager. Second, no woman ever attended a meeting at the Durban Club. Woman weren't even allowed in the front door. If they had to be there, they had to enter from the garage at the back. Third, Pieter would view this very suspiciously.

"Fanie insists on having you there," said an incredulous Pieter as he hung up the telephone. "Heaven only knows why. The rest are all businessmen. Make sure you don't say anything embarrassing!"

I was determined to make an impression. Dressed in a new creatively-financed business suit, I pulled up to the front of the Durban Club, handed the keys to the valet, and walked up the marble stairs as if I belonged there. At the top of the entranceway stood an expressionless Indian doorman, in a formal white uniform with white gloves and a turban.

"Madam, how can I help you? This is a gentleman's club. Are you sure you are in the right place?"

I was now the heroine of my own story, wearing a Chanel suit, rising to the occasion. "I have a meeting in Room 202 with the bank manager and I need to be there now. Could you show me to Room 202 please?" I replied imperiously.

The door to Room 202 opened and before me sat a table full of buttoned-up businessmen talking animatedly to each other. I wondered for a second if I was indeed in the correct place. The room instantly became quiet as all eyes turned to the door. I could read what they were thinking, 'What on earth is this woman doing here?' I searched for the bank manager's face.

"Welcome, *Mev.* Coetzee!" boomed Fanie as he walked up and shook my hand. "*Manne*, this is *Mev.* Coetzee. She will add a woman's perspective to the meeting today," he announced.

He led me to a vacant seat at the polished boardroom table. I greeted one of Pieter's colleagues who had been at our house for dinner with his wife, and then turned to introduce myself to the two men sitting on either side of me. On the table were notepads, bank leaflets, pitchers of water, and pens imprinted with the bank logo. Everyone shifted uncomfortably in their chairs as the atmosphere changed from *Die Manne* to serious businessman.

I introduced myself as Ruchel Coetzee, director of Pieter Coetzee Architects. I *was* my husband's business partner even if he never acknowledged it.

"The reason why I have asked all of you here today," said the bank manager, "is to gain feedback from our valued clients regarding customer satisfaction at the bank. I would like to invite some suggestions from all of you on how to improve our service to our clients."

When it came time to discuss ideas for improvement, there was much squirming in chairs because no one wanted to express an honest opinion in front of the bank manager. No one except yours truly, who had everything to say and nothing to lose. After all, if I sounded like an idiot, the men and Pieter would put it down to me just being a woman.

"Well, first of all," I began. All heads were instantly turned in my direction. "Long lines at the tellers are inexcusable. A better, faster system should be implemented. For instance, those who are only making withdrawals or a few deposits should have an express line with a sign that is posted in all three languages—English, Afrikaans, and Zulu. Then there are certain behavioral skills and etiquette that could help your tellers better serve the client. This would also enhance the experience of going to the bank. It should be a pleasure not a chore to do business with your bank. Word of mouth is a very strong marketing tool. Clients who feel they are at a community bank will encourage their friends to open accounts."

I felt strangely empowered as people nodded their heads and offered additional suggestions to my remarks. After the meeting concluded, Fanie asked to speak with me.

"Ruchel," he said, as we were now on a first-name basis, "I found your comments very valuable today. I would like you to come to some internal meetings over the next few weeks to talk to the staff about these behavioral skills, if you have the time."

"Guess what!" I shouted as Pieter walked through the front door that evening. "Fanie said I made a very valuable contribution at today's meeting and wants me to give some lectures to his staff over the next few weeks."

"I've already spoken to Fanie," Pieter replied. "End of the story."

How did I reply?

With silence. Subject closed.

I delivered the lectures and answered questions from staff at various meetings, for which the bank was very grateful. That gave me new confidence in myself. But dreams need lots of encouragement, and a burning desire to become real. For now, I returned to what made Pieter comfortable—the life of wife, mother, housewife, and business partner. My other self had to have patience.

I returned to real estate sales in the mornings to help Pieter locate new land deals. He was rapidly turning into a property developer. The dream of carrying my briefcase around the world was temporarily shelved. In my heart I knew a time would come to revive it. Soon.

The time was just not now.

CHAPTER THIRTY

1990: *President F. W. De Klerk surprises most South Africans by announcing the legalization of the ANC and the unconditional release of Nelson Mandela. Mandela, who has been living in a house within the prison walls of Robben Island for the past two years, takes his wife Winnie's hand and walks to freedom on February 11. He emerges through the gates to jubilation and dancing by millions of people across the nation and the world. The Sunday Times prints a picture of Mandela and De Klerk standing together. It is the first picture of Mandela that South Africans have seen since 1963.*

Pieter and I watched de Klerk as he mounted the podium on February 2, 1990, to give his live television address. We were rooting for him to make the changes that would end apartheid. Pieter had liked him from the moment he and his buddies threw him into the pool those many years before. Nothing was more exciting than listening to that speech as it happened.

De Klerk ends the ban on the ANC, the PAC, and the SACP, and provides amnesty to those serving prison sentences because they were members of these groups. That was the death knell for apartheid. That meant, that meant...

Yes! Mandela would be released from jail!

Ke hantle! Well done! High fives, hugs, and jubilation not only in our home but also across the world.

Not everyone expressed joy.

Not everyone agreed with Bishop Desmond Tutu who, immediately after the speech, said De Klerk *"took my breath away."* Eugene Terre'Blanche, the fierce leader of the quasi-military, extreme right-wing AWB, said incredulously, *"Just don't tell me that. No, oh no, it can't be true."* Chief Mangasothu Buthelezi was also not overjoyed; his Inkatha party stepped up their fighting with the UDF in the townships in KwaZulu, Natal. And therein lay the problem. On one side there were the ultra-right-wing Afrikaners, many of whom were in the police force or in their own little armies, and on the other side were the unhappy and proud Zulus. Guns and spears raised high in the air as the land bubbled and boiled with trouble. Still, the talks between the government and the ANC continued in earnest throughout that year.

*   *   *

The sense of national hope in 1990 echoed in our home as well.

Together with two of his quantity surveyor buddies, Pieter bought an office building in Sherwood, just behind the Berea. His workload for low-cost housing projects was increasing and the offices had to be expanded. Additional Indian staff were hired, and that meant the stakes for the best curry went way up. Pieter created a competition among the wives of his staff as to who made the best curry. Each Friday a new dish was brought to the office. He was in curry heaven with all the *breyani*, jackfruit curry, *samoosas*, and *bunny chows*.

Only my husband.

"Ruchel! Have you seen my Kevlar jacket? Freddy says the seas might be rougher this year. We have to pack mostly wet gear for this race. Martha! Bring me my gray tracksuit and the Madame Pazzazzz T-shirts. Ruchel! Where are you?" Pieter began pulling clothes from his closet onto the floor.

"I'm here, I'm here!" I called from downstairs.

"I still have to pick up the beer and tin food at the store. See what I need here and put it in my bag. Solomon, fetch the extra sail in the garage and put it in my car!"

"Dad, are you going to win this time?" asked Peter through all the commotion.

"Yes, my boy! Dad is going to win this time. Mommy will bring you and your sister to the harbor when I get back. You can take the trophy to school to show your friends."

"Make sure you sail safely!" I cautioned, dragging T-shirts and tog bag into the bedroom. "I don't want what happened to the other boat a few years ago!"

"What happened, ma?" asked our astute daughter. She would go into an immediate panic at any sign of danger to her family.

A few years back the *Rubicon* was not so lucky to survive this *Vasco da Gama* yacht race that stretched from Durban to East London. Other yachts had seen her signaling for help in the far distance and even heard her crew's mayday call on channel 6. But the treacherous sixty-foot waves triumphed that night, tossing the small yacht high into the air before opening their jaws to swallow it whole. The yacht and her crew disappeared with not a trace forever.

"It got a little lost, Nicky, and they couldn't complete the race," I replied quickly.

"Aagh, your father is tough and strong like this, my sweetheart!" Pieter gave his daughter a huge big bear hug. "Your mother always panics for nothing. When I get back with the trophy we can all celebrate together on the boat! Bring some of your friends with you," he smiled, sneaking a mischievous wink at me.

The animal magnetism that coursed through my husband's body was hard to ignore. I watched from the dock as his muscular arms tidied the sheets on the boom, readying his beloved mistress for the grueling race. His eyes were dancing in the wind and at that moment all I wanted to do amid the festive atmosphere was drag him down into the cockpit and make passionate love to him. He had a powerful effect that I am sure spilled over to those watching from the sidelines. He was hard to ignore and difficult to resist.

My wild and playful lion king.

And no matter the drama, no matter the arguments, when *Madame Pazzazzz* with her raucous crew set sail out of the harbor that day all I could do was get down on my knees and pray that God would return him back safely to me.

It was, as Freddy had predicted, a treacherous storm.

The stretch of coast they sailed that night was called the wild coast because of the way the plates under the ocean threw the waves up in a vicious mass each time they shifted.

Reports from the yacht club were not good. Not good at all. Some of the yachts gave up half way and returned to Durban broken and defeated. I hung onto every word that was posted on the bulletin board at the clubhouse, pressed exhausted sailors for information as they returned from the jetty. I had no sleep that night. I cursed, I cried,

I prayed, and I panicked. What if? What if he met the same fate as the *Rubicon*? I can't do without that crazy idiot. Oh God! Please return him safely to me. Please God!

The phone rang at two in the morning on the second day of the nail-biting nightmare.

Oh God, no, don't let it be bad. I picked up the receiver. "Hello? Hello?"

Static noise.

"Hello—Piet—is that you?"

"We won! We won! We took line honors. We won!" screamed Pieter over the phone from East London.

"I am going to strangle you!" I cried as I thanked God for letting me hear his voice again.

I was in a desert without him, a plant left out to dry under the scorching sun. He quenched my thirst.

We traveled to Cape Town to snap up two vacant properties at the top of Bantry Bay. That was a coup. The owner was a friend of Pieter's from university. Our plans were to move to Cape Town once Nicky had finished school in four years.

Pieter was ready to move to the Cape. Why? Because in his head he was already living in his new architectural creation on the rocks overlooking the Atlantic Ocean. Every design that came to fruition was like an artist's work, always needing another brushstroke added here or there. Most of the times the paint was hardly dry and another empty canvas appeared on the back of a napkin. The napkin pencil marks morphed into working drawings in the flash of an eye. So just as I was about to enjoy freshly baked scones and an early morning sunrise over the Indian Ocean, while relaxing on the patio with my family surrounding me in my beautiful La Lucia home, Pieter was ready to build the next masterpiece.

We even placed Peter's name down at Bishops, the exclusive all-boys private school on the foothills of Table Mountain. Thinking toward retirement, we bought a beachfront property in Betty's Bay, just down the coast on the other side of Hermanus. The plan was to use the beach house to collect seashells on the seashore while eating *perlemoen* (abalone) under the African stars. We had it all mapped out, plotted, and planned as we celebrated the enormous progress our country had made that year.

That year, 1990, was also the year we made our first trip overseas with the children. It was the first time Pieter and the children had stepped out of their country, six weeks in June and July that included a week in Paris, a week at Disney World, three weeks taking in Miami, the Cayman Islands, New Orleans, Washington, and New York, and then a final week in London before heading home again.

Of course, my husband was the most childlike of all the children.

We hardly slept. In Paris we caught a taxicab together with a Frenchman who invited us to Parliament. How strange to hear a female politician moan about all the North Africans coming into France and how measures should be taken to curb the influx. At Disney World I was reduced to jockeying for a coveted autograph from the Ninja Turtles, which I finally obtained to the delight of my son. He himself, too exhausted to traipse through the Louvre, hardly slept at Disney. In the Cayman Islands Nicky and her father were brave enough to enter a sunken ship during a night dive and talk to each other with their masks off in an air pocket in one of the cabins. I was way too scared and just floated outside waiting for them to come out.

In New Orleans I left Pieter on his own to buy camera equipment because he said it was cheaper in America, but I nearly killed him (what's new) when I learned he had spent a small fortune in one of those "going out of business" stores. He also realized he had been royally screwed when he reached Washington and compared prices in a local Wal-Mart we stumbled across.

In Washington, the White House was smaller than I expected, and we literally ran through all the must-sees. I don't know why we tourists do that. Can't we just be satisfied with exploring one or two places fully and leave the rest for another time? No. At least, not the Coetzee family. We had to see everything in two days. Everything!

But New York was different. It was my kind of town.

It was my birthday when we arrived so when Pieter asked me what I wanted, I told him I'd like to walk down Fifth Avenue alone and could he please take the children to Central Park and a movie. He thought the request strange but I promised to be back in time for a special dinner.

Oh the joy!

My other self gasped for air.

We enjoyed London as if it were the first time, taking in shows watching the changing of the Guard. We even saw Denise and her family at the Tower of London, making it truly feel like a small world.

But a sense of foreboding began to overtake me. I couldn't shake it off. I wondered if everything at home was okay.

"Jenny, have you heard from Ruchel?" Mother asked on the phone to my sister in Johannesburg.

"Ma, you ask me this question every three days," she sighed. "I'm sure they're fine. Aren't they due back at the end of this week?"

"Jenny, you aren't lying to me are you?" Mother persisted.

"Ma, why would I lie to you?"

"Ever since Peter's accident I never know if you children are keeping things from me. I had this terrible dream last night. The same kind of dream I had before Gussie died, except this time Ruchel was in the dream. Find out what hotel they are staying at in London?"

"Ma, you're panicking for nothing."

Mother could not sleep. The panic in her bones had set in so that even Father and Evelyn were at a loss to calm her. Mother had extremely keen intuition, and was often correct in her predictions, as if the spirits of past relatives warned her of impending catastrophes.

"I think I will phone Michelle in Durban to find out if she knows Ruchel's travel agent," said Mother to Evelyn as she walked to the phone.

As if on cue, the phone rang. Mother's heart dropped to the floor because she knew immediately it wasn't something she wanted to hear.

"Hello, hello!" Mother answered.

"Shirley, this is Pietie from Durban here. I am afraid I have some bad news—"

"Oh God!" Mother screamed. "Is it Ruchel? Who died, who died?"

CHAPTER THIRTY-ONE

1990: *A right-wing AWB member, angry because of a fallen comrade, exacts revenge by firing his machine gun into a local taxi bus carrying a dozen commuters back to the township. Another AWB member promises to "neuk al die bliksemse swart kaffirs" (kill all the bloody blacks) if they come anywhere near his home or family. Still another AWB member goes on a Sunday drive into the area near a township and takes random potshots at anyone who he decides needs to be killed. A gang of black tsotsis crawls stealthily in the middle of the night through the long grass up to a farmhouse nestled against a small hill. They throw a knife in the barking dog to silence him. Lights are switched on by the elderly white couple inside the house as they peer anxiously out their window. Too late. The gang is already on the porch and through the door. Five men rape the wife while they force the husband to watch. Then both are tied to the bedpost before their throats are slit by the leader. The old couple is left to bleed to death as the gang members walk out with all their possessions.*

Martha. Wonderfully kind hearted and loving Martha had died during an asthma attack in her room. She died two days before we were due to arrive back home.

"How?" I screamed as Mother finally found us in our hotel room in London. "Where was Samson? Oh God, why? This can't be happening. I bought her all these presents. Chose each one carefully because I knew she would be excited to get them. And now she is gone. Gone because no one was there to help. Samson was probably too drunk to hear her fighting for her last breath. And I wasn't there to help her. Oh God, why?"

"I know, it's so sad, so sad," replied Mother tearfully. "I'm flying up to Durban tomorrow to take care of the body, which has to be

shipped back to Kimberley to her family. I've already made all the
arrangements and will fetch you at the airport on Tuesday."

The flight back home was somber.

The children cried all the way back and Pieter and I just sat
silently. Visions of Martha swirled in my head. Martha in her long
blue, carefully ironed church dress walking proudly up the driveway.
Martha in the kitchen taking banana bread out of the oven, Martha
showing Pieter how to cook venison by first soaking it in vinegar,
Martha hugging Peter or whispering a secret to Nicky. Martha, my
friend, my confidant, my calm. Memories collided as tears rolled
down my cheeks.

Sala hantle, Martha. Pelo ea ka e topile. Goodbye, Martha. My
heart is sore.

Mother in her usual take-charge fashion immediately set about
employing one of Martha's friends, Ruby. Ruby was a tall timid Zulu
who had sometimes helped Martha with the housework and who
was currently unemployed. She happily agreed and Mother made
sure she knew exactly how to use which buckets and which cloths for
which kind of cleaning. Some things never change. Ruby settled in
immediately with the family but she never replaced that boisterous
beacon of light we loved so much.

The sorrow didn't end there. Pieter soon received a call from
home to say his father had suddenly died of a heart attack. We all
flew back to Postmasburg where their tears awaited our tears as we all
tried to comfort each other.

"He was so young and handsome," whispered one elderly lady
as we stood around the grave in the dry veld. "Only fifty-eight, you
know."

The Dominee stood under the sparse acacia tree beside the grave
reading from the Bible, dust whirling around his polished black shoes.
Freshly cut flowers were laid about on the ground.

"I feel so sorry for poor Mabel, she really loved her husband,"
said the old lady.

"I know. The poor children as well, especially the younger one,"
whispered another. "Such a shame."

Pieter was outwardly strong, but griefstricken, and often went for
walks in the veld to be alone with his thoughts. Losing a brother and

now his father was hard to bear. I tried to comfort him but I could not fully grasp the pain that drove my brave lion to solitude.

Our country looked strangely different after traveling. Questions arose that never before had been asked. Why did we barricade ourselves in our homes when homes in America had no dividing walls? Why did we look over our shoulders every time we walked into a store or climbed into our cars, when in America we did not even feel scared? And the trash. In America there was no trash. People vacuumed the streets! Amazing! We took photographs to show at home how the Americans lived. Clean, with not a mound of trash in sight.

But traveling overseas does that to you, makes you compare how you live, makes you wonder whether living in a war zone is normal or not. Time faded our memories of other countries, but the questions never left us.

Time is also terrific healer and life simply has to go on.

Pieter became involved with a consortium of colleagues to develop a multiple-unit holiday resort on the coast of Natal that would rival the best in both design and consideration for the environment. The two-story wooden chalets would have three bedrooms and an expansive balcony overlooking the crashing waves. It was a deal that would accelerate our plans to move to the Cape, where our hearts lay.

Why the Cape? Anyone who has been to Cape Town and its environs would never ask that question.

The Cape was the crown jewel of Africa, with its majestic Table Mountain sweeping down to the icy blue waters of the Atlantic Ocean. The Cape danced to a beat so different, so vibrant, so magical that anywhere else paled in comparison

So we had a plan, all laid out, as we worked toward our inevitable move to the Cape.

Nicole in the meantime entered her teenage years. With that came the parties with boys from the private schools of Michaelhouse and Hilton in the Natal midlands. My daughter, who had a better and less angst-filled teenage life than yours truly, received numerous love letters from smitten teenage boys. She was a vibrant and popular member of the tightly knit group of girls whose brothers attended these schools. They did everything together: played tennis together, went to weekend holiday cottages with one of the parents together, listened to music in each other's homes together, and generally never left the cocoon of each other's friendship. She came home once with a hickey, which almost gave Pieter a heart attack, but overall it was innocent teenage fun. Life was the high and drugs were never part of the picture.

Sometimes we were drawn into the oh-so-English activities, such as the annual Michaelhouse and Hilton rugby match. This was a day that made you think you were sitting in England.

"You *souties* have no sophistication!" Pieter laughed.

"What does a dutchman know about sophistication!" Carole's husband laughed as he grabbed one of the bottles.

"Just listen to those idiots!" said Denise as she sat out the knives and forks on the foldout picnic table. "You would think they are children the way they act!"

"Men are children—look at those lunatics in the AWB!" bemoaned Carole between shouts of "go Michaelhouse!"

"I know," I replied. "Who does this Terre'Blanche think he is, starting that little army with those brute bullies of his? Can't they just accept that apartheid is dead and gone?"

"Oh, didn't you hear?" interjected Denise, who was now slicing a lemon pie. "There are these right-wing Afrikaners who want their own state. I think they have designated a spot near where your husband comes from. They call it Orania or something like that."

"Near Postmasburg?" I asked in disbelief.

"It is further up from Postmasburg, near the Kalahari Desert," Pieter said, slicing himself another piece of *biltong*. "They want an area where the whites will run the town and where no blacks can live. Blacks, if they want, can only work there."

"And that's going to happen?" I asked, even more amazed.

"Not as far as I know," said Pieter, who was now more interested in the score on the field and drinking champagne with The Boys.

Here you had the moderate right-wingers who thought, okay, if the government wants to give the country to the blacks, then at least they can carve us a piece of land so we can barricade ourselves within its all-white walls. Militant right-wingers like the AWB were hellbent on fighting to the end no matter the consequences. To most rural right-wing whites, De Klerk was the most hated public figure in South Africa.

President de Klerk in the meantime had to contend not only with the threats of the AWB but also with continued attacks from the media.

So De Klerk began to purge suspected right-wing militants from the police force while continuing talks between his government and the leaders of the other parties. At the Convention for a Democratic South Africa (known as the Codesa talks), a declaration of intent was signed for a new democratic order in South Africa. Absent from this meeting were not only the right-wing parties but also Chief Buthelezi with his Inkatha Party and the head of the militant Pan-Africanist Congress. Still, Mandela and De Klerk forged ahead, a bold and precarious move considering all the opposition from centuries of distrust and hatred. Russian roulette? Almost.

De Klerk took another gamble by calling a referendum in early 1992. In a turnout of almost eighty percent of registered whites, nearly sixty-nine percent voted "yes" for De Klerk to continue his quest for a more democratic South Africa. The people had spoken, us included, and had given the government the green light.

*   *   *

Energized by the results of the referendum, we forged ahead with our plans.

We spent the summer on Clifton Beach in Cape Town.

If life could only stop for a moment for us to reflect on what we have, we could enjoy it even more. But life doesn't permit the luxury of that reflection. Only time does and then it's often too late, especially in a country plunging ever deeper down a dark ravine.

*   *   *

The situation in the townships was worsening, especially in the Transvaal and KwaZulu, Natal. Rivalries between local activists heated to a boiling point. Counteraccusations of being a traitor immediately called for a brutal death. Methods of killing took many forms: burning tires, stabbing, slicing the head off, shooting, stoning, poisoning, and more. Multiply that by the hundreds of townships across the country.

No one could come to a consensus. One tribe hated another tribe and neither thought the other worthy of more power than the next. Even on commuter trains, gangs would board at one station, stab and kill a few innocent passengers, then hop off at the next station. Police records show that over a three-year period, more than six hundred people died and another fourteen hundred were injured just on trains alone. No place was safe. There were even taxi wars, in which one taxi owner would kill another over territory disputes. More innocent adults and children died in those battles.

Mandela tried to create a peaceful, unified front against the government but some, like the general secretary of the PAC, encouraged the violence. Looting of rural shops and farms increased tenfold, and it became an everyday occurrence to rape or beat someone to death, black or white.

*   *   *

Trying to keep a positive attitude proved challenging.

One morning I was at Pieter's office picking up plans to take to the local authority when one of his vendors stopped me outside by my car to chat.

"This friend of mine had quite the experience yesterday morning, you know," he responded.

"What happened?" I asked, curious.

"Well, he left for work early yesterday but an hour later he remembered he had left something behind. So he drove home again. When he arrived he saw that his front door was half open. He could swear he had closed it that morning, so he took his gun out of the car and proceeded cautiously to the front door."

"Took his gun out of the car?" I asked incredulously. "Who carries a gun in their car?"

"Don't you carry a gun in your car? You should because you never know when you are going to be attacked," he replied.

"Oh, that's nonsense," I argued, forgetting my own incident for a moment. "Anyway, your friend went to the door and then what?"

"Well, as he opened his front door he saw two black men dismantling his TV set. One of them turned around with a gun in his hand but before he could pull the trigger my friend shot the guy dead in his living room."

"Shot him dead?" I asked, horrified.

"Well, my friend was not just going to stand there while the black man shot him," he replied, probably thinking you couldn't find a dumber blond at that moment.

"So what happened to the other man?" I asked.

"He ran into the bathroom and locked the door. My friend phoned the police while aiming his gun at the bathroom door. The police arrived, handcuffed the guy, and put him in the back of the van."

"Wow," I said. "I don't know how I would have reacted."

"Oh, that's not the end," said the vendor. "Wait till you hear the rest. While my friend was thanking the policeman, the captured black man in the back of the van turned to him through the bars and said, 'I know where you live. We will come and get you later.'"

"And so?" I asked.

"Well, the jails are so overcrowded and the police would have probably released this man in a week, so my friend just shot him point blank in the van. Dead. Just like that."

"He couldn't do that!" I said, even more horrified.

"Of course he could," said the vendor. "He knew the guy would come and kill him at a later time. I'd do the same. The policeman had a fit and dragged the dead man back into the house because you're only allowed to shoot a man if he's on your property. After that the policeman phoned for backup to report the crime and to fetch the two bodies."

That made me wonder what kind of wild country I was living in.

A few weeks later after I dropped the children off at school, I raced back toward La Lucia realizing I forgot the minutes to a meeting I was attending. In between I had to pick up some plans for Pieter. It was easy to swing by the house to pick up my minutes before returning to the Berea, but it was a lot of driving. I decided that it wasn't worth the detour to go home.

I had just arrived at Pieter's office to drop off the plans when I saw him running out the door.

"Something has happened at the house!" he shouted.

The entire house was ransacked. Mattresses were torn, drawers were wide open, and broken glass lay everywhere. The robbers had tried to carry everything out.

"Where's Ruby?" I panicked. "Ruby! Ruby!" I shouted while Pieter went through each room assessing the damage.

"Ruchel, I found her!" called Pieter from our dressing room. "She's tied up in the wardrobe shaking and bleeding from a head wound. Fetch some bandages!"

"Madam!" she cried as Pieter untied her. "The *tsotsies* came with guns. Lots of them and they hit me over the head. I am scared, Madam, very scared, they will come back to kill us!"

While I comforted Ruby, Pieter called from downstairs in the living room.

"They took the videotapes of the children growing up and of our vacations. I don't like that. Even the children's photos are missing. What would they do with photographs?"

"Not good, Madam," cried Ruby. "Not good. They come back for the children! Witchdoctors want the children for *muti*!"

I did not even pause to ponder that I would likely have been killed had I stopped back at the house when I was fetching the plans. That my children's safety was now endangered superseded all other thoughts.

"They have our house marked!" I told Pieter while I looked through my drawers to find what little jewelry they might have left. None.

The robbers did not place value on art, and our vast collection of South African art remained intact on the walls.

Pieter said, "We'll sell and move to a smaller house on the Berea until we move to Cape Town in two years. This house is becoming an invitation for robbers because it's impossible to secure properly. Where's Samson, Ruby?"

*   *   *

Our beautiful and avant-garde house was not long on the market before being snapped up by an Afrikaans family from out of town. It was a painful time for all of us, especially Pieter, as the house was his dream, built with his sweat and tears. He was uncharacteristically quiet as he sat in the cellar below the deck contemplating how to move all the wine we had accumulated.

"I am going to miss this house and my pool and my wine cellar," he sighed. Hundreds of bottles of South African wine lay in their special brick wine holders in the circular room. "The buyer wants the old street lamp we found in Cape Town. Remember how we bargained with the guy to buy it? You know, I never really got to enjoy the full area of my studio and wine cellar below the pool because there was never enough time to do what I planned to do. Never enough time to just paint and listen to my music with a good bottle of Cabernet beside me. Never enough time."

I had mixed emotions. I was sad because the house had finally reached its potential, and because it held many happy memories, but the safety of our family was far more important. I was becoming less and less attached to material possessions. The only exceptions were the huge canvas artworks that evoked a different emotion each time I passed from one room to another.

Samson, more remorseful than ever after we had located him passed out in his bedroom the morning of the robbery, sprang into action and helped with the enormous task of packing everything up.

We bought a small three-bedroom sixties-style Durban house in the ritzy part of the Berea, just above Mentone Road and down the street from the children's schools. It was a question of location, location, location and Pieter immediately set about drawing plans to tear the house down and build anew. Of course, I just nodded and said fine as long as we could get a contractor from the start. In my heart I knew not much would happen if we were going to move to the Cape in two years' time. I wasn't up to the dust and chaos of renovation after the previous trauma. Gone were the days when we could sleep with no front door for a month.

Three months after we moved in we all flew to Europe to ski in Verbier, Switzerland, for two weeks. The past few months had been exhausting and we felt the children's minds needed relief from such constant drama. Now, we had never skied before because South Africa gets hardly any snow and no ski slopes exist anywhere in the country.

We flew back questioning once more whether we were wise to continue living in such a country when many of our friends were leaving. Our answer was the same. We were South Africans and our soul was attached to the soil. Why would we leave?

"Phone for you, madam!" called Ruby from the bedroom, "The madam's mother is on the phone. She says you must hurry!"

"What's wrong, ma?"

"Oh it is so sad, so sad," Mother was in a state. "Poor Uncle Dudley. His son was killed in the township this morning!"

"What was his son doing in the township?" I hadn't had much contact with them since I still very young.

"He was in the police force and his unit was called into the township to quell the violence when a bullet hit him right in the head. The funeral is tomorrow. You have to send flowers."

"That is too terrible," I replied sadly. "What did daddy say?"

"Your father just walks around shaking his head. He says you can't be driving around at night like you do. Natal is as violent as the Transvaal and you might as well kill your father and myself if you continue driving by yourself at night."

Well, if the angst of the country was not bad enough!

But my parents were not far off. It was no longer safe for a woman to drive alone at night. Stories abounded about women who stopped at traffic lights only to find a gun pointed at them. Some were lucky to escape with no car while others were killed and left on the side of the road. And the threat of violence was not restricted to certain spots. It happened randomly—in a town, a suburb, a driveway.

A few months later we woke up to the glaring headlines of the assassination of the charismatic SACP leader, Chris Hani. We read that he died in a hail of bullets as he entered the front door of his home in Johannesburg, while clutching a newspaper. Further down the column we learned how his fifteen-year-old daughter opened the front door, saw her father bleeding on the floor, and collapsed in hysteria over his lifeless body. "'It was pitiful. The child was wailing. I quickly took her away from the sight of her dead father bleeding all over the patio,'" said the neighbor, who did not want to be named for fear of reprisals..."

It was a shock but not a surprise. The right wingers had long threatened to strike down any communist making inroads in the country. Police discovered that the order to kill had come from one of the more prominent Conservative Party members, Clive Derby-

Lewis. That did come as a surprise, because he was not some militant renegade AWB but a respected member of the community. It meant that the virulent hatred of the right had seeped into more souls than we thought possible. Was this going to be an all-out war?

It certainly seemed like war in parts of the country. After Hani's death, black youths ran into the central commercial district of Johannesburg, pillaging the stores in protest. Anyone who happened to be walking downtown that day was caught in the crossfire between the rioters and the police. Five people were killed and two hundred fifty injured that morning.

The anger did not stop there. Eight days after the assassination, gunmen in a car went on a rampage, shooting innocent passersby in the street. Nineteen people were killed. The next day, during the funeral of Hani at a stadium in downtown Johannesburg, an angry mob burned two men to death in their homes and set several other homes on fire. Even family pets were torched alive.

Attack after attack occurred across the country. Police could not keep up. They were running out of paper just to log the reports.

Then the chanting began.

Kill the Boers! Kill the farmers!

There were even more reports of farmers and their families being killed.

Kill the Boers! Kill the farmers!

We were all horrified at this new call for the killing of Boer farmers. It was especially disturbing considering the odds: eighty-twenty in favor of the black population. Granted, the chanting came from a small minority but Zimbabwe sat on our doorstep. Their history of killings was not comforting.

"I'm having trouble guarding one of my developments under construction," Pieter began complaining. "Material is starting to disappear and the guards we employ say they are helpless in catching the thieves because there are so many of them. If it carries on like this, we won't make any profit. Actually, forget profit, we are now starting to work out how much we are losing."

"Can't the police in the area patrol around the development?" I asked.

"The police?" laughed Pieter. "Please. The police don't know which way to turn right now. The whole country is upside down. If neither the ANC nor the government can quell some of their people, then I'm not sure living in this country makes any sense."

Whoa! My husband? My salt of the earth, macho South African Afrikaner husband is telling me that he is doubting whether we should continue to live in South Africa?

Nicole was half way through her junior year, Pieter and I had already booked and paid for two weeks in Asia for his fortieth birthday in August. Cape Town was still in the master plan. I wasn't going anywhere. Surely a country that had just released Mandela was well on its way to a happy ending?

"I think you are just panicking right now," I repeated.

"I have to phone my lawyer to see what we should do. I had a suspicion the area would become volatile."

"Mom!" called Nicky, "Leelee's mom is taking us to the party. Can you fetch us tonight?"

"Where again is the house?" I asked from the kitchen.

"In Kloof," said my daughter from her bedroom. "It's one of David's friends from Michaelhouse. Everyone is going!"

"Well, make sure you get the correct directions from Lee's parents!"

I thought of asking Pieter to drive with me but he was in such a major funk these past few days that any expedition out of the ordinary would have elicited either a huge lecture or an outright "no." It was easier to just go alone. I also didn't have the courage to explain to him why our daughter was going to a party out in Kloof. It was all harmless fun. My daughter and I had a very close relationship. Often we'd sit on the bed after one of her parties and discuss who said what and who kissed who.

As it took a good half hour to go from the Berea to Kloof on the highway I decided to leave at least an hour before the 11:00 PM pick-up time.

"I am just going to fetch the girls!" I called out to the living room where Pieter was watching television.

"Where are they?" he asked.

"Oh, just up the road. See you just now," I said, grabbing my car keys and walking out the door.

CHAPTER THIRTY-TWO

1993: *A year earlier, the majority of the white electorate had given De Klerk a resounding "yes" vote in a referendum to negotiate with the ANC the last apartheid relic, the Constitution. Many of them are fearful for their safety and the security they had known but they view De Klerk with optimism that he can lead them through these uncharted waters. De Klerk envisions a federal type system with some power sharing for the next ten years. The ANC is totally opposed to that and wants majority rule. The Codesa talks are deadlocked as the struggle for power is argued back and forth between De Klerk and the ANC for a new South Africa. The talks are also boycotted by the Zulu chief Buthelezi and his Inkatha Freedom Party (IFP), which as the largest tribe is fighting to gain power over the ANC and their Xhosa supporters. The IFP joins up with the white Conservative Party to form a strong opposition against the talks. Outside the talks the violence increases exponentially. The right-wing AWB and the left-wing PAC independently continue their struggle for power through the barrel of a gun. Racial hostility heightens as South Africa plunges into a violent abyss.*

I could see the woman was bleeding heavily as she was rushing closer to my car. Just as I opened the door, a hand grabbed my shoulder.

"No!" I screamed. "Don't hurt me! Please don't hurt me!"

"*Wat die donner doen jy hier alleen, Mevrou* [What the hell are you doing here alone, Madam]?" came the voice from behind.

I turned around and found myself staring at an agitated, angry policeman. Another policeman jumped out of the van behind me and began searching my car.

"*Hoekom is jy hier*? Why are you here?" he repeated in English.

"I, I, I don't know!" I wailed. "I'm supposed to be, sob, in Kloof, but this, gulp, this, this, sob, does not look, sob, like, like, sob, Kloof."

"Further down this road is the township!" he shouted at me. "The township!" Veins threatened to burst in his face. "Do you understand? If you went further down this road you would be killed. There are *tsotsies* fighting down there, killing each other! *Verstaan jy, Mevrou?* You understand, Madam? This is not a place for a white woman alone! Jannie," he turned to the other policeman who was at the side of his van and shooting in the direction from which the bleeding woman had come. "*Vat hierdie vrou die bliksem hier uit* [Get this woman the hell out of here]!"

"What about the poor woman!" I wailed even as the second policeman pointed for me to shift over into the passenger seat.

"*Ons sal haar na die donnerse hospitaal kry* [We'll get her to the bloody hospital]," he muttered, turning the car around and speeding up the road like a bat out of hell.

"Why are you so late, Ma? It's already midnight," Nicky demanded as she rushed up to the car with her friends. "Lee's mom has already phoned Daddy, he didn't even know you were going to Kloof. He said to Lee's mom that you told him you were just going up the road. Daddy is very mad. He was shouting on the phone. Why did you drive to Kloof by yourself?"

I could not bring myself to tell my daughter or her friends what had just happened so I told them I had just gotten lost. Also, I was now in a major panic as to what would confront me when I got home. On a scale of one to ten, with ten being the worst, I had been an eight a few moments before and a twenty right now. I knew Pieter would be extremely angry.

I didn't know how angry.

He was boiling. No, scrap that. He was about to burst a vein. How dare I lie to him and tell him I was just going up the road. How dare I think I can drive by myself at night to fetch his daughter in a remote location. How dare I allow her to go to this remote location in the first place. How dare I…. How dare I…. And to top it all, the policeman had phoned him to tell him what had happened, which made him want to strangle me. Did I realize I could have been killed?

He was going to phone my mother to tell her how irresponsible I was.

Mother was worse. She even put Father on the line, which translated into supreme anger.

"Pieter is right," she admonished me on the phone the next day. "You had better not think of driving alone at night again, I am warning you! Forget the book club. Let your husband fetch the children. That is what men are supposed to do. I do not know why you think you have to do everything yourself. The children need their mother alive. Your father wants to speak with you now!"

"Hello?" I answered.

"My Ruchie, I don't want you driving alone at night. Mommy tells me that you were nearly killed. That does not make me happy. Not happy at all! You know how much I love you and if you were killed I don't know what I would do. Maybe we should get you a driver?"

"No, Daddy," I replied, now in tears. "I don't need a driver, I'm fine, Daddy...."

* * *

It was the catalyst, the chemical reaction that set in motion what happened next.

"We are leaving the country!" Pieter announced. "I can't have my family in danger anymore. Enough is enough. The blacks and the whites can take what they want to take. I can't fight any longer trying to keep a business operating here. I'm losing money faster than I could ever have imagined!"

"How! Where?" I demanded, knowing full well that if my husband announced a plan with such conviction that such plan was already in motion. Experience had taught me well.

"America!" he announced. "We will go to America. It's safe there and it's easier to start all over again there than in Europe. I spoke to some friends who are also moving there. We have to start selling things right away."

"But we are supposed to go to Asia in three weeks' time for your birthday!" I shot back. "We've already paid for the whole trip. If I cancel now, we lose all of it!"

"Ruchel, the money I'll lose for the trip is a tenth of what I'm losing each day on the projects. Johan told me that the daughter of a friend of his was raped the other day by a gang who broke into the girl's hostel on campus. On campus! Do you want that to happen to your daughter? Do you? And Pietie said that his neighbors were killed by the garden boy yesterday. Their own garden boy!"

"Michelle didn't tell me that!" I said quickly, wondering how come I never heard anything.

"That's because all you and Michelle talk about is her company. I hope she is not giving you any bullshit ideas!"

Well, it was true. Michelle and I did talk about how well she was doing in the public relations company that she had started in Durban after quitting her job at the newspaper. How she flew to Johannesburg and Cape Town and met with people in boardrooms and how she made deals in her office. I loved hearing all about it. It was water to my dream and I drank in the information like a lone flower in the middle of a desert. But this was not Utopia. This was now. After hearing that we might be moving to America, I jumped into the car and drove to Michelle's office on Florida Road in the Berea.

"I don't know what to say!" I cried as I plunked myself onto one of her paisley sofa chairs. Her office looked more like a psychiatrist's reception room than the busy public relations office that it was. "Oh, and I'm not supposed to tell anyone we're leaving. He says he is not waiting five years to file for formal emigration. We are just going to go on tourist visas and stay! That's what he says his friends told him to do."

"Your husband is going to do what?" asked Michelle, horrified. "Are you telling me he's just going to uproot the whole family and move to America with no plan, no sponsor, no job, no formal papers? The government isn't going to let him have the visa you need to live in America! You know that, right? He is crazy! How does he think he's going to pull this off? What about the children? What do you think your mother will say?"

"I don't know… America is not easy to get into. I know friends who have waited for years to file formal emigration papers and then another few years more before they were actually allowed to move. Then we had friends who were lucky enough to win a green card lottery. But Pieter wants to move now. Not later, now! So waiting around to win the lottery is not even an option."

"Well, how does he think he's going to find a sponsor for a visa to work in America if you guys don't even know anyone living in America?" continued Michelle in her logical way.

"His friends say that you just have to arrive there and find a lawyer who'll introduce you to someone who could sponsor you," I said, not even trusting my own answers. I mean, what lawyer would do that? All they have time to do is file papers on your behalf, not find sponsors. "Oh, I don't know, Mali!" I sighed. "All I know is that he wants us to start selling everything. The properties, the shares he has in other properties, the furniture, everything!"

"And how do you propose taking the money out of the country?" Michelle probed further. "And how much money you'll get in this volatile market is questionable anyway. You'll be lucky to get even a quarter of the value."

"Don't tell me, I know!" I said. "We can't even exchange our currency anywhere in the world because of the controls the government has imposed on South Africans. So, yes, hard cash is not going to give us dollars, I know. Pieter is trying to buy some dollars on the black market but you pay at least twenty percent just to get a couple of hundred dollars. That's not going to get us far. We can take our annual allowance for travel use each year, it is documented in our passports, but I think that's only about two thousand dollars per person. Some of that has to be documented for flights and hotels that have already being paid for, so even that's not much use."

But Pieter was on a mission. He had made up his mind to leave, and although I was taken aback in the beginning, I finally began to see his point. What was the use of staying in South Africa if we were constantly in danger? And the possibility of Nicole being raped at university was all I needed to push me over the edge.

What university in South Africa could guarantee my children safety and a good education? Every week the newspapers had something to say about violence and rape in the universities. If that meant I had to change countries and start all over again, so be it. I could send my daughter to Harvard. Imagine. Harvard.

"Ruchel, you can't tell anyone what we are doing!" Pieter instructed. He was trying to divest his shares in certain properties.

Some that he could not sell he just wrote off, saying the partners could spread his portion among themselves once he left the country. As far as his office was concerned, he announced he was winding down his operations and moving to the Cape to be more involved in property development there and less in designing for others in Durban. Each night I found him on the phone, talking and planning with a select few friends who were advising him. We shared a cloak-and-dagger atmosphere while the children and our parents remained in the dark.

By November of that year the wheels were set in motion. The year 1993 was already one of the most violent in the country's history and the picture was looking grimmer by the day.

"Ruchel, we have to fly to America for a week to see where we can settle," said Pieter one night after the children were in bed. "Ask your mother if she can come and look after the children."

"Then I have to tell my mother what we are doing because if she comes here she will know immediately that we're up to something."

"Last night I pretty much sold the house for what we paid for it. I'd like for us to fly out in December, so I suppose we can't hold off telling the parents any longer. I'd like to tell the children only when we get back from America, though, because I don't want to run the risk of them telling their friends. I'm flying out tomorrow night and have booked a flight for you three days later. That will give your mother time to pack and fly out here."

"Ma, Piet and I are thinking of moving to America." I said hesitantly on the phone the next day. "We need for you to come up and look after the children for a week while we go and scout out where to live."

The statement and request was so loaded, I was surprised Mother didn't have a heart attack on the spot.

"What!" Mother shouted. "What are you saying? Moving to America?"

"Ma, I'm flying out to meet Piet in New York on Sunday. Can you come up and look after the children for a week?"

"I'm coming up immediately!!" Mother said. "I can't seem to make any sense of this over the phone! Where on earth did this sudden decision come from? I hope your husband is not forcing you to move." Mother slammed the phone down and arrived in Durban the very next morning.

"Why do I know nothing of this?" she demanded in the car on the way back from the airport

"Ma, both Piet and I agree that it's now too dangerous to live here any longer. Even universities are no longer what they once were. It'll be better to educate the children in America."

"Where are you going to live?"

"I don't know, ma," I replied. "That's why I'm meeting Piet in New York on Sunday. You can't say anything right now to the children or to anyone. Right now the children think we'll live in America in the future but they don't know we want to leave in December."

"You know, Ruchel, this is too much for my body. It is all too up in the air," Mother complained. "I don't like it. I don't like it at all!"

Mother had a right to worry because this move was indeed all up in the air. Pieter and I had no formal plans, no job waiting for us on the other side, no idea where we were going to live, no friends, no family, no nothing there.

Due diligence? What due diligence?

After visiting several cities up and down the east coast, our final destination was Fort Lauderdale. People told us that Fort Lauderdale, with its small town atmosphere and gleaming yachts, was a great place to live. They were right. It was a pretty town and the weather was far nicer than up north. Fort Lauderdale was just right.

What excellent due diligence.

We flew back to Durban and told Mother we had seen some places but had not finally made up our minds. We didn't want her to be subjected to hundreds of questions from people who could alert the government that we had left with no formal papers, which could ruin our chances of becoming legal in America. We felt it best if we quietly went ahead, seeing if we could achieve legality there before attempting to come back to South Africa for a visit. It was a daunting decision because it meant that, should the process take five years or more, it would be that before we could set foot in our country again.

We sat the children down a week later and explained to them that we were moving to America in three weeks' time and that they could not tell any of their friends they were going. Peter took it quietly and stoically. Nicole burst into tears.

"How can we leave before I finish my senior year?" she cried. "I'm going to miss the Matric Dance with all my friends I've known since I started school. I'm going to miss all my friends, period. How can you do this to me? This is so unfair! What school do I have to go to? I am going to tell Gansi!"

"Gansi is coming to help pack up the house," I replied, half in tears myself. My heart broke for my daughter. It was all so unfair, I knew, but I also knew that in the long term, if we managed to pull it off, the children would be safer and better educated. Our flame of hope to stay in South Africa had already died.

Tears flowed as I asked Denise, Carol, and Michelle to meet me at a restaurant for coffee.

"We are going to miss you, my friend," they all cried as we hugged each other in the restaurant.

"I am going to miss you guys too," I cried. "Who knows when I'll ever see you all again. Just phone my mother regularly and tell her you guys are okay. I'll try to phone her at least once a month. I don't know where we'll eventually settle, it's all so up in the air. Carol, tell the book club girls that I'm sorry I never said goodbye but that one day I'll make it up to them."

The crying never stopped. Peter and Nicole both disobeyed orders to not tell anyone and chose to huddle instead with their close friends at recess, saying how much they would miss each other. Items of clothing were exchanged in remembrance and small teddy bears with friendship notes were tucked into satchels.

But the most copious tears and broken hearts were reserved for family. That was harder than we'd imagined, because we didn't know when we'd see them again. It was not as if we were leaving with a promise to come back and visit at some future time and date. We were leaving without being able to make such a promise.

Pieter and I phoned my sister and then my brother in Bloemfontein and heard every reaction from disbelief to anger to tears to acceptance. But even that did not prepare us for the call to Pieter's mother in Postmasburg. We spoke long into the night. We promised to phone her when we arrived in America. We asked her to look after herself and Pieter's younger brother and to be careful to lock the doors at night. We told her we'd miss her and that we'd send lots of photos. Then we phoned each of his sisters and his brother to say goodbye. They all thought we were out of our minds.

Mother arrived in Durban to help pack up the house.

"What happens if you don't make it in America?" she argued. Newspapers were everywhere as Ruby wrapped one bone china teacup after another. "I will keep everything for you. At least all your furniture, books, children's toys, and bicycles will be here if you decide to come back."

"Ma, we are going to make it in America. I promise you!" I replied, still trying to convince myself..

* * *

It was time to say goodbye.

Each of us had packed two suitcases and one overnight bag. It was a sobering experience. What was important and what was not? A few winter and summer clothes. What was too painful to leave behind? Photo albums, of course, memories on pages that might give us strength during uncertain times. The children's school reports and birth certificates, of course. How else could we obtain legal status and get them into schools? In my case, I packed the pillow that had been with me since childhood, and in Pieter's case, I packed two albums filled with all his professional achievements. There isn't much of your entire life that you can fit into two suitcases and an overnight bag. Not much at all.

It was a sad goodbye to Samson and Ruby, both of whom stood next to the car with tears running down their cheeks. For all his intoxicated moments Samson was still a loyal friend and I was glad that Michelle had agreed to take him on permanently. Our neighbor had a friend who wanted to hire Ruby, so I was relieved that both would not be lost without money or a job owing to our sudden departure. "Madam and *Baas* must come back soon." They both waved. "*Sale kahle* [Go well)]!"

"Your father will meet you at the airport in Johannesburg," Mother instructed in the car on the way to the airport. Her eyes were already red from seeing the tearstained faces of Ruby and Samson. She was hugging both of the children, who were on either side of her in the back seat. "Don't forget to leave the power of attorney documents with me so that I can sort out matters for you here at home. And your last will and testament in case anything happens, God forbid, to either one of you."

At the departure gate we all broke down and cried as Mother hugged the children over and over again. The call for final boarding blared over the speakers.

"Come on, we have to go!" said Pieter as he grabbed the children's hands. "Say goodbye to Gansi, kids."

"Bye Gansi, we love you, Gansi!" the children cried and waved as Pieter led them through passport control.

"Dear child," Mother turned to hug me. "I am going to miss you so much!" I was rooted to the spot. I could not move for fear of being torn from my mother forever. I tried to tell her how much I would miss her too but the tears were choking me up. My resolve to leave was beginning to waiver as I hugged Mother's trembling body.

"Hurry up, Ruchel!" called Pieter from the other side of passport control.

"Look after the children, do you promise me?"

"I will, mom, I will," I sobbed. "I'm coming!" I yelled at Pieter. "Mom, I have to go. I will"—I sobbed harder—"phone you when we arrive in America."

I tried to be brave but fear was in my heart. Mother would now be an ocean away. Once I stepped through that passport control area, I would not see her again for a long long time.

"Ruchel! Hurry up. There is no time left!" called Pieter.

"I am going to miss you so much, mom. Please be safe. I love you."

"I love you too, dear child!"

My last memory of Mother before I boarded the plane was her standing in her favorite black pants and white shirt, wiping tears from behind her large brown sunglasses as she tried to wave enthusiastically with her handkerchief. It was the most devastating moment of my life.

"Do you have all the money you drew from your stocks?" Pieter asked on the plane to Johannesburg.

"Yes," I replied, wiping tears from my eyes. "It's at the bottom of the overnight bag. How are you going to change the money into dollars?"

"I have to give it to a guy who is meeting me at the airport. He'll take the rands for us to Switzerland," Pieter said.

"Do you know this guy?" I asked, a little worried. The cash from all the stocks my grandmother had put in my name many years before, together with the money Pieter had left, constituted our entire life savings.

"No, I was told just to meet him at an arranged spot and hand the bag over to him," replied Pieter. "From there this guy will, for a fee, take it to Switzerland and convert it to dollars. All I have to give him is the name and phone number of the hotel where we are staying when we land in America. My contact said the money should be transferred within two weeks."

"How can you trust such a transaction when you can't even get a name from this man?"

"It's the only chance we have when we arrive there to have some money to buy a car and pay the lawyer's fees. The exchange rate is horrendous, nearly four rand to one dollar, and on top of that these people take twenty percent. But there's nothing else we can do."

At the airport in Johannesburg I rushed into my father's arms as he swooped down to hug the children. By the time Pieter joined us his face was white. I knew that he had just handed all our money over to an anonymous person with no receipt and no guarantee.

"He just nodded, took the money, and walked in the opposite direction," whispered Pieter nervously into my ear. "He disappeared into the crowd before I could change my mind."

It was hard to digest but we were committed to leaving and starting all over again, with or without the money. It was a chance we had to take. Besides, my emotions overtook any rational thought that day.

Pieter and I reviewed our travel documents and other papers at an airport restaurant while my father hugged and played with the children. All around us people moved to and fro, backward and forward, South Africans of all colours and races speaking different languages but with the same mannerisms that made them all so African. I tried to imprint that moment in my mind to savor later but it was hard to capture through the fog that clouded my brain. Not long after that, the final boarding call for South African Airways to New York blared over the speakers.

"That's us!" declared Pieter. "Let's go. Children say goodbye to Oupa." Everyone hugged everyone as tears rolled down our sad, tired faces.

"Make sure you phone us and tell us where you are!" instructed Father. "I am going to miss you lots, all of you."

"I am going to miss you too, dad. I am going to miss you every day!" I cried as I hugged my father for what felt like the last time.

"Just remember that you can do anything you want if you just work hard at it. America is the land of hope and dreams!" My father smiled.

"I know, I know." I smiled back through the tears. "I promise I won't disappoint."

"My Ruchie!" said Father. "Be careful in America, do you hear! Always remember to hold your head up high and don't let anyone take advantage of you!"

"I will, dad, I promise," I cried as he held me close.

"And remember," he called out as I slowly walked to the passport gate, "remember that you can always come home. Just phone your mother and we will send you a ticket home."

"I will, dad, goodbye, dad, I love you. Tell mommy I love her too, and be safe all of you!"

It was our last goodbye, our last farewell to the country that gave birth to us.

I climbed the stairs into the plane and paused to smell the air for the last time. It was filled with jet fuel but it was nevertheless African air, warm humid African air that filled my lungs for the last time. Would I ever again see the deep red sunsets over the dry bushveld, ever again hear the turtle doves cooing in the blue gum trees, ever again smell the wood burning in the cold mountain air, ever again see the smiling face of an African child dancing in the street, ever again see my family, hug my family, be comforted by my family?

As I sat silently waiting for takeoff, memories of the time when everything was all so carefree and innocent flooded my mind.

Memories of when fairies beckoned me to have tea with them at the bottom of the garden. When Evelyn cradled me on her back singing *Thula thula, thula thula, baba.* When ice cream dribbled down my cheeks on hot sandy beaches by the sea. When leaves rustled and birds sang while the aromas of *kibi* and *baba ghanoush* and the sounds of laughter swirled through the air. When clouds puffed up like faces while Michelle and I giggled in the tall dry grass. When Martha laughed as she sliced her warm banana cake. When wildebeest and giraffe grazed in the distance while we joined hands and sang *Kumba ya* around campfires. When crickets and beetles tap-danced under starry, starry nights. When the sweet smell of rain falling on the dry veld filled your soul, and the yawn of a lion made the world pause, reminding you that this was his land. This was your home…

Goodbye, Mother Africa.

One day I will return and I will make you proud. One day I will return and you will make me proud. We will grow up and change, the both of us, and one day I will return and we will be happy as we dance to the beat of the African drum.

Sala hantle! Se ntebale.

Goodbye. Don't forget me.

AUTHOR BIOGRAPHY

Ruchel Louis Coetzee was born in Bloemfontein, South Africa, a city known for an abundance of colorful flowers and the 2010 FIFA World Cup soccer matches. She grew up during the last turbulent days of Apartheid, and saw her country and her life change forever. Pulani is her African name. It means 'rain.'

Ruchel and her family moved to the United States in 1993. In 1995 she fulfilled her dream, and founded a film and video production company called Successful Images, Inc. rebranded to Ruchel LLC. Her corporate and nonprofit videos have won numerous Addys, Auroras, and Telly awards, and she is known for her skills as an interviewer. Ruchel produced her first feature film "Gringo Wedding", a romantic comedy geared towards the Latin American community. It received two film festival awards. She has written several articles for newspapers and magazines and has been a guest speaker at various corporate networking groups. "Pulani" is her first novel.

A full-time producer and writer, Ruchels next release is her cookbook. "PULANI'S KITCHEN – Simple Healthy Meals Inspired By Life In South Africa". The cookbook is a result of the numerous requests for her famous carrot cake, "afriscotti" (South African version of biscotti), mamoul (Lebanese date cakes) and other recipes mentioned in "PULANI". More than just a collection of recipes, "PULANI'S KITCHEN" is geared to those who have no time to spend in the kitchen or who are just learning to cook, and presents the process of meal preparation so it fits easily around a busy life.

For more, visit her website at www.PULANI.net

ACKNOWLEDGEMENT

When I had embarked on a journey to write this book my desire was to give a voice to those who silently loved their land with the burning intensity of a blood red African sunset. What transpired was a journey that led me to the knowledge of the woman I am today. We can only begin to have this understanding and open dialogue when we can appraise the road we have walked in life. The road we travel will include battles and apprehensions but these battles allow us to exonerate our fears and to courageously endure any impending storm.

I am deeply indebted to those who have contributed advice, time, friendship and a rich experience to my life. There are far too many to mention by name in this book but their presence will always be inscribed in my heart.

A special tribute needs to be paid to those who were unwavering in their support to get the book to its published form—you know who you are.

Special thanks to copy editor Peggy Ann Chevalier whose patience, warmth and friendship will be treasured always.

To my editor and publisher Cheryl Smith whose extraordinary calm, rationality and efficiency kept me going in the last difficult weeks. She asked the right questions and continues to be a constant source of support and encouragement. Her friendship holds a special place in my heart. I am truly indebted.

To my lifelong best friend Michelle Maliepaard, our laughter and shared secrets will always carry us across the oceans together.

I want to express my profound thanks and love to my family. My mother continues to be my strength. Her love and bravery are a divine guidance even in my darkest hours. My father, who always upholds me as his princess; my sister Jenny, whose sage and loving advice never ceases to amaze me and my brother Wayne, whose humor and take charge nature helps ease the pain of having my family live so far away.

To my adoring beautiful children, Nicole and Hendrik Peter, who keep me alive each and every day, you will always occupy my whole heart. Finally to my husband and soul mate Pieter, who constantly encourages me to passionately dance across the African veld while holding me in his arms.

FAMILY TREE

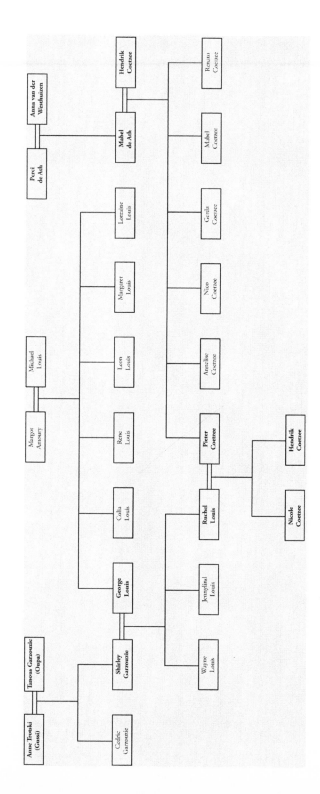

POLITICAL ACRONYMS

ANC - African National Congress

AWB - Afrikaner Weerstand Beweging—extreme right wing party

COSATU - Congress of South African Trade Union

FNLA - Frente Nacional de Liberatacao de Angola - Angola's National Liberation Front—a democratic party

IFP - Inkatha Freedom Party—majority of the members are from the Zulu tribe

IZWE - Izifundazwe ZaseNingizimu Afrika (antiapartheid meetings and literature)

MK - Umkhonto we Sizwe (Spear of the Nation)—military wing of the ANC during apartheid. In 1994 they were incorporated into the South African National Defense Force

MPLA - Moviemento Popular de Libertacao de Angola— Angola's Labor Party

NGK - Nedenduitse Gereformeerde Kerk—Dutch Protestant Church

OAU - Organization of African Uunity—International organization founded as the organization of African unity to promote cooperation among the independent nations of Africa

PAC - Pan-Africanist Congress—South African liberation movement during apartheid—now a minor political party

SACP - South African Communist Party (SACP)—the SACP is a partner in the tripartite alliance consisting of the ANC and COSATU (Congress of South African Trade Union)

SADF - South African Defense Force

SWAPO   -   South West Africa People's Organization SWAPO—
            the governing party and former liberation movement
            in Namibia Union of South Africa- historic forerunner
            to what is now known as the Republic of South
            Africa

UDF   -   United Democratic Front—anti apartheid organization
            during the 1980s

UOFS   -   University of the Orange Free State—Afrikaans
            speaking University

GLOSSARY

A

acacia – a type of tree

Addis Ababa – capital city of Ethopia

Afrikaans – South African language originating from the 17th Dutch
   settlers

Afrikaner – a South African of European descent whose native
   language is Afrikaans – see Boer

Apartheid – segregation, sanctioned by law, was widely practiced
   in South Africa before 1948, but the National Party, which
   gained office that year, extended the policy and gave it the
   name apartheid. The Group Areas Act of 1950 established
   residential and business sections in urban areas for each
   race, and members of other races were barred from living,
   operating businesses, or owning land in them.

apteek – pharmacy

assegais – slender spear

Aunty (not Auntie) – a true relative or a family friend

A Wimba Weh – a traditional African song also known as "The
   Lion Sleeps Tonight" [see also "ohi'mbube, ohi'mbube]

B

baas, or Baas – boss

baba ghanoush – eggplant dish

Basotu – The South Sotho tribe living in Lesotho and the Orange
   Free State province

biltong – beef jerky

bioscope – movie house

biskuit (pronounced 'bis-kate')- dried-out sweet bread – like
   biscotti

bliksem – damn, hell; exclamation

bliksemed – killed

Bloemfontein – capital city of the Orange Free State

bobotie – a delicious South African meatloaf made with curry, chutney, raisins and other spices

Boer – "farmer" a South African of Dutch, German and French descent

boetie (pronounced "bootie") – brother

bosbefock(ed) – "bush crazy," crazy or irrational mental state

braais – barbecue

braaivleis – roasted meat

bundu – veld

bunny chow – hollowed out bread loaf filled with curry lamb or beef stew

Bushman – the oldest and now extinct tribe of South Africa—they were nomadic and short statured

C

Cape Flats, the – flat and windblown area of Cape Town

Cape Town – capital city of the Western Cape

catty – catapult

Coloured -a person of mixed European ("white") and African ("black") or Asian ancestry, as officially defined by the South African government from 1950 to 1991.

Commonwealth, the – a political community founded for the common good.

Cyril – Mother's friend.

D

De Oog – "the eye"—a hot springs resort in the Northern Cape

doek – headscarf

dolmades – grape leaf rolls

donnerse – stupid, "bloody"

dooses – idiots

dop – a drink

dorp – small town

draughtsman – a person employed in making mechanical or
    architectural drawings
droe wors -dried sausage to resemble jerky
dumela – Sotho for hello
Durban – capital city of Natal province
Dutchman – stereotype of an Afrikaner

E/F

Eisteddfod – annual performing arts competition
Engelse – English

G

gatval – mad, angry
gekuis – going steady
General Botha – first Prime Minister of the Union of South Africa
    in 1910
goeie donner – damn, exclamation
Group Areas Act – an act of parliament created under the apartheid
    government of South Africa in 1950 that established
    segregation – see apartheid)

H

hamba – Sotho word meaning "go" or "let's go"
hauw – wow
hardegat – stubborn
homelands – a territory set aside for the black inhabitants of South
    Africa
Hottentot Mountains – mountain range in the Western Cape

I/J

Ikeys – University of Cape Town
impis – group of Bantu warriors
ingekruip – in bed with

ja – yes
Jan van Riebeeck – Dutch pioneer founder of Cape Town 1652
Johannesburg
joi de vivre – joy of life
jou – you

K/L

Karoo – semi-desert South African region
karringmelk biskuit – dried buttermilk bread—similar to biscotti
kea laboha – Sotho for thank you
kibi – Lebanese lamb and corn dish
Kimberley – city of diamonds in the Northern Cape
klaar – finish
kloofnek – mountain pass
kloosterkoek – nun
kocksisters – sweet deep-fried bread
kos – food
kudu – large South African deer
kuised – going steady [also see gekuis]
Kyalami – South African premier race track - similar to the Indy
     500
lekken biltong – great jerky
Lesotho – landlocked country surrounded by South Africa
Ltd (no period) – limited company incorporated under the English
     law

M

mamoul – a traditional Lebanese date cake
Mandela, Nelson – president of South Africa from 1994 - 1999
manne – men
meisie – girl
mevrou – madam
mielie meel – maize flour
moer – kill
moerse – bloody
Monica – sister's nursemaid

N

naam – name
Natal – One of the four provinces of South Africa created in 1910
neef – cousin
nogal – as well, also

O

Ohi'mbube… ohi'mbube (pronounced "A Wimba Weh") – Zulu
    word meaning "lion" or "you're a lion"; also the title of a
    Xhosa song commonly known as "The Lion Sleeps Tonight"
Orange Free State – one of the four provinces of South Africa
    created in 1910

P/Q

pakisa – Sotho for hurry
pannekoek – South African crepes, sweet pancakes
pap – porridge
Parliament – a legislative body
pass book –the non-white population of South Africa were required
    to carry these government issued ID books outside of their
    work or home. If they failed to do so and were caught they
    were locked up in jail.
pass laws – the Pass Laws were introduced in South Africa in 1923
    to regulate the movement of the non-whites in the urban
    areas. They were repealed in 1986
perelemoen – abalone
phakisang – Sotho for hurry up
poep – shit
poeswyn – cheap wine
Port Elizabeth – known as the "windy city", it is one of the largest
    port cities in the Eastern Cape

R

Raadsaal – justice building

Rand – South African currency

Red Jerepigo – a sweet red South African wine; the name is derived
from the Afrikaans "Rooi Herepik my" meaning "God's
biting me"

Republic (the Republic of...) – a type of government where the
citizens choose the leaders of their country

rondavels – round clay huts with thatch roofs

rooinek – English person, derogatory

S

samoosa – Indian dish—triangular phyllo pastry with filling

shoh – Sotho for "wow!" "OMG"

skiem – gather

snoek – type of fish

sorghum – a beer made from maize and grain

Sotho – there are three distinct groups of the Sotho tribe. The
Basotho (southern Sotho) live in Lesotho and Orange Free
State. The other two are the Pedi (northern Sotho) and the
Tswana (many of whom live in Botswana)

South African Act – an act of the British Parliament which created
the Union of South Africa in 1910. The Act was the South
African Constitution until 1961 when South Africa became a
Republic and left the Commonwealth

sousboontjies – beans in sauce

souskluitjies – dumplings in sauce

souties – English people, derogatory

snaakse – strange

syringa tree – lilac tree

T

tannie – aunt

thokolosi – scary, imaginary man

tlo – Sotho for come here

tok-tokkie – a child's game similar to "ring and run"
township, or Township (proper noun) – often underdeveloped
    areas usually outside urban living areas set aside for non-
    whites during apartheid
Transkei, the – means "the river Kei". It was an area in the Eastern
    Cape of South Africa set aside as a homeland for the Xhosa
    tribe under the apartheid policy of "separate development". It
    is now reintegrated into the Eastern Cape province.
Transvaal – One of the four provinces of South Africa created in
    1910
Tweespruit – small town outside Bloemfontein
Tweetoring Kerk ("two-tower" NGK church) – Dutch Protestant
    Church
Thula – Sotho for hush, quiet

U/V

uitlander – foreigner
vrying – kissing

W

Western Cape – One of the four provinces of South Africa created
    in 1910
windbuks – air rifle
windgats – show offs

XYZ

Xhosa ("Khosa") – the Xhosa tribe come mainly from the Eastern
    Cape and speak by clicking their tongues. Most famous
    Xhosa is Nelson Mandela.
zigzag – pattern of small corners at different angles

HEROIDES

"Stories of the Heroes of Our Times"

For more visit our website at:
www.heroides.com

LaVergne, TN USA
22 October 2010

201865LV00002BB/2/P